D1175125

CHALLENGING THE ORTHODOXIES

Challenging the Orthodoxies

Edited by

Richard M. Auty
Senior Lecturer, Department of Geography, Lancaster University

and

John Toye
Director, Institute of Development Studies,
University of Sussex, Brighton

338.9009172
C 437

First published in Great Britain 1996 by
MACMILLAN PRESS LTD
Houndmills, Basingstoke, Hampshire RG21 6XS
and London
Companies and representatives
throughout the world

A catalogue record for this book is available
from the British Library.

ISBN 0–333–65474–9

First published in the United States of America 1996 by
ST. MARTIN'S PRESS, INC.,
Scholarly and Reference Division,
175 Fifth Avenue,
New York, N.Y. 10010

ISBN 0–312–16017–8

Library of Congress Cataloging-in-Publication Data
Challenging the orthodoxies / edited by Richard M. Auty and John Toye.
p.   cm.
"First published in Great Britain 1996 by Macmillan Press Ltd.,
Houndmills, Basingstoke, Hampshire"—T.p. verso.
Includes bibliographical references and index.
ISBN 0–312–16017–8 (cloth)
1. Developing countries—Economic policy.   2. Economic
development.   I. Auty, R. M. (Richard M.)   II. Toye, J. F. J.
HC59.7.C338   1996
338.9'009172'4—dc20   96–14480
                                                          CIP

10   9   8   7   6   5   4   3   2   1
05   04   03   02   01   00   99   98   97   96

Printed in Great Britain by
The Ipswich Book Company Ltd
Ipswich, Suffolk

MIC

Contents

III   Rural and Environmental Responses

List of Acronyms

AID	Agency for International Development
BMAS	Botswana Medical Aid Society
BPOMAS	Botswana Public Officers Medical Aid Scheme
CITES	The Convention on the International Trade in Endangered Species of Wild Fauna and Flora
CMC	Calcutta Municipal Corporation
CMDA	Calcutta Metropolitan Development Corporation
CNC	Comision Nacional Campesina [Chile]
DNPWC	Department of National Parks and Wildlife Conservation [Nepal]
DSR	Debt Service Ratio
GDP	Gross Domestic Product
GNP	Gross National Product
HPAE	High Performing Asian Economy
IBRD	International Bank for Reconstruction and Development
IDS	Institute for Development Studies
IMF	International Monetary Fund
ISR	Interest Service Ratio
IUCN	World Conservation Union
LDC	Less-Developed Country
NAFTA	North American Free Trade Agreement
NDP	National Development Plan
NGO	Non-Governmental Organisation
OECD	Organisation for Economic Cooperation and Development
R&D	Research and Development
SADC	South African Development Community
TDS	Total Debt Service
ULUS	Uluguru Land Usage Scheme
UNCED	United Nations Conference on Environment and Development
UNDP	United Nations Development Programme

Notes on Contributors

Richard M. Auty is Senior Lecturer in Geography at Lancaster University.

Stephanie Barrientos is Senior Lecturer in Economics at the University of Hertfordshire.

Anu Bose is a postgraduate student completing her PhD at the Department of Development Administration in the University of Birmingham. She formerly worked as a bureaucrat in the NGO and trade union sectors.

Katrina Brown is a Lecturer in Natural Resource Management in the School of Development Studies at the University of East Anglia and Senior Research Fellow at the Centre for Social and Economic Research on the Gobal Environment (CSERGE).

Jacqueline Charlton is Head of the Department of Law and Public Administration at Glasgow Caledonian University.

Jan Kees van Donge is Senior Lecturer in the Department of Public Administration, Chancellor College, University of Malawi, Zomba.

Nigel Dower is Director of the Centre for Philosophy, Technology and Society and also Senior Lecturer in the Departments of Philosophy and Politics and International Relations at the University of Aberdeen.

Jerry V. S. Jones is Director of International Economic Policy Research at Kings College, London.

Tony Killick is Professor of Economics in the Overseas Development Institute in London.

Renee Prendergast is Senior Lecturer in Economics at the Queen's University, Belfast.

Kunibert Raffer is Associate Professor in the Economics Department, University of Vienna.

John Toye became President of the Development Studies Association in 1994. He is Professor of Development Studies and Director of the Institute for Development Studies at the University of Sussex.

John G. Williamson is Senior Fellow in the Institute of International Economics, Washington, DC.

Jim Winpenny is Research Fellow at the Overseas Development Institute in London.

1 Challenging the Orthodoxies

Richard Auty and John Toye

IDENTIFYING ORTHODOXY

Orthodoxy originally meant simply 'true opinion' or 'right judgement'. If this were still its meaning, our title *Challenging the Orthodoxies* might seem a little foolish, or even perverse. Who in their senses would want to challenge true opinions and right judgements? This is not our purpose, however, or that of the contributors to this book. Orthodoxy has since taken on an extended meaning. Today it carries the implication of imposing an opinion or judgement *as if* it were true and right. It also implies dissuading dissenters, by emphasising the established or accepted character of the orthodox opinions or judgements. It encourages the use of the social sanctions of scorn or ridicule to deter those who might be inclined to think themselves a little wiser than the rest of humankind from saying so. Orthodoxies are no longer just sets of beliefs. They are beliefs to assent to which one feels some kind of social and psychological pressure.

Such pressure is hardly measurable. This poses a problem. In the welter of views and writings on development studies, different claims about where the pressure is coming from can be made, and have been made. Identifying orthodoxies can become a rhetorical device to advance a particular set of beliefs, by claiming that its contrary is oppressive. The counter-revolution of the 1980s not only said that believers in planning and intervention were wrong, but that they were intellectually corrupt, a clique who defended 'dirigisme' while knowing that it rested on bad economics. On the other side, there were many who criticised this counter-revolution for its ideological basis, and its unwillingness to confront the real problems inherent in trying to achieve development by simply applying free-market nostrums.

So this talk of orthodoxy faces a recurring difficulty. What is an orthodoxy, and what is an intellectual challenge to orthodoxy? One person's orthodoxy is another's Aunt Sally, a concoction of views that no one actually holds, set up only for the purpose of being demolished, and to make the contrary view seem more brilliant than it would if it were plainly stated. Despite this general difficulty of identifying genuine orthodoxies, and distinguishing them from others manufactured only for the purpose of debate, no such problem exists for development studies in the 1990s. A particular set of key beliefs has been distilled from the counter-revolution of the 1980s, and declared to be the basic credo of all serious economists of development. This is the 'Washington consensus'.

The origins of the Washington consensus, its key elements and its subsequent evolution form the theme of Chapter 2 by John Williamson (Institute of International Economics, Washington DC). Williamson acknowledges himself as the father of the Washington consensus although, like many parents, he has had second thoughts as to whether he gave his progeny the most appropriate name. Williamson makes it clear that the Washington consensus was an attempt to identify the lowest common denominator among the views of the right and the left in the 'development establishment' in Washington concerning appropriate policies for Latin America in the late 1980s.

Critical elements within the consensus identified by Williamson include:

- fiscal discipline, a tighter prioritisation of public expenditure and tax reform to broaden the tax base and sharpen incentives;
- more market-sensitive interest rates along with a competitive exchange rate and trade liberalisation;
- deregulation to promote competitive enterprise through privatisation and the removal of barriers to foreign direct investment;
- the securing of property rights, including those in the informal sector, through an appropriate legal system.

Williamson stresses that the consensus should not be construed as a neoliberal manifesto and that he himself has reservations about some points which are included in it. He would also prefer to add others (of a more socially responsive nature) but doubts, however, that they would be accepted within the constraints entailed in maintaining the consensus.

Williamson points out that there has been some evolution in the consensus in a direction of which he approves because it espouses greater social concern. Two possible candidates for inclusion are, first, priority within public expenditure for social expenditure with a high pay-off in poverty alleviation and improved income distribution through policies such as targeted welfare payments and the provision of piped water or low-cost, self-help housing. The second area for inclusion in the consensus is the rapid dissemination of universal access to birth control.

Yet the inclusion of social concerns within the Washington consensus appears to go unheeded in some quarters where one of its roles appears to be that of a symbol of a repressive and uncaring establishment. Worse, this establishment might be one which is less than careful with the truth as Robert Wade implied in a critique of the East Asian Miracle study by the World Bank. Unfortunately, Wade's intriguingly titled paper, 'The World Bank and the art of paradigm maintenance: The East Asian Miracle study' cannot be reprinted in the present volume due to copyright difficulties.

SOME ECONOMIC CRITIQUES OF ORTHODOXY

In Chapter 3, Kunibert Raffer (University of Vienna) challenges the orthodox assumption that the debt crisis is over. He argues that, just as the leading international financial institutions prematurely hailed an upswing in the fortunes of sub-Saharan Africa in 1989, so a couple of years later they have mistakenly signalled the passing of the debt crisis in Latin America. Raffer contends that the World Debt Tables take too little note of the impact of debt rescheduling on the debt service ratios of debtor countries. Consequently, the World Debt Tables tend to underestimate the burden which Latin American countries must still bear.

Raffer's warning of the need for caution was subsequently underlined by the dramatic collapse of confidence in the Mexican economy which took place between the drafting of his paper in June 1994 and its final editing in the spring of the following year. If Mexico can suffer such a relapse, what then of other Latin American debtors which have hitherto been accorded less assistance with debt relief and have conformed less to the role of a model debtor?

The orthodox perspective is again taken to task in Chapter 4 by Renee Prendergast (Queen's University, Belfast) who queries the faith which the leading international financial institutions place in markets. While acknowledging the greater economic success of capitalist countries compared with socialist ones, she queries the orthodox assumptions about the optimality of market competition under conditions of innovation. She notes the importance in successful capitalist countries of market and non-market institutions of which the most notable are the opportunity and incentive to pursue economic experimentation and the intense rivalry between domestic firms as a spur to innovative activity.

In applying these considerations to developing countries, Prendergast concludes that strongly market-oriented reforms may encourage firms to exit (and scrap the accumulated human and physical capital) rather than to innovate. She notes that state intervention in East Asian countries has been more successful than in Latin America because of greater discipline over the provision of incentives. She interprets the World Bank East Asian Miracle study as reluctantly recognising a role for governments in coordinating entry, provided non-market targets, such as export goals, are retained to spur innovation. Because competition may create a conflict between innovation and learning, the East Asian experience (supported by institutional economics) provides examples for follower countries to resolve that conflict.

Tony Killick (Overseas Development Institute) pursues Prendergast's theme in a somewhat broader context in Chapter 5. He uses the concept of the flexibility of national economies in order to tease out some of the institutional features which differentiate countries' abilities to adapt to change. He draws a distinction between short-run (responsive) and long-run (innovative) flexibility and discusses the differences in the ease of adjustment experienced by individuals, firms and institutions. He argues that in the process of aggregating from individuals to institutions, flexibility becomes harder to achieve.

A second interesting broad hypothesis emerges concerning the relationship between per capita income and flexibility which Killick postulates to resemble an inverted U-shape. Low-income countries have lower flexibility because of poor information, cultural resistance (in some cases) to change, the vulnerability of mono-product economies to external shocks and the absence of economies of scale and effective markets. Meanwhile, as economies mature it is assumed that vested interest groups contest resources and outcomes so that transaction costs rise while an ageing population exercises more resistance to change and a deteriorating dependency ratio depresses incentives. Such speculations underline the contention that society provides a rich and changing matrix within which economic transactions take place. They caution against the excessively economic reductionism of the orthodox perspective.

BROADER CRITIQUES OF ORTHODOXY

Nigel Dower (University of Aberdeen) takes fundamental issue with the whole concept of development in Chapter 6. From a philosophical standpoint, orthodoxy reflects a very narrow and Eurocentric view of development which is overly-concerned with a few qualitative indices of economic welfare. But Dower stops short of siding with the views expressed by Wolfgang Sachs and others in *The Development Dictionary* which reject development as an unwelcome homogenisation of cultures based on a western model of economic growth, science, technology and bureaucracy. Instead, Dower seeks to tease out a number of widely-recognised characteristics of development which have at their core the view that development is a process of social change from worse to better that can be controlled by human beings working within some rationally conceived social order. He emphatically concludes that development is a social imperative for any society which recognises that there is a collective responsibility for practical improvement. Such improvements concern basic elements of well-being, a healthy natural environment, a properly functioning culture with basic values concerning human conduct and the world view of society, and a commitment to continuity.

A critical assumption of the orthodox perspective is that people basically respond rationally to experience. In this context, an important orthodox prescription for, for example, sub-Saharan Africa has been to get the prices right so that farmers are provided with effective indicators concerning the efficiency of alternative uses for resources. This view is challenged in Chapter 7 by survey work undertaken in Tanzania by Jan Kees van Donge (University of Malawi). His study of primary school leavers in a rural area subject to mounting land shortages and environmental deterioration reveals a sharp contrast between professed lifestyle preferences and actual experience.

The school leavers surveyed strongly agreed that education was a key asset although very few were likely to derive much career benefit from it. More significantly, the most preferred way of making a living after teaching was cited to be farming, with trading, whether local or with Dar es Salaam, not favoured by many. Most respondents felt strongly that farming was preferable to trading and traders were portrayed as exploitive of farmers. Yet, in reality, few school leavers would be able to make a living in the region from farming and most would be involved in trade. Moreover, there was little evidence that school leavers understood the problems which local farming faced. Instead, they looked to government intervention and fertiliser to retrieve the situation rather than more specific measures within their own control. Local economic problems were denied and ideological notions took preference over the interpretation of actual social practices. Consequently, not only orthodox economists looking to market-driven solutions, but also advocates of recent *sociological* orthodoxies (such as participatory procedures, bottom-up approaches and tapping local knowledge) also need to question their basic assumptions.

The social underpinnings of development remain the theme of Chapter 8 in which Stephanie Barrientos (University of Hertfordshire) draws attention to the importance of female labour to Chilean fruit production. Fruit has become an important contributor to the success of that country's export-led growth model and accounted for 13 per cent of Chilean exports in the early 1990s. But fruit production relied heavily on female labour to meet the peak labour demand in this highly seasonal industry. Yet the conditions of work demand long hours with little job security and very few safeguards in the absence of union representation.

Although the women workers welcome the opportunity to participate in non-household activity which fruit picking and packing provide, and they would not wish to return to their previous situation when they were largely confined to household chores, their conditions of employment could be significantly improved. For example, one estimate places rates of remuneration in the Chilean industry at one-twentieth those for equivalent work in California. Surprisingly little change has occurred under the democratic presidencies of Aylwin and Frei, even though the job conditions of female Chilean fruit workers emerged under the Pinochet dictatorship. Instead, the imperative of the export-led economic growth model has meant that any improvements have been concentrated on facilitating female labour participation (through help with child minding). The suggestion is that specific groups in society pay disproportionately for the 'success' of the orthodox model.

In Chapter 9, Jacqueline Charlton (Glasgow Caledonian University) turns to a different sort of challenge to the new orthodoxy, namely that of making its own confident policy prescriptions work within a relatively favourable economic environment. The example chosen concerns health care provision in one of sub-Saharan Africa's economically most successful countries, Botswana. Here, a government commitment to equalising access to health care has combined with sharply rising expectations to seriously strain the public sector's capacity to meet its commitments.

The Botswana government embarked on a rather ambitious expansion of tertiary health facilities in the public sector as part of a market acceleration of mineral windfall expenditure in the late 1980s. Although the rate of investment expansion was subsequently scaled back, there remained formidable recurrent expenses at a time when the country's economic prospects appeared to be weakening and there were serious shortages of qualified manpower for the medical sector. In this context, interest has turned to the role of the private sector.

Some private provision already existed in terms of the facilities within the mining company compounds, use of facilities in neighbouring South Africa, and also small private schemes. The latter are expanding rapidly with the construction of a private hospital and the development of corporate health schemes. This latter development provides the nucleus for a growing fraction of the population to ease the burden on public medical care. The private sector also provides a yardstick for the public sector in terms of service provision and cost effectiveness, with some possible synergies in shared services. Finally, the private sector addresses Botswana's shortage of medical skills by attracting into the country trained personnel who would otherwise not have considered such a move. There are also potential conflicts arising out of replicating facilities, the poaching of staff and introducing a differentiated system of health care. The experiment will be watched with interest.

THE RURAL/ENVIRONMENTAL DIMENSION

The environmental dimension is an important omission from the Washington consensus which is addressed in Chapters 10–13. Perhaps this omission occurs because some would have dissented from its inclusion in the consensus on the grounds that, like Nordhaus, they see the 'reification' of a single issue like the environment, as an unnecessary restriction on the ability of conventional growth economics to deal with the natural capital stock and its depletion. Indeed, many of the tenets of the so-called weak sustainability approach discussed in the World Bank's *World Development Report 1992* are formal extensions of that approach which, at the very least, serves to draw attention to an issue within the development process which has hitherto been inadequately addressed.

In Chapter 10, James Winpenny (Overseas Development Institute) welcomes the potential contribution which environmental economics can make to the sustainable development of low-income countries. He argues that such countries tend to be especially dependent on their natural resource endowment because of the dominance of agriculture and paucity of industrial skills. In a review of five such countries which are already at, or rapidly approaching, the elimination of their land frontier, Winpenny notes that in four of them institutions tend to continue to encourage land-extensive farming practices with increasingly adverse consequences for environmental degradation. The four countries comprise Cameroon, Ecuador, Uganda and the Philippines. Winpenny's fifth case study, Kenya, is the exception.

The required intensification of the farming system has been achieved in the Machakos District of Kenya, south-east of Nairobi, an area carefully studied over several decades by Winpenny's colleagues at the Overseas Development Institute. He argues that it is no coincidence that Kenya is the only country in his sample which has not been beset by 'urban bias', the neglect of rural areas in favour of the rapid build-up of urban-based activity, much of it of dubious efficiency as far as the investment of scarce capital resources is concerned.

More specific conditions favouring land use intensification in the region include increased market-orientation (facilitated by the growth of rural infrastructure, notably roads); a wide range of technically and economically feasible land use options; an open society with a broad and well-educated, development-oriented leadership; the complementary growth of non-farm opportunities to provide alternative employment, a source of savings for rural investment and a market for crops; and finally, a land tenure system which gives sufficient security for farmers to invest in land improvement and conservation. Winpenny concludes that by helping to identify both market and government failures, and measuring the benefits from their correction, environmental economics can help reduce the obstacles to the land use intensification which is needed in order to minimise the degradation of rural environmental resources.

In Chapter 11, Jerry Jones (Kings College, London) examines the industrialisation of the countryside in densely-settled Asia with reference to the experience of seven 'villages', six in China and one in Taiwan. He describes the dramatic changes in the physical environment which were undertaken initially in order to raise farm productivity and subsequently in order to diversify into non-farm activities. By the 1990s, farming no longer dominated the economy of any of the villages and, in fact, in several of them it accounts for less than one-fifth of the area's income. An important consequence of the rural industrialisation process has been the sharp increase in the productivity of farm labour as alternative forms of employment have eliminated surplus labour and placed a premium on labour conservation. Moreover, there has been an increasing tendency for land to be contracted out for farming purposes. This provides one means of overcoming the fragmentation of holdings which has historically hampered agriculture in such societies.

However, the geographical dispersal implicit in rural industry creates problems in terms of the adequate provision of infrastructure and also of controlling pollution. As far as environmental degradation is concerned, given scarce administrative resources there is the risk that regulations will be less rigorously enforced so that pollution will be the worse in consequence. However, as Jones and others have pointed out, the fact that the polluters also have to live within the polluted areas may be expected to bring pressure to bear on the development of informal agreements to curb industrial effluent. Interestingly, Jones argues that such informal agreements may be more forthcoming where communal institutions have survived than where there has been a sharp break between industry and farming. For example, despite some a priori expectation that the higher per capita income of Taiwan would prompt earlier measures to curb pollution, this had not occurred in the village that Jones examined. Instead, pressure to restrain a privately-owned firm from polluting irrigation channels had achieved little success.

A second theme running through Chapter 11 is the survival in China of communal endeavour, not so much in farming as in the rural industries. There are major regional differences in the extent to which this is so and, in general, those regions where cooperatives were most successful are the ones in which they continue most to flourish. One unexpected danger raised by this situation is of sharp inequalities emerging in neighbouring communities, one of which supplies labour to the enterprises of the other. This occurs because although all workers might be paid according to a common wage scale, the distribution of profits tends to enrich the 'employing' village and to result in the accumulation of capital and skills which the village supplying labour lacks.

In Chapter 12, Katrina Brown (University of East Anglia) also deals with the rural environment in criticising the 'disciplinary shortsightedness' of the economic (orthodox or other), social or natural science perspective in failing to integrate human socio-economic and ecological aspects of environmental conservation and resource use. She advocates a political ecology approach which concentrates on the livelihood strategies of local resource users, identifying the interest groups and analysing the conflicts between them. She applies her approach to a study of the grasslands in the Terai region of Nepal and sets it in the context of the country's changing property rights and conservation policy.

The Terai region has experienced a massive influx of migrants over the past quarter-century while at the same time land has been set aside in a number of national parks, conservation areas and game reserves. The net result has been to squeeze the natural resources in an area where they were hitherto considered to be in abundant supply. The chapter identifies no fewer than eight separate groups with an interest in using the resources and it reviews measures for resolving their differences. The movement towards a constitutional monarchy in Nepal strengthens the prospect of engaging the hitherto marginalised groups in the decision-making process. Such a trend is, of course, in line with the general push to engage people more fully in the development process.

The final chapter by Anu Bose (University of Birmingham), like many others in this book, draws attention to the social relationships of production, a factor all too easily neglected by the simplifying assumptions and high levels of aggregation favoured within the orthodox perspective. Chapter 13 analyses the way in which low-caste *mazdoors* in Calcutta are able to secure a living and to interact with the rest of society by virtue of the monopoly they have in handling waste material. The dynamism of this social relationship is illustrated with reference to the adaptation of the *mazdoors* to technological developments in waste disposal. As the Calcutta housing market changed during the 1980s and demand for the *mazdoors* traditional 'private sweeping' services contracted, so the more enterprising among them entered new markets which dealt with the waste collected in an expanding system of roadside waste containers.

The *mazdoors* therefore currently participate in three markets. The traditional market for public and private waste management remains, but the newer markets include one for the right of access to waste from the new system of roadside containers and a further market for the recycling of wastes in those containers. In all three markets, competition is strictly defined according to caste, and roles within the markets are also assigned along gender lines. Bose concludes that none of the markets she has analysed conforms to the perfect markets so beloved of neo-classical economists, rather they are socially constructed and work within a set of local, social, political and cultural contexts.

The dialogue between orthodox and unorthodox perspectives which provides the theme of this book has shown sharp differences of opinion. Yet in one sense at least those divergences stem from a misunderstanding about the objectives of each approach. The orthodox perspective has sought to define a powerful paradigm for analysing fundamental economic parameters which seeks to summarise the lessons of the various post-war economic experiments with a view to discarding those which have failed. In the process, the simplifying assumptions which it has made leave it open to attack from those economists who dispute the lessons drawn and also from those non-economists who doubt the utility of the 'economic' approach in the first place.

Such a dialogue is to be welcomed because there is much of merit in both sides of the debate and the exchange of insights presents a challenge to both sides to limit the extent to which their perspectives merit criticism. It may be that some integration of the differing views can be achieved. For example, the orthodox economists might seek to improve the objectivity of their approach and to demonstrate more clearly how the characteristics and values of differing societies can be incorporated within it. For their part, the critics of orthodoxy might recognise that economics is not simply the intellectual apparatus of greed and exploitation and profit and loss, but rather about improving social welfare based on the efficient allocation of scarce resources and, as such, is capable of embracing a much wider set of values than many of its critics might suppose.

Part I:
Economic Responses

2 Lowest Common Denominator or Neoliberal Manifesto? The Polemics of the Washington Consensus[1]

John Williamson

When Dr Auty invited me to address the annual conference of the Development Studies Association in 1994, he told me that the intent of the conference organisers was to challenge orthodoxy. He also told me that he would like me to talk about what I somewhat unfortunately dubbed the 'Washington consensus' when I first attempted to assemble a list of the reforms that mainstream opinion in Washington believed the Latin American countries needed to make in order to emerge from the debt crisis and join East Asia on the path of catch-up growth. I protested that these were mutually contradictory specifications since the Washington consensus was a lowest common denominator of orthodoxy. He replied that deriding orthodoxy was such a common practice in the Development Studies Association that defending it would be a true challenge to orthodoxy, thus leaving me with no option but to accept his invitation.

I start this chapter with a brief summary of the ten points of the Washington consensus, more or less as I first laid them out in 1989. I then proceed to describe why I though it would be useful to do this. The next section contains a discussion of whether subsequent developments would suggest a need to modify the original list. I conclude with some conjectures on why the Washington consensus became interpreted in some quarters as a neoliberal manifesto.

THE WASHINGTON CONSENSUS

In my original presentation (Williamson, 1990, ch. 2) I laid out ten specific policy prescriptions as commanding a consensus in Washington. These may be summarised as follows:

1. *Fiscal discipline*. Budget deficits, properly measured to include provincial governments, state enterprises and the central bank, should be small enough to be financed without recourse to the inflation tax. This typically implies a primary surplus (that is, before adding debt service to expenditure) of several per cent of Gross Domestic Product (GDP), and an operational deficit (that is, the deficit disregarding that part of the interest bill that simply compensates for inflation) of no more than about 2 per cent of GDP.

2. *Public expenditure priorities*. Expenditure should be redirected from politically sensitive areas which typically receive more resources than their economic return can justify, like administration, defence, indiscriminate subsidies and white elephants, toward neglected fields with high economic returns and the potential to improve income distribution, like primary health and education, and infrastructure.

3. *Tax reform* involves broadening the tax base and cutting marginal tax rates. The aim is to sharpen incentives and improve horizontal equity without lowering realised progressivity. Improved tax administration (including subjecting interest income on assets held abroad – flight capital – to taxation) is an important aspect of broadening the base in the Latin context.

4. *Financial liberalisation*. The ultimate objective is market-determined interest rates, but experience has shown that, under conditions of a chronic lack of confidence, market-determined rates can be so high as to threaten the financial solvency of productive enterprises and government. Under that circumstance a sensible interim objective is the abolition of preferential interest rates for privileged borrowers and achievement of a moderately positive real interest rate.

5. *Exchange rates*. Countries need a unified (at least for trade transactions) exchange rate set at a level sufficiently competitive to induce a rapid growth in non-traditional exports, and managed so as to assure exporters that this competitiveness will be maintained in the future.

6. *Trade liberalisation*. Quantitative trade restrictions should be rapidly replaced by tariffs, and these should be progressively reduced until a uniform low tariff in the range of 10 per cent (or at most around 20 per cent) is achieved. There is, however, some disagreement about the speed with which tariffs should be reduced (with recommendations falling in a band between three and ten years), and about whether it is advisable to slow down the process of

liberalisation when macroeconomic conditions are adverse (recession and payments deficit).

7. *Foreign direct investment.* Barriers impeding the entry of foreign firms should be abolished; foreign and domestic firms should be allowed to compete on equal terms.

8. *Privatisation.* State enterprises should be privatised.

9. *Deregulation.* Governments should abolish regulations that impede the entry of new firms or restrict competition, and ensure that all regulations are justified by such criteria as safety, environmental protection, or prudential supervision of financial institutions.

10. *Property rights.* The legal system should provide secure property rights without excessive costs, and make these available to the informal sector.

THE PURPOSE OF THE EXERCISE

The origins of the Washington consensus lie back in 1989, when I was expressing my support for the Brady Plan in front of a US Congressional Committee. I argued that many Latin American countries had started to make overdue and profound changes in their economic policies, which deserved support by the industrial countries in the form of a measure of debt relief. A few weeks later I found myself at a seminar at the Institute for Development Studies (IDS) at Sussex describing what I had argued before that Committee and defending my support of the Brady Plan: I was challenged by Hans Singer to identify the policy changes that I regarded as so welcome. In an attempt to respond to this challenge I made a list of the ten reforms laid out above, which I thought both did and should command general support in Washington, which is what I christened the 'Washington consensus'.

In November 1989 the Institute for International Economics convened a conference focused on that list. The conference first discussed whether I had accurately reported the opinions prevalent in Washington. Stanley Fischer (who was then the Chief Economist at the World Bank) agreed that there had been a substantial convergence in policy recommendations but suggested an alternative taxonomy that seemed to me to be less specific but largely to overlap in substance, with the important exception that he wanted to include the social agenda in a far more explicit way than my mention of health and education in the second point. Richard Feinberg also agreed that there had been a major convergence but argued that my term 'Washington consensus' both overstated the degree of agreement within Washington and understated the geographical range over which convergence had occurred, and argued that I should have called it the 'universal convergence' instead. I agree that this would have been a better term, although I regret it is now too late to change it.

My main concern as to the accuracy of my reporting of what commands a consensus in Washington concerns point 5, the need for a competitive exchange rate. In retrospect I worry that my reporting may have been clouded by wishful thinking. At the height of the debt crisis there may have been a dominant concern that exchange rate policy, at least in Latin America, should be guided by concerns to establish adequate competitiveness, but already by 1989 the International Monetary Fund (IMF) (especially its EC Executive Directors) was beginning to succumb to nominal anchor theology, while the US Treasury has almost always been dominated by gung-ho floaters. Those of us who want to see exchange rates managed, with a dominant concern being to maintain adequate competitiveness, may well be a minority.

Having constructed my list and reassured ourselves that it was a reasonable portrayal of mainstream thought, we then had a number of papers that examined particular Latin countries with a view to establishing the extent to which local opinion was on the same wavelength and the extent to which policy had been modified. In very broad terms, one can say that the opinions of Latin economists had also converged, perhaps as much as in Washington, and that political opinion had also changed quite a long way, but that public opinion was still hostile. There had been quite a bit of action, although the record was distinctly spotty.

I gathered enough material to confirm the case that I had been making in support of the Brady Plan in the spring of 1989, although it was a bit late in the day for that purpose. On the other hand, the battle to modernise economic policy in Latin America was still very much in progress. It is certainly true that my list was invoked by some of those urging such reforms, albeit with complaints that the term 'Washington consensus' did a disservice to the cause by suggesting that the reforms were being made in response to pressure from Washington rather than because of local recognition that the changes were desirable. Enrique Iglesias (the President of the Inter-American Development Bank) told me that I should have called it the 'Latin American consensus' to emphasise the extent of the change in attitudes within the region. I take the point that it was a very bad name from the standpoint of making propaganda within Latin America in favour of economic reform, but can only plead that my original propaganda intention, to the extent that there was one, was to make propaganda in Washington in favour of debt relief, from which standpoint the name is surely a rather good one.

AN UPDATING

To what extent would 'Washington' (meaning essentially the US government and the international financial institutions) still endorse this agenda? And are there additional policy issues on which consensus has since coalesced?

It is in my view wrong to interpret the advent of the Clinton administration as marking any general weakening of support for the range of reforms summarised in the Washington consensus. There were of course changes of emphasis: for example, somewhat less hypocrisy was involved in the support for fiscal discipline on the part of other countries. There was surely more enthusiasm for increasing public expenditure on basic education and health, and less concern to achieve fiscal discipline by cutting public expenditure rather than by increasing taxes. But by and large I would judge that there is about as much support for the programme as a whole as there was before, which is hardly surprising inasmuch as I had drawn up the list on the basis of the lowest common denominator of what could command a consensus and the Clinton appointees were not a bunch of Washington outsiders in the way that the original Reagan appointees were.

Similarly, the advocacy of what were termed 'market-friendly policies' by the 1991 *World Development Report* marked an attempt to give a more positive emphasis to the role of the state implied in my list by the remarks on public expenditure priorities, rather than any rejection of what I intended the Washington consensus to comprise. Other changes in view regarding the role of the state, such as greater sympathy for industrial policy on the part of the Clinton administration than its predecessor, relate to topics that I had deliberately excluded from my list because I did not believe they commanded a consensus.

The important changes since late 1989 in what commands a consensus in Washington concern not the abandonment of anything that was then accepted but rather additions to the list. Until the end of the 1970s it was generally taken for granted that policy should be concerned not just with the level and growth of income, but also that income distribution mattered (with a more egalitarian distribution being presumptively better). That view was self-consciously rejected by the first Reagan administration, but concern with the social dimension of economic policy gradually re-emerged. As already mentioned, Stanley Fischer raised this topic spontaneously when discussing my original paper:

> Emphasis on poverty reduction has increased in recent years and will continue to do so. The concern with poverty reduction goes beyond the belief that economic growth will reduce poverty, to the view that specific policies, such as targeted food subsidies as well as the medical and educational programs to which Williamson refers, can reduce the number of poor people in a given country and should be used for that purpose.

I was delighted that Fischer felt that the World Bank had got back to the point where such a view could be expressed by its Chief Economist, but I doubted nonetheless whether his inclusion of poverty reduction in the wider consensus was justified at that time.

However, his prediction that the issue would become increasingly salient proved to be correct. The World Bank devoted the 1990 issue of its *World Development Report* to poverty. The Inter-American Development Bank held a major conference on Social Reform and Poverty in early 1993, and now devotes a large portion of its lending programme to socially oriented projects. Concern with the social dimension was fully reinstated with the advent of the Clinton administration. Both the Agency for International Development (AID) and the World Bank now explicitly include 'sustainable development' among their priorities.

Can this concern be summarised by any propositions comparable to the preceding ten in terms of their scope and the breadth of the consensus that they can command? Two possible candidates would be:

1. *Social expenditure.* Public expenditure priorities should include social expenditures with a high pay-off in terms of assisting the most disadvantaged and improving income distribution, such as targeted welfare payments and the provision of piped water and low-cost, self-help housing.[2]
2. *Birth control.* Universal access to birth control should be provided at the earliest possible date.

I doubt that one could go further by claiming a consensus in favour of more progressive taxation or land reform. These strike me as among the many important topics on which differences of view persist among those who think of themselves as part of the broad middle-ground that takes mainstream middle-brow economics seriously.

A 'NEOLIBERAL MANIFESTO'?

I have repeatedly emphasised that the Washington consensus was first drawn up as a lowest common denominator rather than as a manifesto. It lacks (or at least lacked) many planks that I would have included had I been intending to draw up a manifesto, notably those regarding the social dimension. It also lacked a number of points that most conservatives would want to see included in a manifesto, such as the abolition of capital controls, the absence of incomes and industrial policies, and the minimisation of taxation. The reason that these topics were excluded is that I did not believe that conservatives would have endorsed the social agenda or that others would have endorsed the anti-statist agenda, so that neither was eligible for inclusion in a lowest common denominator.

I was therefore surprised and discomfited when I discovered that people I would normally expect to be my intellectual friends were interpreting the Washington consensus as something pernicious and describing it as a neoliberal manifesto. My initial puzzle was to discover what the term 'neoliberal' meant. Since I have always regarded myself as a liberal in every sense (for example, both to the east of the Atlantic where its antonym is 'socialist' and to the west where its antonym is 'conservative'), I assumed that I must be a neoliberal too, but this did not seem to square with the way the term was being used. I eventually tracked down a definition somewhere in Mario Simonsen's latest book (Simonsen, 1994) along with the analysis of relativity and Beethoven's ninth symphony. He identifies it with the economic policies pursued by Ronald Reagan and Margaret Thatcher under the inspiration of Friedrich Hayek and Milton Friedman. Since I have never seen much historical continuity between the humanism of the classical liberals like John Locke, Adam Smith and John Stuart Mill and the hostility to social action of Hayek and Friedman, let alone of their political admirers, this struck me as an abuse of language.

But if 'neoliberalism' means what I would have thought it more natural to call 'conservative' or 'neoconservative', then I am clear that I am not a neoliberal and I would deny that the Washington consensus, in the form that I invented it, can reasonably be interpreted as a neoliberal manifesto. It avoids any hint of the taxation phobia that characterises the right of the political spectrum, nor does it call for abolishing capital controls and avoiding incomes and industrial policies. How, therefore, can one explain the fact that it became widely interpreted as a neoliberal manifesto?

One hypothesis is that this is a consequence of the name that I pinned upon it. I do not believe that the way things are named is as immaterial as suggested by Shakespeare's 'What's in a name? A rose by any other name, Would smell as sweet...'. Had the rose been called 'thornflower', which is a rather accurate description, would it have been as big a commercial success? And the suspicion is that mentioning Washington suggested to many the imposition of economic correctness by Washington, or dependency, or the arrogance occasionally displayed by employees of the IMF and World Bank in their dealings with member countries, or the triumphalism of the American right at the collapse of communism. Indeed, I suspect that many of those who most fervently denounce the Washington consensus as a neoliberal manifesto have never actually read what I wrote, but that the hostility to what is associated with Washington was sufficient to persuade them that I must be an apostle of what they disliked.

Another hypothesis is that the wording of some of the propositions may have given rise to the misconception. 'State enterprises should be privatised' is, it is true, a little bald. It can be interpreted in the sense that it was written, to say that all Latin American countries in 1989 had a number of state enterprises that were strong candidates for privatisation. But it can also be read to say that every state enterprise everywhere should be privatised, including the water works and British Rail, which is a proposition that would be unconvincing to many reasonable people.

A third hypothesis is more worrying: that it was labelled a neoliberal manifesto in an attempt to discredit the paradigm change that has occurred in thought on development over the past quarter-century. For, while the ten points on my list may seem to be 'economic common sense'[3] to many of us, they do represent a sharp break from the import substitution, nationalisation, planning, and use of the inflation tax to raise savings that were once standard policy recommendations among development economists. The old paradigm said that development demanded a strong state able to mobilise savings, direct investment, and assure a market for the additional output the investment permits. The new paradigm says that development demands that individuals be empowered through education and that society provide enough physical and social infrastructure (meaning a stable money and laws governing contract and so on, as well as law and order) to enable individuals to plug themselves into the world economy. One has to expect that someone who still believes the old paradigm will resist enthroning the second as common sense.

CONCLUDING REMARKS

I was once told that the mere fact that I invented the term 'Washington consensus' does not give me any particular right to dictate what the term means. I accept that language is a living thing and that meanings change over time. All I have a right to do, on this view, is to dissociate myself from a meaning that I find offensive. If I cannot change the meaning of the term back to what Thatcher and Reagan have in common with Blair and Clinton (to include what survived to be absorbed into the mainstream from the original set of policies pursued by Thatcher and Reagan, which is not negligible, but to exclude monetarism and supply-side fantasies), then I will have to join in denouncing the Washington consensus.

But I am reluctant to make such a semantic surrender. As long as I am called the 'father of the Washington consensus' (as I was in the Brazilian press in mid-1994), I think I have a special right to say what the term means. It is not a neoliberal manifesto, but rather a list of what a certain group of people believed at a certain point in time would have been good policy for a certain group of countries. That leaves several issues, all more productive than semantic controversy, that can sensibly be debated. One is whether I accurately reported on what the certain group of people actually thought, which corresponds to John Toye's first interpretation of the Washington consensus as 'the outcome of an opinion survey' (in Williamson, 1994, p. 39). A second is whether they were correct in their assessment, which would cover debate between the two paradigms sketched above and roughly corresponds to John Toye's second interpretation of the Washington consensus as 'a statement of what "serious" economists ought to believe'.[4] A third is not Toye's neoliberal manifesto, an interpretation that I have already rejected, but rather focuses on the application of those rather general principles to specific situations, and on the issues that are not claimed to be resolved. This actually strikes me as the most interesting agenda, although it is the one about which I have said least in this chapter. But it will have been worth indulging in these semantic elaborations if they clear the way for substantive discussion on the topics where debate can prove most fruitful. (I do not endorse John Toye's insinuation that an attempt to focus debate in this way amounts to censorship that will threaten the further advance of knowledge.)

NOTES

1.   A paper presented to the annual conference of the Development Studies Association at Lancaster on 8 September 1994 and to be published by Macmillan in the conference proceedings. Copyright Institute for International Economics. All rights reserved.
2.   This goes further than the second entry in the earlier list, in endorsing social expenditures with a high equity pay-off even if they cannot be rationalised

by a presumption of an increased rate of growth. It retains the basic view that equity concerns should be addressed through fiscal measures, primarily the composition of public expenditures, rather than through directed or sub-sidised credit, trade policy, or populist macroeconomics.

3.   As another Brazilian economist, Marcílio Marques Moreira, suggested I should have called the Washington consensus.

4.   Oral comment by John Toye at the 1994 DSA conference.

REFERENCES

Simonsen, Mario Henrique (1994), *Ensaios Analíticos* (Rio de Janeiro: Editora da Fundacão Getulio Vargas).

Williamson, John (ed.) (1990), *Latin American Adjustment: How Much Has Happened?* (Washington, DC: Institute for International Economics).

Williamson, John (1994), *The Political Economy of Policy Reform* (Washington, DC: Institute for International Economics).

World Bank (1990), *World Development Report 1990* (Washington, DC: World Bank).

World Bank (1991), *World Development Report 1991* (Washington, DC: World Bank).

3 Is the Debt Crisis Largely Over? A Critical Look at the Data of International Financial Institutions

Kunibert Raffer

Latin America
016
019
F34

INTRODUCTION

While the 1980s became known as the decade of the debt crisis, the 1990s have been heralded as the years of hope and recovery, if not for all debtors then at least for those having adopted 'prudent' economic policies. In other words, the present situation of Latin America is used – with cautious caveats regarding sustainability – as the practical vindication of Bretton Woods-type adjustment policies.

As early as 1991 the Inter-American Development Bank's report *Economic and Social Progress in Latin America* titled its first part 'The Nineties: A Decade of Hope'. In spite of a Gross Domestic Product (GDP) per capita at the level of 1977 and a drastic fall in standards of living not experienced in the region for half a century it thought greater optimism for this decade justified (Inter-American Development Bank 1991, p. 5). The following report of 1992 starts with the ominous formulation 'The Recovery Begins' (Inter-American Development Bank 1992, p. 1), strongly recalling the famous 'Recovery has begun' (IBRD & UNDP, 1989, p. iii), used by the International Bank for Reconstruction and Development (IBRD) and the United Nations Development Programme (UNDP) to herald the economic recovery of sub-Saharan Africa in 1989.

In its *World Debt Tables 1992/93* the IBRD concludes with regard to 'a number of' Latin American countries: 'With debt indicators now back to pre-1982 levels, most of these countries are emerging from the debt crisis, helped in some cases by the catalytic effects of reductions in their commercial bank debt' (*World Debt Tables 1992*, p. 3). It is also fast becoming general wisdom according to the IBRD (*World Debt Tables 1992*, p. 41) that the recent resumption of large capital flows into some Latin American countries heralds the end of the debt crisis. For 'commercial

23

banks and some of their middle-income developing country borrowers, the debt crisis ... is largely over', as proved by 'renewed portfolio flows [which] are part of a wider (albeit still fragile) return to market access' (*World Debt Tables 1992*, p. 7). In short, Latin America has dealt with its debt overhang (cf. *World Debt Tables 1993*, p. 5). Pointing at over two dozen low and lower-middle-income countries still under debt pressure, the IBRD sees a growing dichotomy between middle-income and poor debtors. It is generally agreed that the debt crisis is still felt in some countries, notably in sub-Saharan Africa, or by Severely Indebted Low Income Countries, a group largely identical with sub-Saharan Africa. These countries, the argument goes, have not embraced 'sound' policies as eagerly.

The IBRD takes care to place caveats more visibly than in 1989 – possibly a fine example of learning by doing. It warns, for example, that complacency might be premature as 'The newer portfolio flows are generally more volatile and their marked redirection to a few developing countries is to some extent an outcome of low interest rates in their home markets, as well as one-off adjustment in the composition of individual and institutional investor portfolios' (*World Debt Tables 1992*, p. 3). Similarly, strong concerns about the sustainability of some of the new capital flows are noted (*World Debt Tables 1993*, pp. 4ff).

This chapter examines to what extent this cautious vindication of success can be justified by data and indicators published by the International Financial Institutions, mainly the IBRD and the International Monetary Fund (IMF), themselves. It analyses the debt situation of Latin America (Latin America and the Caribbean in IBRD terminology) in general, and of the countries with so-called 'Brady-restructurings'. As it is generally agreed that the crisis is not over in Africa, this region is not dealt with. This chapter concludes that a closer look at the IBRD's own publications does not show that the debt overhang has been overcome in Latin America, nor does it justify the vindication of successful 'adjustment policies' at the moment. A new indicator of debt overhang is proposed, reflecting the actual debt burden better than the traditional debt indicators used by International Financial Institutions.

ANALYSING LATIN AMERICA'S DEBTS

The literature defines debt overhang as a situation where the debt burden is so disproportionately large that conceivable efforts to pay according to contract could not ameliorate the debtor's situation. The fruits of such efforts would thus accrue exclusively to creditors. Krugman (1988) defines it as the expected present value of potential future resource transfers being less than a country's debt, or – less formally – existing debts 'sufficiently large that creditors do not expect with confidence to be fully repaid'. Similarly, *World Debt Tables 1992* (p. 11) defines the 'reduction of debt obligations in line with ability to pay' as removing the debt overhang. According to both definitions, arrears (that is, incapability to service debts in line with obligations) are a clear and undeniable proof of a debt over-hang. Furthermore, arrears should make creditors cautious.

The IBRD's *World Debt Tables* warn readers that conclusions drawn from debt indicators will not be valid unless accompanied by careful economic evaluation (cf. *World Debt Tables 1992*, vol. II, p. v). The claim that debt indicators are now back to pre-1982 levels should thus be evaluated with this 'necessary caveat' in mind. As Table 3.1 shows, the IBRD's traditional debt indicators have actually declined. However, as the IBRD measures payments on a cash basis (payments made), not on the basis of payments due, low ratios of debt service or interest payments to exports or Gross National Product (GNP) can result from two very different situations. A country without any debts would logically have ratios of zero. So would a country with huge debts but not paying a single penny. If used to describe a country's indebtedness these indicators might be misleading. Using payments contractually due, calculated by adding arrears to actual payments, rather than the IBRD's traditional indicators, is thus more meaningful. Calling debt service obligations 'the real measures of debt burden' the IBRD (1989, p. 21) recognised this fact some time ago.

This real measure of debt pressure might escape notice unless one follows the IBRD's caveat to look beyond its traditional debt indicators. As the IBRD started to publish data on arrears some years ago, this correction – already suggested by Raffer (1993a) – can be done easily. Table 3.1 shows the differences in debt indicators resulting from the two approaches. As the figures differ between *World Debt Tables* issues, it should be added that latest available data were used.

Interest and principal arrears are only available on long-term debt. Actual arrears will be higher unless short-term debts – which were around 18.5 per cent during 1989–91, or around US\$ 67 billion in 1990 and 1991 – are always serviced fully on time. This might not be as assured as with regard to the other component of total debts, IMF drawings, which exploded between 1980 and 1991 from slightly less than 0.6 per cent of total debts to nearly 4 per cent. IMF drawings multiplied (in current dollars) by 12.3 times. Furthermore, total debt service does not include principal repayments of short-term debt.

TABLE 3.1: *Latin America's Arrears and Debt Service 1980–93* (Million US$/%)

	1980	1982	1983	1984	1985	1986	1987	1988	1989	1990	1991	1992	1993ᵖ
Arrears of:													
Interest	66	332	1 198	3 286	2 873	3 711	8 554	9 014	17 077	26 019	27 782	21 625	14 995
Principal	623	n.a.	n.a.	n.a.	6 969	9 563	12 394	15 073	18 495	25 933	26 460	25 484	23 694
Sum	689	n.a.	n.a.	n.a.	9 842	13 274	20 948	24 087	35 572	51 952	54 242	47 109	38 689
Actual Payments:													
INT*	24 580	37 572	34 760	35 254	34 750	30 371	28 850	33 834	26 313	22 830	24 082	22 931	23 946
TDS†	46 265	59 045	50 237	51 627	47 691	48 373	47 019	55 464	51 307	46 094	45 816	54 284	57 342
Payments Due (Arrears + Actual Payments):													
INTᵈ	24 646	37 904	35 958	38 540	37 623	34 082	37 404	42 848	43 390	48 849	51 864	44 556	38 941
TDSᵈᵗ	46 954	n.a.	n.a.	n.a.	57 533	61 647	67 967	79 551	86 879	98 046	100 058	101 393	96 031
DSR and ISR (Cash Base):‡													
ISR	19.7	30.3	29.8	27.2	27.9	27.4	23.4	24.3	16.9	13.3	13.6	12.6	12.3
DSR	37.1	47.6	43.0	39.9	38.2	43.7	38.1	39.8	32.9	26.9	25.9	29.8	29.5

TABLE 3.1: *Continued*

	1980	1982	1983	1984	1985	1986	1987	1988	1989	1990	1991	1992	1993[p]
Contractual DSR and ISR:[§]													
ISR[d]	19.8	30.6	30.8	29.7	30.2	30.8	30.3	30.8	27.8	28.5	29.3	24.4	20.0
DSR[d]	37.7	n.a.	n.a.	n.a.	46.1	55.7	55.1	57.1	55.7	57.1	56.6	55.6	50.4

* Interest
[†] Total Debt Service = Interest payments plus principal repayments (cash base: actual payments irrespective of contractual oligations)
[‡] DSR = Debt Service Ratio: (actual) total debt service/exports of goods and services
ISR = Interest Service Ratio: (actual) interest payments/exports of goods and services
[§d] indicates that payments contractually due (not actually made) are used in the numerator
[p] projected
SOURCE: *World Debt Tables*, various issues; calculations based thereon.

For 1992 only estimates of interest arrears are available in *World Debt Tables 1992*. The US$ 21,625 million interest and US$ 25,484 million principal arrears of *World Debt Tables 1993* would mean a slight increase of arrears to US$ 47,109 million. Adding these (26 per cent of export earnings) to the 29.8 per cent debt service ratio of the *World Debt Tables 1992* the real ratio in 1992 would be 55.8 per cent, well above the ratio of 1980. The contractual interest service ratio (ISR^d) would be 24.4 per cent, nearly double the 12.6 per cent or 12.1 per cent of the *World Debt Tables 1993* and *1992*, respectively. Taking the estimates for 1992 published in *World Debt Tables 1992* a contractual interest service ratio of 24.6 would result, also well above the 19.6 per cent of 1980. The IBRD's opinion on lower debt indicators quoted above thus only holds for the region if one disregards arrears.

According to the newest *World Debt Tables* (1993) the projected 1993 figures for interest payments show a contractual interest service ratio which is actually equivalent to 1980 (as no arrears are published for 1981, this is the only pre-debt-crisis year that can be used). The contractual debt service ratio, however, the more important indicator for foreign exchange needs, is still well above 50 per cent, and also above the level of 1980.

It is of particular importance to note that arrears of interests have been perceptibly higher than actual interest payments in 1990 (113.6 per cent) for the first time, in 1991 (115.4 per cent), and nearly as big in 1992 (94.3 per cent). Principal arrears were higher than repayments in 1990 (111.5 per cent), 1991 (121.7 per cent) and 82 per cent in 1992 (*World Debt Tables 1993*). Not surprisingly – considering the privileged position of some official lenders – private creditors accounted for most of these arrears, between 83 and 87.8 per cent in the case of interest, and from 69.7 to 73 per cent in the case of principal.

Until 1991 Latin America's contractual debt service ratio was markedly worse than sub-Saharan Africa's (*World Debt Tables 1993*). As no arrears are shown for the big debtor Mexico (nor for Chile and Uruguay) the situation for Latin America excluding Mexico (LA–M in Table 3.2) is even more drastic. Its contractual interest service ratio was 27.2 in 1992, its contractual debt service ratio 59.5.

The sharp drop in interest arrears projected for 1993 accounts for the relatively favourable interest service ratios. Interest and principal repayments are somewhat higher than in 1992, and total and long-term debt increase. Theoretically this decline can thus only be explained by:

(a) a fall in interest rates during 1993 large enough to reduce arrears by one-third and interest due (defined as arrears plus interest paid) by 12.6 per cent, a reduction of the average interest rate by one-eighth;

(b)   capitalisation of interest arrears; or,
(c)   forgiving arrears.

The first explanation can be ruled out. Two possibilities remain, both of which disguise the actual incapability to service debt. Actually, 'Interest capitalised' increased dramatically in the region during the last years: it more than doubled from US$ 606 million in 1989 to US$ 1.312 billion in 1990, grew to US$ 2.857 billion in 1991 and US$ 9.278 billion in 1992. For 1993 US$ 8.6 billion are projected in the IBRD's explanation of debt stock changes (Debt Stock-Flow Reconciliation), which easily accommodates the fall in arrears of US$ 6.629 billion. In 1992, most of the reduction resulted from the clearance of arrears, especially by Brazil. However, its US$ 9 billion settlement was immediately followed by new arrears of US$ 2.7 billion in the same year (*World Debt Tables* 1993, p. 32). In other words, according to the *World Debt Tables* the reduction of arrears is not due to an economic improvement, but simply to capitalising unpaid interest. Adjusting arrears for capitalised interest for the region in the 1990s (when it exploded), renders:

	1990	*1991*	*1992*	*1993*
INT Arrears* ($ mill.)	27 331	30 639	30 903	23 595
ISR[d]*	29.2	30.9	29.5	24.4
DSR[d]*	57.9	58.2	60.7	53.8

* adjusted for capitalised interest
[d] indicates that payments contractually due (not actually made) are used in the
   numerator

In other words: the perceived end of the debt crisis in Latin America is often due to the toleration of extremely large non-payments, or breaches of contract. Mostly private creditors have to carry the burden. Rather than a recovery these figures recall Maddison's (1985, p. 28) description of Latin America in the 1930s when 'debt default eased payments constraints', and creditors acquiesced in the situation.

Naturally the global decline in interest rates since their apex in the 1980s has had beneficial effects, lowering interest service ratios perceptibly. The importance of interest rates is immediately clarified by pointing out that average rates of new commitments were 11.6 per cent in 1980 and 7.2 per cent in 1992. As 53 per cent of long-term debts were at variable rates in 1992, an increase to the level of 1980 would mean about US$

9 billion more to pay. Eventually this shift would also be reflected in higher interest rates of non-variable rate loans. Each percentage point increase of the average interest rate is equivalent to roughly US$ 5 billion. Contractual debt service ratios, however, which are most important from the point of view of foreign exchange needs, have remained nearly constant during 1986–92, above 55 per cent. Even with the optimistic projection of interest arrears for 1993 every other Latin dollar would have to go to creditors if contractual obligations were honoured.

Although it is not possible to analyse the special case of Mexico here in depth, some remarks are necessary. The country benefited from a unique, special relation to the US. Already under Baker the US abandoned insisting on full repayment in the case of its Southern neighbour. The subsequent Brady Plan was executed most generously there because expectations of the North American Free Trade Agreement (NAFTA) and higher oil prices during the last Gulf War benefited Mexico. In 1982 huge reschedulings took place. As early as 1985 Mexico could reschedule a debt stock equivalent to 54.3 per cent of its long-term debt. Between 1985 and 1992 Mexico was allowed to reschedule every year. The cumulative amount of these reschedulings is US$ 136.4 billion, or 120.3 per cent of its total debt stock in 1992. Mexico rescheduled soon after the beginning of the debt crisis, a fact recognised by *World Debt Tables* (1992, p. 47) in a graph. Nevertheless *World Debt Tables* statistics on the country state that data on restructuring for this time is not available.

By contrast the region of Latin America excluding Mexico rescheduled a total amount of US$ 226.507 billion (1986–92), or 45.6 per cent. Mexico's debt was reduced by US$ 17.677 billion during 1988–92, or 15.6 per cent of its total debt stock, while the debts of the rest of Latin America were reduced by only 9.9 per cent. Briefly put, Mexico did face particularly sympathetic creditors and a most helpful environment. Still it has had to reschedule or capitalise some interest payments every year since 1986 (except in 1988). Nevertheless its debt service ratio was 44.4 per cent in 1992, well below the 49.5 per cent of 1980, but much higher than the 26.3 per cent of 1990. In spite of principal repayments of US$ 13 billion in 1992, total debts diminished by less than US$ 2 billion. Finally 30-year 'bullet' maturities of both par and discount bonds mean no debt service until repayment will be due, a considerable reduction of debt service. The IBRD calculated a net debt service effect of Mexico's Brady package during 1990–94 of US$ 1.8 billion on average (*World Debt Tables 1990*, p. 33), a substantial relief that has to be taken into account when evaluating Mexico's relatively good performance as a debtor.

PROPOSING A NEW DEBT INDICATOR

It is possible to reflect a debt overhang relatively well by one single indicator. As arrears are the clearest sign of a debt overhang, the relation between payments effected and all payments due

$$0 \leq DSR/DSR^{d*} \leq 1$$

is a good index. It is 1 if payments are made on time, zero if the debtor does not pay. It does not suffer from the ambiguity of the interest service ratio (ISR) and the debt service ratio (DSR), which are equally low if a debtor has small debts or if a heavily indebted country simply does not pay. Theoretically DSR^{d*}, which we may call the *real* debt service ratio, must include all payments due but not effected, including interest arrears and amortisation of short-term debt (which are not available) plus capitalised interest. Furthermore, it should include rescheduled principal arrears for every year. Unfortunately data on rescheduling of principal in one year, as provided by the *World Debt Tables*, may (and apparently does) cover more than repayments due in that particular year. Relevant data permitting the allocation of rescheduled principal to the years when it was originally due, are not available. For these practical reasons the real debt service ratio (DSR^{d*}) is defined as the contractual debt service ratio (DSR^d) plus interest capitalised. While an improvement on traditional debt indicators, it, too, understates the burden of debt service.

According to the *World Debt Tables* arrears have increased dramatically during the debt crisis. While the share of interest arrears was negligible in 1980, 0.2 or 0.27 per cent of interest due – depending on whether the data of *World Debt Tables* 1992 or 1993 are correct – this share was projected as 38.5 per cent for 1993, 49.6 per cent including capitalised interest. Principal arrears were supposed to be zero in *World Debt Tables 1992*, but US$ 623 million (2.8 per cent of repayments due) a year later (*World Debt Tables 1993*), increasing to US$ 23.7 billion (41.5 per cent of repayments due) in 1993. The ability to pay has apparently deteriorated substantially. Even if it were not the ability but the willingness to pay, this, too, should make creditors equally cautious.

The evolution of our debt overhang index is depicted in Table 3.2. For 1980 no data on capitalised interests are available, but it may be deduced from historical facts that such capitalisations – if they occurred – must have been very small. Uruguay is not shown among the 'Brady countries' because it had – like Chile – always an index of 1.

TABLE 3.2: *Evolution of the Debt Overhang (DSR/DSR^{d*})*

	1980^a	1988	1989	1990	1991	1992	1993^p
Latin America	.9853	.6918	.5865	.4639	.4452	.4905	.5480
LA–M	.9809	.6181	.4979	.3950	.3606	.3736	n.a.
Argentina	1	.5493	.3501	.3328	.2860	.2606	n.a.
Costa Rica	.9944	.2829	.2044	.5536	.5854	.8097	n.a.
Mexico	1	.9999	.9917	.9825	.9885	.9963	n.a.
Philippines	1	.8876	.9068	.8957	.8705	.8979	n.a.
Venezuela	.9915	.9946	.9871	1	1	.8422	n.a.
Brazil	.9691	.9023	.7337	.3800	.3321	.3449	n.a.

^{a} capitalised interest not available
^{p} projected
SOURCE: *World Debt Tables 1993*.

Some interesting facts emerge from this presentation of the IBRD's data. First, one need not be a 'good' debtor to be eligible for so-called Brady-type (or one should rather say Miyazawa-type) relief, as is proved by Argentina, Costa Rica and Brazil (agreement in principle reached on 9 August 1992). Second, except in the case of Costa Rica these time series do not reflect positive impacts by Brady-type reductions on debt servicing in the early 'Brady-countries' so far, not even in the Philippines that had a second helping. Costa Rica and the Philippines still cannot service their debts correctly. Third, if a region honours only about half its contractual obligations (34.97 per cent if one deducts Mexico, Chile and Uruguay) one can hardly call the debt crisis over or the debt overhang overcome. The IBRD's statement 'Latin America has benefited from strong inflows of foreign direct investment and portfolio investment thanks to reforms and dealing with its debt overhang' (*World Debt Tables 1993*, p. 5) is definitely not supported by its own figures.

Finally, Argentina, Brazil, Mexico and Venezuela are the main countries in the region able to place bonds (*World Debt Tables 1993*). Brazil, honouring only one-third of its contractual obligations, got large reschedulings in 1992 and was second in attracting new bonds, right after Mexico and before Argentina in 1992 and 1993 (*World Debt Tables 1993*, p. 9). Apparently new bonds worth billions of dollars can be placed by debtors with huge arrears.

A CAVEAT ON DATA

The reliability of (particularly recent) data is another important point. Detailed data submitted to the IBRD by reporting countries form the basis of the *World Debt Tables*. A comparison of time series shows that the following values for the ratio Total Debts/GNP were published for Latin America:

	1986	*1987*	*1988*	*1989*	*1990*	*1991*	*1992*
World Debt Tables 1990	62.0	64.2	53.6	46.7	47.9ᵖ	–	–
World Debt Tables 1992	63.2	64.9	55.6	47.8	42.6	41.4	37.6ᵖ
World Debt Tables 1993	66.7	68.8	43.5	51.0	46.7	45.0	41.7

World Debt Tables 1993 displays a more pronounced improvement, which can be interpreted as more successful 'adjustment' policies. Comparison with other *World Debt Tables* suggests that the *World Debt Tables* 1993 figure for 1988 results from an error regarding Gross National Product (GNP). More interesting still are the slightly different time series in the IMF's *World Economic Outlook* (WEO) on ratios of external debt (total debt without liabilities to the IMF) to GDP:

	1984	*1985*	*1986*	*1987*	*1988*	*1989*	*1990*	*1991*	*1992*	*1993*
WEO89	46.3	45.4	44.1	43.8	38.8	37.0	35.8	–	–	–
WEO93	53.0ᵃ	53.6	51.6	57.3	50.6	43.9	41.1	43.6	37.3	36.5

ᵃ from IMF, *World Economic Outlook* (WEO) 1992.

Values for 1989 and 1990 in *World Economic Outlook 1989*, as well as the figure of 1993 are estimates or projections, naturally subject to estimation errors. The substantial difference for years long gone by such as 1985 or 1986, though, and the very different picture drawn by the two time series, do justify questions. The first line displays a constant (and monotonously falling) reduction of the debt burden, while the second peaks in 1987, falling afterwards. The value of 1989 displayed by the *World Economic Outlook 1989* is again reached in 1992 according to the *World Economic Outlook 1993*. If one assumes a necessary time-lag until 'adjustment' policies can show effects, the lower line would by coincidence more readily support claims of successful 'adjustment' policies.

Suffice one more illustration for the problem of data. The Chilean situation improved drastically between *World Debt Tables* 1992 and *World Debt Tables* 1993. While the former publishes a debt service ratio of 33.9 for 1991, the latter shows 23.1. The interest service ratio nearly halved from 24.3 to 13.3 for 1991. These differences are not easily explicable by usual adjustments of recent data, particularly so as Chile never had any arrears.

Regarding repatriated flight capital, Chile is a good example too. *World Debt Tables* 1993 (p. 4) particularly stresses the importance of repatriation as contributing to the recovery in Latin America. Capital is now flowing back because of sound economic policies (ibid., p. 11). Naturally statistics on capital flight cannot be very precise, and there is certainly reason to believe that repatriation does occur.

During the 1980s when capital flight was – quite correctly – seen as a sign of wrong economic policies, statistics on Chile showed no capital flight, even a slight inflow into the country. This was repeatedly quoted as a proof of the military junta's sound economic policy. All estimates of the 'atypical' Latin American country, for example Pastor (1990) using IMF and IBRD data, or Duwendag (1986), rendered essentially the same result. Duwendag pointed out that existing data showed the opposite of capital flight for Chile, arguing that one could therefore not classify Latin America sweepingly as a capital flight region. A detailed case study on Chile by Arellano and Ramos (1987), estimating capital flight in several ways, finds relatively clear outflows for a very limited period (1982 and partly in 1983). But the sum amounting 'in all likelihood to no more than US\$ 1 billion (or 5 percent of foreign debt)' (ibid., p. 153) is more than compensated by inflows in either 1985 alone or during 1979–80. The authors regret that Chile will not be able to benefit from repatriated capital: 'Unfortunately the modest size of capital flight means that its repatriation – even if it all returned – could reduce Chile's debt no more than 5 percent' (ibid.).

Fortunately Chile was nevertheless able to benefit massively from repatriation as soon as repatriation became the characteristic of sound economic policies. After serving as a model of how to avoid capital flight, it could serve as a model of repatriation. A logical explanation of how money that had never left could return is still needed.

As these examples show, a great deal of caution regarding the data base on which conclusions of recovery rest is indicated. Also, they justify more research into the reliability of these data.

CONCLUSION

The substantial increase in official debts may pose grave problems in the future. In contrast to private banks, the International Financial Institutions neither reschedule nor reduce their claims – a fact which means a 'hardening' of conditions. The present incentive system of the International Financial Institutions allows them to gain from their own errors at their clients' expense, a fact that is at the root of grave management shortcomings (cf. Raffer, 1993b). Also, official debts are not necessarily cheaper than private debts: in 1992 Mexico (0.1 percentage points), Argentina (0.1), the Philippines (0.2) or Uruguay (1.8!) paid higher interest on new official commitments than on private commitments (*World Debt Tables 1993*).

New flows come from new sources of finance, namely bonds (as in the 1930s) and foreign direct investment. In other words, commercial banks handle securities for clients to earn fees, but do not consider recovery secure enough to put substantial sums of their own money into the region again. According to the *World Debt Tables* (1993, p. 5) the region's 'flows to private banks have actually been negative because of voluntary repayments'. Inflows of foreign direct investment are to a considerable part due to privatisation, that is the selling of public companies, and therefore singular, irreproducible events. Once those state enterprises are sold, inflows cease and repatriation of profits soon becomes the preponderant balance of payments effect.

The improvement in developing country access to international capital markets 'has been supported by regulatory changes, particularly in the Japanese bond market. Quality guidelines for Samurai bond issues ... were relaxed further in 1992 and the minimum credit rating ... was lowered from A to BBB' (*World Debt Tables 1993*, pp. 21). Changes in regulation regarding equities making private placement in general more attractive occurred in the US too (cf. IMF, *World Economic Outlook 1993*). These regulatory changes, and a trend towards explicitly rating developing country borrowers at least partially triggered by such changes, allowed institutional investors to place money there.

The volatility of portfolio investments has been repeatedly emphasised also by the IBRD. Calls for a new IMF facility to help countries facing problems due to sudden withdrawals of capital could already be heard. This is all the more important as foreign exchange provided by substantial present inflows seems to be used to service debts. One might suppose that arrears would even be higher without them. To the extent that new foreign exchange has been used for payments to banks or the International

Financial Institutions it is no longer available to cover sudden with-drawals. Some of the risk of being 'stuck' with a debtor nation is being shifted away from private banks and from multilaterals having increased their exposure considerably during the 1980s. This is similar to the larger process of risk-shifting during the 1980s, when inflows by public institutions allowed commercial banks to receive higher (re)payments than otherwise would have been possible. It can be interpreted as a trend of returning to the situation prior to the 1930s, when Latin debt was held by private creditors and banks saw themselves mainly as fee earning intermediators. As Southern debts played the role of junk bonds until the 1930s, the opinion of the IMF that Third World bonds in the 1990s are the new 'junk bonds' (cf. IMF, 1992, p. 31) combines well with this interpretation. This shift to (or bail-out by) new creditors occurred with official support and possibly because of optimism by the International Financial Institutions.

Shifting from predominantly sovereign to mainly private borrowers may well be a reason for concern. During the debt crisis some debtor countries were forced by creditor banks to socialise ex post already de facto insolvent private debts. No International Financial Institution has even criticised this practice, nor was any mechanism constructed to keep this from happening again. Thus these new private-to-private flows may finally end up as a burden on governments.

Growing deficits of current account balances – from US\$ 3.1 billion in 1990 to US\$ 38.5 billion estimated for 1993 (*World Debt Tables 1993*) for Latin America, or an increase of 230 per cent per annum – do not suggest stabilising influences. This sharp deterioration did not happen everywhere in Latin America – Chile and Costa Rica held their current account deficits roughly constant between 1990 and 1992, the latest year available. Mexico's deficit more than trebled during this period (179 per cent per annum). Argentina, Venezuela and Uruguay changed considerably from surpluses to deficits, and Brazil, not a model debtor, changed from US\$ –3.8 billion to a surplus of US\$ 4.1 billion.

The debt overhang, or unserviceable debt, is not gone, with very few possible exceptions such as Mexico. While debt reduction has certainly contributed occasionally and to some extent, the present situation is explained by tolerated non-payment rather than by 'sound economic policies', successful 'structural adjustment' or 'reforms and dealing with its debt overhang'. Pointedly put, if creditors had been prepared to accept much lower (let alone similar) arrears in 1982, be it in percentages of long-term debts or in current dollars, there would have been no debt crisis. Detailed analysis of the data of the International Financial Institutions thus gives at least as much reason for strong scepticism as for cautious optimism.

One final qualification of debt optimism must be made. During 1981–90 gross domestic investment in Latin America fell by 3.1 per cent per annum (Inter-American Development Bank 1992), or from 100 to 73. A growth rate of not less than 8 per cent per annum over four years would be necessary to reach the level of 1981 again.

EPILOGUE

The Mexican crisis of 1994–95 vindicated the call for strong scepticism so clearly, that no qualification of this chapter, which was written in June 1994, is necessary. The only 'success' of orthodox debt strategies seems to have been shifting some risk on to mutual funds, pension funds and retirement accounts – or on to the public at large. Lured by regulatory changes and official optimism they had replaced banks and the International Financial Institutions to an extent that these 'tens of millions of little-guy investors' (*Time*, 13 February 1995) were one reason, if not *the* main argument, for the new US\$ 50 billion bail-out. The fact that the crisis broke in the very country always enjoying privileged treatment as a debtor and showing excellent debt indicators, should be taken into account when evaluating other debtors. The Mexican crisis also strengthens the case for an international insolvency procedure for sovereign borrowers modelled on the US Chapter 9 as an efficient and durable solution with a human face (cf. Raffer, 1990).

REFERENCES

Arellano, J.P. and J. Ramos (1987), 'Chile', in D.R. Lessard and J. Williamson (eds), *Capital Flight and Third World Debt* (Washington DC: Institute of International Economics), pp. 153ff.

Duwendag, D. (1986), 'Kapitalflucht aus Entwicklungsländern: Schätzprobleme und Bestimmungsfaktoren', in A. Gutowski (ed.), *Die internationale Schuldenkrise; Ursachen – Konsequenzen – Historische Erfahrungen*, Schriften des Vereins für Socialpolitik, NF Bd. 155 (Berlin: Duncker & Humblot), pp. 115ff.

Inter-American Development Bank (1991), *Economic and Social Progress in Latin America, 1991 Report* (Washington, DC).

Inter-American Development Bank (1992), *Economic and Social Progress in Latin America, 1992 Report* (Washington, DC).

International Bank for Reconstruction and Development (IBRD) (1989), *Sub-Saharan Africa – From Crisis to Sustainable Growth* (Washington, DC: IBRD).

International Bank for Reconstruction and Development (IBRD) & United Nations Development Programme (UNDP) (1989), *Africa's Adjustment with Growth in the 1980s* (Washington DC: IBRD).

International Monetary Fund (IMF) (1992), *Private Market Financing for Developing Countries* (World Economic and Financial Surveys) December.

International Monetary Fund (IMF), *World Economic Outlook* (WEO) (Washington, DC), October (various years).

Krugman, P. (1988), 'Financing vs. Forgiving a Debt Overhang', *Journal of Development Economics*, 29(3), pp. 253ff.

Maddison, A. (1985), *Two Crises: Latin America and Asia in 1929–38 and 1973–83* (Paris: OECD).

Pastor, M. Jr (1990), 'Capital Flight from Latin America', *World Development*, 18(1), pp. 1ff.

Raffer, K. (1990), 'Applying Chapter 9 Insolvency to International Debts: An Economically Efficient Solution with a Human Face', *World Development*, 18(2), pp. 301ff.

Raffer, K. (1993a), 'Entwicklung und Verschuldung im Lateinamerika der Neunzigerjahre', *Zeitschrift für Lateinamerika*, Wien, No. 43/44, pp. 149ff.

Raffer, K. (1993b), 'International Financial Institutions and Accountability: The Need for Drastic Change', in S.M. Murshed and K. Raffer (eds), *Trade, Transfers and Development, Problems and Prospects for the Twenty-First Century* (Aldershot: E. Elgar) pp. 151ff.

World Debt Tables, IBRD: Washington DC, various years [*WDT 1993–94* quoted *World Debt Tables* 1993].

4 The Environment for Entrepreneurship

Renee Prendergast

LDC's
Ō17
M13

In his *Theory of Economic Development* (TED) (1961), Schumpeter defined development as a distinct phenomenon involving discontinuous change in the channels of flow which forever altered the equilibrium state previously existing (TED, p. 64). According to Schumpeter, such change was a rule initiated by producers rather than consumers of final products. It involved such things as the introduction of a new good or new method of production, the opening of a new market, the conquest of new sources of supply or the fundamental reorganisation of a particular industry (TED, p. 66). Schumpeter labelled the carrying out of these changes or new combinations as enterprise and the individuals who carried them out as entrepreneurs.

While Schumpeter accepted that some environments were more favourable towards entrepreneurial activity than others, at least in his theoretical work, he did not provide much guidance on the precise features of such environments and how they might be cultivated. Some recent commentators have been less reticent. In the 1991 issue of the World Bank's *World Development Report*, we are told that an appropriate environment has three key ingredients: the right market incentives, the right institutions and the right supportive investments. How do we know what the 'right' incentives, institutions and supportive investments are? For the authors of the *World Development Report* this presents no real difficulty. The institutions required are those of the free market. The right incentives will be revealed in the process of market operation and the need for supportive investments will become evident where market failures are uncovered.

The authors of the World Bank report do not attempt to supply any theoretical support for their views. Some empirical 'evidence' is provided but, in several cases, it is rather difficult to connect the evidence presented with the analyst's comments. The plausibility of the Bank's argument, therefore, rests mainly on our acceptance as an indisputable fact: the superiority of the innovation performance of the advanced capitalist countries compared with that of the former socialist countries. This can be granted but, of itself, cannot be regarded as proof of the superiority of free-market

39

institutions since governments in all the advanced capitalist countries have intervened in their economies in various ways. Moreover, from our point of view, conclusions reached on the basis of empirically based comparison of innovation performance in the more advanced countries cannot be assumed to hold for less developed economies where the content and context of innovative activities may be quite different.

MARKETS AND ENTREPRENEURIAL ACTIVITY

Schotter (1989) makes an interesting distinction between two different forms of belief in the market that can sustain a market culture. The first of these is belief in the optimality properties of the market equilibria which result from the voluntary actions of self-interested rational agents. The second form of belief in the market does not rely on the optimality of equilibrium outcomes. Instead the emphasis is on the freedom of rational agents to exploit their own creative resources and to seek out entrepreneurial opportunities wherever they see them. Neo-classical general equilibrium analysis can provide support for the first form of belief. Conversely, it also serves to qualify such beliefs given the recognition that various forms of market failure can give rise to non-optimal results. As far as the second form of belief in the market process is concerned, Schotter sees this as exemplified in the work of neo-Austrians such as Kirzner. It can also be seen in the writings of the classical economists whose emphasis on the supply side of the economy and on innovation means that in many ways their work is a better exemplar of the second form of market belief than that of the subjectivist Austrians.

Given the nature of its assumptions and its structure, the neo-classical general equilibrium theory does not provide us with a suitable vehicle for an examination of entrepreneurial activity. As Loasby (1991, p. 43) has pointed out, the neo-classical system requires the specification of a closed set of possibilities whereas the purpose of innovation is precisely to extend any such set. In most cases, he argues that what purports to be an analysis of Research and Development (R&D) does not formally deal with the emergence of novelty but is better described as the analysis of a treasure hunt (ibid., pp. 44–5). Moreover, as Casson has shown, work such as that of Kihlstrom and Laffont (1979), which attempts to deal with entrepreneurship within a competitive equilibrium framework, operates by removing all genuine uncertainty and replacing it by measurable risk (Casson, 1990, p. xv).

At first sight at least, neo-Austrian theories such as that of Kirzner are much more promising. In order to understand the Austrian concept of social equilibrium, it is useful to begin with von Hayek's (1937) application of the concept of equilibrium to the actions of a single individual. Von Hayek conceives of the individual as drawing up his plan of action on the basis of his given tastes and his perception of the facts. The individual will be in equilibrium, that is, he will have no reason to change his plan and will act according to it as long as his anticipations (perception of the facts) prove to be correct. If we now extend this definition to cover all members of the society, we can say equilibrium exists when all members of the society are executing their respective individual plans. For this to be the case, it is necessary that these plans are mutually compatible and that there is a conceivable set of external events which will allow people to carry out their plans and not cause any disappointments. If external events turn out to be different or if plans are not compatible, a state of disequilibrium will pertain. This is the normal state of affairs. As Kirzner puts it, markets do not achieve perfect dovetailing because of the deep fog of ignorance that surrounds each and every decision made in the market (Kirzner, 1973). The market's achievement is seen as its ability to generate discovery by producing the incentives and opportunities that inspire market participants continually to push back that fog of mutual ignorance (ibid.).

The Austrian insistence that the information which is relevant to the making of economic decisions never exists as integrated knowledge but is dispersed in incomplete and often contradictory form among the individual decision-making units of the society is the foundation of their rejection of a possible role for state planning. In their view not only is the problem of the central planner made difficult by the dispersed and incomplete nature of knowledge, but planning is also seen as frustrating the operation of those spontaneous market forces which allow agents to become aware of errors in their conjectures.

Thus in the Austrian vision, prices emerge as a result of the transactions of the individual participants on the market. These prices convey information about various disequilibria in the market and so also convey information about business opportunities. Alert entrepreneurial types take advantage of these opportunities and in so doing make money for themselves and improve coordination in the economy. The conception of the entrepreneur here is, of course, quite different from Schumpeter's. Schumpeter's entrepreneur is a destroyer of equilibria whereas the activities of the Austrian entrepreneur contribute to the equilibrating process.

The precise status of the Austrian equilibrium is a difficult matter about which little seems to be known. Questioned about it in a recent interview, Kirzner responded that while he would not claim that there was a built-in tendency for entrepreneurial activity to equilibrate the market under all circumstances, it was a fact of life that economic order was generally achieved (interview with S. Boehm, 2 May 1989). This is all very well but the implication of much of the Austrian writing is that the order so achieved is better than what could have been achieved by other means. A criticism made by Lombardini (1989) directed at Walrasian type equilibria is also relevant here. Lombardini's argument is that the fact that some kind of equilibrium is always restored in capitalist economies does not imply that there exists some kind of mechanism that has as its essential feature the role of maintaining the order of society. According to Lombardini, the process by which equilibrium is restored is often the result of some political decisions provided neither by the market nor as a consequence of normal activities carried out by existing institutions (Lombardini, 1989, p. 32). In any case, Lombardini continues: 'the positive essential role of the market is not to keep and restore equilibrium ... but to create the most favourable conditions for economic development' (ibid.).

While some of the claims of the Austrians with respect to the efficiency of the market system cannot be sustained theoretically, their perspective helps us to focus on important features of real market systems. Like the Austrians, the classical economists took the view that the allocation of resources achieved by the free market would be superior to that produced by state intervention because each individual capitalist was a better judge of how to apply his capital in his own local circumstances than any statesman. But, while the classical economist took it for granted that it was advantageous to allocate resources to their most profitable uses and linked this to faster accumulation of capital, the main impetus to growth was seen to derive from technical progress rather than accumulation. Accumulation and growth could facilitate technical progress but technical progress was primarily driven by 'the competition of the producers, who, in order to undersell one another, have recourse to new divisions of labour and new improvements of art which might never otherwise have been thought of' (Smith, 1976, v, 1e, 26).

As envisaged by the classical economists, competition had little to do with the modern concept of perfect competition. Large factories were generally seen as the product of a competitive process and, in general, they were regarded as possessing greater capacity for innovation than small firms. Some of the flavour of the classical analysis is captured in the following passage from Babbage in which he discusses the consequences of oversupply which he regarded as a natural and almost inevitable consequence of competition:

When too large a supply has produced a great reduction in price, it opens the consumption of the article to a new class, and increases the consumption of those who previously employed it ... it is also certain that by the diminution of profit which the manufacturer suffers from the diminished price, his ingenuity will be additionally stimulated; – that he will apply himself to discover other and cheaper sources for the supply of his raw material, that he will endeavour to contrive new machinery that shall manufacture it at a cheaper rate, – or try to introduce new arrangements into his factory that shall render the economy of it more perfect. (Babbage 1963, p. 286)

While the occurrence of a glut and the consequent fall in profits provided an impetus for innovation to drive down costs, Babbage acknowledged that in some cases efforts to innovate would not bear fruit so that some capital was eventually obliged to leave the trade in question. A process of competition along similar lines was also described by Babbage's contemporary Nassau Senior. According to Senior, powerful motives compelled every manufacturer to endeavour to increase the amount of his production and sales and lessen the interval between them. The initiative was usually taken by a manufacturer who thought that he possessed some advantages of skill and situation. He lowered his prices thereby attracting his rivals' customers. They, in turn, tried to recover themselves by following his example.

Every one tries to extend his sales and lower his cost of production. ... The smaller and weaker men withdraw, their place is taken by those who can stand the contest. The trade after having been for a time unprofitable becomes good. Further improvements take place at first without any lowering of price. It is then unusually profitable. Fresh capitalists are attracted to it, they endeavour to obtain business by lowering prices; and there is another interval of contest. (Senior, 1928, vol. II, p. 22)

For the classical economist, the overriding achievement of the market was its ability to generate technical change which was beneficial to all classes of society. They also believed that the market itself operating within a framework of laws and institutions normally had the ability to coordinate the decisions of individual producers. The market processes involved had something in common with those of the Austrians, though the basis for their equilibrium conception was quite different being based on cost of production rather than subjective evaluations. Little explicit attention was given to the coordination of innovation as such, the analysis of the market process being confined to already functioning markets. From this point of view, it is perhaps worth noting that, for long-run classical equilibria to be stable, neither disequilibria nor the reactions to them should be excessive (Duménil and Lévy, 1989). This suggests that Lombardini's comment may be relevant here also and that, in some cases, the restoration of economic order may require intervention by the political authorities in addition to the innovative processes which the classicals saw as integral to the operation of the market.

CREATING FAVOURABLE CONDITIONS FOR ECONOMIC DEVELOPMENT

The central point emerging from the above discussion of the classical system is the key importance of competition in the stimulation of economic development. Competition also had a role to play in the generation of an economic order with some desirable properties[1] but the system was not 'justified' in terms of these. The classical emphasis on the role of competition in providing an impetus for technological change as well as its stress on innovation rather than the properties of a particular order has found resonances in some recent empirical work on international competitiveness. In this section, a number of such studies are considered, beginning with Michael Porter's *The Competitive Advantage of Nations*.

If there is one overwhelming message in Porter's book, it is the importance of vigorous domestic rivalry for the creation and persistence of competitive advantage in an industry. Rivalry is important because once advantage is gained, it can be sustained by a continual search for new things to do and new ways of doing them. According to Porter, powerful forces work against this, particularly in successful firms. Past approaches become institutionalised in procedures, management controls, personnel policy and so on. Information that would challenge current approaches is screened out or dismissed. It takes powerful pressures to counteract such forces and these rarely come exclusively from within the organisation. Companies seldom change spontaneously; the environment jars or *forces* them to change (Porter, 1990, p. 581).

If rivalry creates the pressure which forces firms to improve and innovate, won't foreign rivalry do just as well? Porter argues that domestic rivalry is particularly important because of its visible nature and because it can be personal and emotional. Domestic rivals also face the same basic conditions so there can be no excuses such as accusations of unfair advantages. Moreover, since the presence of domestic rivals nullifies the advantages that come simply from being in the nation, it forces firms to seek higher order and perhaps more sustainable competitive advantages. In the process of seeking these advantages, firms help to create advantages for the entire national industry that are external to any firm. Domestic rivalry also pressures domestic firms to compete abroad in order to grow.

This thesis on the importance of domestic rivalry is supported and amplified by various case and country studies in Porter's book. In the Japanese case, for example, Porter notes the intensity of competition was enhanced by the fact that it was between equals or near-equals. This in turn encouraged careful watching of the competition and matching of competitive moves (ibid., pp. 412–3). In Porter's view, early protection of Japanese industry could not have resulted in world-class competitors without keen local rivalry based on concrete timetables for liberalisation known in advance. Where such local rivalry was not forthcoming, foreign rivals were often encouraged to enter. An example of this was Caterpillar's joint venture with Mitsubishi which led to the renaissance of Komatsu, which at the time was a low-quality producer of construction equipment (ibid., p. 415).

As in Japan, Porter finds that the real driver of Italian success in many industries is extraordinary rivalry. Almost every internationally successful Italian industry, he claims, has large numbers of domestic competitors which are often located in the same one or two towns. Rivalry is personal and emotional. There is constant innovation and specialisation. Innovations and ideas diffuse at amazing speed. Market positions change frequently. At the same time, however, local associations exist to perform limited joint functions such as export promotion (ibid., pp. 445–7).

Despite the dominance of the *chaebol* in Korean economic life and the dangers they pose in terms of the concentration of economic power, Porter finds that 'an essential underpinning of Korean competitive advantage is the fierce and even cutthroat rivalry that characterises every successful Korean industry' (ibid., p. 473). At least four or five companies, often including subsidiaries of the leading *chaebol*, compete in every significant sector of industry. Again the rivalry is said to be intense and emotional. The firms meet head to head not only in the Korean market but also abroad. The competition creates pressure to invest, to improve productivity and to introduce new products and it also mitigates any tendency for the firms to compete solely on the basis of the now fast eroding labour cost advantage.

Enough has been said to spell out the importance of direct and intense competition from rivals facing the same basic production conditions in encouraging the upgrading of a firm's products and processes. What we now have to consider is whether or not domestic rivalry always has such salutory results. Is it not possible for the competition to go under or at least move out of the particular sector? Is it not possible for competition to become so intense that it is destructive and prevents firms from keeping an eye on long-term goals?

While he appears to discount the possibility of destructive competition and expresses concern that intervention to prevent such competition may be counterproductive, Porter nonetheless takes the view that the economists' traditional thinking about the merits of perfect resource mobility is flawed. Such thinking, he argues, assumes that the productivity of resource utilisation in a given industry is given and that consequently it is better for resources to flow to wherever productivity is higher. However, innovation can often boost the productivity of resources employed in a particular trade much more than the gains from reallocating them. It is important to emphasise that the gains from innovation are usually not simply there for the taking and may well require a major investment in restructuring at a time of low current returns and in the face of substantial risk (Porter, 1990, p. 116). 'The alternative, giving up, must be unthinkable if improvement and innovation are to take place' (ibid.). This is not to say that commitment is any guarantee of success. Commitment is a necessary condition for innovation but it is by no means sufficient.

The issue of whether industry responds to competitive threats by innovating or by engaging in cut-throat price-cutting has been discussed independently by Lazonick (1991) and also in his 1993 review of Porter's work. Lazonick takes the view that the key determinant of whether or not the firm's decision makers choose an innovative strategy is the extent to which 'they control an organizational structure that they believe provides them with the capability of developing productive resources that can overcome the constraints they face' (Lazonick, 1991, p. 328). Such structures include not only the internal organisation of firms themselves and their relationships with the public authorities but also networks of relationships between the firms in a particular industry or cluster of industries. In his 1993 review of Porter's work, Lazonick notes the emphasis placed by Porter on the importance of domestic rivalry in pressuring innovative change. He argues, however, that a close examination of Porter's own documentation and analysis shows that any emphasis on competition to the exclusion of cooperation is unwarranted and that it is the balance between domestic rivalry and domestic competition that yields global competitive advantage (Lazonick, 1993).

In exploring further the issue of coordination, it will be useful to introduce a distinction made by Teece between two types of innovation, namely autonomous (stand-alone) and systemic (Teece, 1988, p. 268). An autonomous innovation is one which can be introduced without requiring modifications to other parts of the system.[2] A system innovation, on the other hand, requires significant readjustments elsewhere in the system. Teece argues that where there are significant technological interdependencies, coordination between independent parties may be difficult to achieve because the introduction of an innovation will often result in differing costs and benefits for the parties involved. One way of solving this problem is through integration. This facilitates information flow and the coordination of investment plans and removes institutional barriers to innovation where this requires the allocation of costs and benefits and the making of specialised investments in several parts of the industry.

Teece's analysis of vertical integration emphasises the importance of the firm as a mechanism for overcoming differences of interest and for co-ordinating change. But while vertical integration may be essential if progress is to be made, it may not be a desirable long-run solution. As Richardson (1972) has pointed out, activities which are closely complementary may also be highly dissimilar and thus best carried out in different organisations (see also Loasby, 1991, p. 81). Consequently, once a nucleus of capability exists within the firm, it may be efficient to encourage the spinning-off of subcontracting businesses to carry out the relevant activities in separate organisations.

Where an innovation requires the coordination of activities with a high degree of 'technological strangeness',[3] forms of long-term relationship between independent firms may be superior to vertical integration. As Gomes-Casseres (1994, p. 63) has recently argued, 'the growing complexity of products and services, and of their design, production and delivery' is a major factor favouring formation of alliance groups. Finding and assembling all the relevant technologies and skills under a single roof may be difficult and, in any case, may not be desirable given that the greatest advantages of specialisation and of scale are often realised at the component level rather than the system level. While there is evidence that new forms of alliance are being developed in high technology industry involving competition between groups of firms (Gomes-Casseres, 1994; Moss Kanter, 1994), forms of inter-firm cooperation are not new. The more traditional geographically based cluster of firms involved elements of both market and non-market mediated cooperation. What the older and newer forms of inter-firm cooperation have in common is that they contribute most to innovative performance when they involve a dense network of interpersonal relationships and internal infrastructures that enhance learning, unblock information flows and facilitate coordination by creating trust and mitigating perceived differences of interest (Porter, 1990, pp. 152–3; Moss Kanter, 1994, p. 97). It is widely recognised that Asian companies have been particularly adept at developing and using inter-firm relationships and that failure to do so is a particular weakness of North American firms. Thus, Moss Kanter (1994, p. 97) refers to American firms as taking a narrow, opportunistic view of relationships. Similarly, Porter (1990, p. 527) refers to relationships between US firms as being opportunistic and notes that skill transfers and the sharing of market insights take place only sporadically.

The planned coordination of change that takes place within the firm and between firms working in close cooperation sooner or later has to be brought into contact with the wider system of which it is to form a part – be subjected, so to speak, to the test of the market. The innovation may prove successful or otherwise. It may require modification as a result of customer feedback or it may itself create the impetus for modifications in the larger system which in turn react back on itself. The innovation may compete with innovations performing broadly similar functions. It may share the market with them, it may capture the entire market or it may lose out to a product which is in no way superior to itself. As Nelson (1988, p. 313) has remarked, the process of technical change in capitalist societies at least with the vision of hindsight appears to be extremely wasteful.

> Looking backward one can see a litter of failed or duplicative endeavours that probably would never have been undertaken had there been effective overall planning and co-ordination. Economies of scale and scope that might have been achieved through R&D co-ordination are missed. Certain kinds of R&D that would have a high social value are not done. Also, because technology is to a considerable extent proprietary, one can see many enterprises operating inefficiently, even failing sometimes at considerable social cost, for want of access to the best technology. (Nelson, 1988, p. 313)

Since innovation processes in capitalist economies are so wasteful, why they have performed so well compared with the socialist economies is something of a puzzle. Nelson takes the view that what makes effective central planning difficult if not perhaps impossible is the uncertainty which surrounds the question of where R&D resources should be allocated in a field where technology is fluid (ibid.). There are always a variety of ways in which existing technologies can be improved and ways of achieving any particular improvement. Often, there will be no agreement even among experts about which of these ways is likely to be best. In such circumstances, any attempt to get ex ante agreement on the matter may be futile and even counterproductive. It may be best to let the market decide ex post which were the good ideas.

The issue of the comparative performance of capitalist and socialist economies in terms of innovation touched on by Nelson is discussed in some detail in Rosenberg (1992). Like Nelson, Rosenberg emphasises that technological innovation is fraught with uncertainties so that there is no way of knowing a priori which alternatives are worth pursuing and which are not. In such a situation experimentation may be valuable provided means are available for terminating searches in directions which have proved unpromising and limiting the costs of failure. According to Rosenberg, the history of capitalism involved the progressive introduction of institutional devices which facilitated the commitment of resources to innovation by keeping the costs of being wrong within tolerable bounds while at the same time holding out the prospect of large personal gains if decisions turned out to be the right ones. These devices included business firms with limited liability for their owners and ownership shares that were easily marketable (1992, p. 190). In addition to the incentive structure, Rosenberg pointed to the importance of the freedom to conduct experiments. For such freedom to exist, it was necessary that the economic sphere should attain a degree of autonomy from external forces, especially arbitrary and unpredictable interventions by government (1992, pp. 191–2). Such autonomy is never absolute and other conditions must also be fulfilled if there is to be freedom to conduct experiments. The most important of these according to Rosenberg is the existence of a large number of decision makers each with insufficient power to influence the outcome of the market evaluation of the new product (ibid.).

Rosenberg argues that the most decisive failure of twentieth-century socialism was its failure to allow experimentation. He attributes this failure primarily to the centralisation of decision making. Any central authority, he argues, will have a strong motivation to withhold resources from those who might prove that the authority had made the wrong decision (1992, pp. 192–3). Moreover, in the Soviet case, there was a strong belief in the efficiency of giant firms and this together with a sellers' market meant that firms were insulated from all forms of competition. The threat of competition thus being absent, plant managers lacked a strong sanction against the failure to innovate. At the same time, there were penalties for failing to fulfil the annual plan while successful innovation was poorly rewarded. In Rosenberg's view, the structure of the incentive system was such that it not only discouraged experimentation but also discouraged the successful adoption of new technologies generated elsewhere.

Arguments in a similar vein to those of Nelson and Rosenberg have been put forward also by Pelikan. Like them, he argues that economic self-organisation cannot be optimally planned in advance and must involve experimentation through associative trials and errors (Pelikan, 1988, p. 390). Three elements are, therefore, of crucial importance: the generation of trials, the elimination of errors and the selection of successes. Pelikan argues that a too lax selection will enable errors to survive whereas a too constrained trial generation will cause absent successes. But while selection processes should not be too lax, they should not be too severe either or they may prematurely eliminate future successes in temporary difficulties. Consequently there is a role for competent hierarchies which can improve on the short-sighted selection of product markets. Pelikan argues that socialist systems are likely to be characterised by absent success because of too few trials; because entry is constrained in various ways; and because of too many surviving errors due to monopolistic privileges and soft budget constraints. The strength of capitalism, according to Pelikan, derives not from markets but from 'the potential for efficacious experimentation with both market and non-market structures at all levels of economic organization' (p. 393).

RECAPITULATION OF THE ARGUMENT SO FAR AND CONSIDERATION OF ITS RELEVANCE FOR LESS DEVELOPED COUNTRIES (LDCs)

The welfare theorems of competitive equilibrium analysis enable us to make claims about the optimality of the allocations which can be achieved by a system of perfect markets when preferences and production possibilities are taken as given. Such claims do not carry over to more open systems where new goods and new methods of production are being introduced as a result of innovative activity. In such open systems, any claims on behalf of the market system are necessarily quite different. They involve arguments to the effect that innovative activity benefits from the freedom of individuals to use and develop their own creative abilities and that competition acts as a spur to innovative effort. No a priori claims about optimality can be made and the success or otherwise of the system ultimately becomes an empirical question.

Recent historical experience has shown that some capitalist economies have performed better than any of the socialist economies in terms of innovation. This has been interpreted widely as the triumph of the market and conclusive proof of the value of market-oriented economic reforms. The analyses reviewed here suggest that two features have been especially important in those capitalist economies which have been successful at innovation and that these features are supported and cultivated by a wide array of market and non-market institutions. The first of these features is the provision of the space and incentives for economic experimentation. The second is intense rivalry between firms which encourages them to engage in innovative activity.

The importance of economic experimentation derives from the fact that at the frontiers of technology nobody agrees where the next innovation lies or how best to achieve any particular technological objective. However, as Rosenberg (1992, p. 194) recognises, an environment exhibiting hostility towards experimentation may not be a huge disadvantage if the option of acquiring advanced technology from abroad exists. This is generally the case for developing countries whose industrialisation in the present century has tended to be based on learning or the borrowing of foreign technology (Amsden, 1988, p. 38). Although the forms of experimentation which are important at the technological frontier are not relevant in this case, this does not mean that entrepreneurial or innovative activity is unimportant in LDCs. The problems associated with the adoption of foreign technology are by no means trivial and there is abundant evidence that the pace and direction of adaptation are influenced by the competitive environment.

It seems, therefore, that as far as developing countries are concerned, the main argument for the market system relates to the importance of competitive pressure. The question of whether in practice agents respond innovatively to competitive pressure emerged as the key issue in our discussion of international competitiveness. As we saw, for Porter, the chief determinant of whether or not the response would be innovative was the degree of commitment to the industry concerned. Lazonick, on the other hand, emphasised the importance of accumulated capability and access to appropriate organisational structures, whereas Pelikan emphasised the existence of non-market institutions which keep alive long-term opportunities that market forces would tend to eliminate. In short, the response to any competitive threat depends on the nature of the options available or as Boulding (1981, p. 81) put it, what adjusts when the system is subject to strain is the adjustable. This has important implications for the reform process in developing countries because there is a danger that strongly market-oriented reforms designed to increase exposure to competitive pressures may increase flexibility in ways which favour exit rather than innovation as the appropriate response to competition (Chang, 1993, pp. 15–18). The really difficult thing is to expose firms to competition at the same time as ensuring that innovation is the most attractive response. As argued below, experience suggests that this may require non-market forms of competition.

Everybody accepts that learning takes time and that there is a theoretical case for protecting or subsidising new industry. Arguments against support for new or infant industries are not generally against the principle *per se* but concern the practicalities of implementing support policy in such a way that the infants do in fact mature into competitive industries. There is now a considerable body of evidence that this was achieved in the East Asian economies by making receipt of support conditional on the fulfilment of various performance targets (Amsden, 1988, 1989; World Bank, 1993). As Amsden puts it, governments in the East Asian economies intervened with subsidy to support private enterprise. They often instigated investment activity by deliberately getting prices 'wrong'. What differentiated their interventions from less successful interventions in Latin America and elsewhere was not the degree of distortion but the degree of discipline to which subsidy recipients were subject.

The World Bank's study of economic growth and public policy in the high-performing Asian economies (HPAEs) shows that the Bank now accepts that government intervention in many of these economies was substantial although it continues to question the extent to which the documented interventions actually accelerated growth or contributed to structural change. Markets, on the other hand, seem to have nothing to prove. 'The fundamental market-oriented policies can be recommended without reservation' (Page, 1994, p. 5). According to the Bank, there is, however, a role for 'effective but carefully limited government activism' as long as this addresses failures in the working of the markets (World Bank, 1993, pp. 10–11). The main class of market failures to be overcome is coordination failures. According to the Bank, some effective interventions in East Asia were efforts to overcome coordination failure by promoting cooperative behaviour among private firms and between firms and government (ibid.). In Japan and Korea especially, the benefits of this cooperation were combined with those of competition by means of various forms of non-market based contest, for example making certain forms of support conditional on export performance. This reluctant admission that, in developing economies, the coordination and incentive functions of markets can be achieved (more effectively?) by other means is immediately qualified by the argument that it is only possible in situations where honest and efficient public bureaucracies exist and is consequently not to be recommended widely.

CONCLUSION

As Schumpeter long ago recognised, the optimality theorems of Walrasian general equilibrium theory apply primarily in economies in which development and entrepreneurial activity are absent. When we talk about the developing economy, arguments in favour of markets cannot, therefore, derive their support from these theorems. In this chapter, I have argued that two features of what is popularly called the market economy are important for development. These are, first, the ability to provide the space and incentives for economic experimentation and, second, a competitive environment which spurs innovative effort. For most developing countries, the second of these features is the more important since the option of industrialising using foreign technology exists.

Within a purely free-market framework, the desire for a competitive environment to encourage innovation may conflict with the need to provide the time and space necessary for learning. The East Asian experience, however, suggests that it is possible to create frameworks within which reconciliation may be achieved. No hard and fast rules can be laid down for such frameworks. In large part, they are the product of trial and error. They may involve a variety of organisational forms and relationships between organisations all of which may vary over time as objectives and capabilities change.

NOTES

1. For example with prices equal to costs of production.
2. Sometimes an innovation is autonomous because the degree of novelty is such that it is necessary to create *ab initio* an entirely new set of activities within the firm. Issues relating to this problem are discussed in Marx (1977, p. 361) and Dahmen (1970, pp. 64–5).
3. The term 'technological strangeness' is attributed to Hirshman (1977, p. 77).

REFERENCES

Aitken, H.G.J. (ed.) (1965), *Explorations in Enterprise* (Cambridge: Harvard University Press).

Amsden A.H. (1988), 'Private Enterprise' – The Issue of Business–Government Control', *Colombia Journal of World Business* 23, Spring, pp. 37–42.

Amsden, A. (1989), *Asia's Next Giant* (Oxford and New York: Oxford University Press).

Babbage, C. (1963), *On the Economy of Machinery and Manufactures*, reprint of 4th edn, 1835 (New York: Augustus M. Kelly).

Boehm, S. (1989), 'Interview with Israel Kirzner', *Review of Political Economy*, vol. 1.

Boulding, K.E. (1981), *Evolutionary Economics* (Beverly Hills and London: Sage Publications).

Casson, M. (ed.) (1990), *Entrepreneurship* (Aldershot: Edward Elgar).

Chang, H.J. (1993), 'Explaining Flexible Rigidities in East-Asia'. Paper presented at ODI Workshop on Nature, Significance and Determinants of Flexibilities of National Economy, 4–6 July 1993, Bisham Abbey, Marlow, England.

Dahmen, E. (1970), *Entrepreneurial Activity and the Development of Swedish Industry 1919–1939*, trans. A. Leijonhufvud (Homewood: Richard D. Irwin inc. for the American Economic Association).

Dosi, G., C. Freeman, R. Nelson, G. Siverberg and L. Soete, (eds) (1988), *Technical Change and Economic Theory* (London and New York: Pinter Publishers).

Duménil, G. and D. Lévy (1989), 'The Competitive Process in a Fixed Capital Environment: A Classical View', *The Manchester School* vol. 57, no. 1, pp. 34–57.

Eatwell, J., M. Milgate and P. Newman (eds) (1987), *The New Palgrave* (London: Macmillan).

Gomes-Casseres, B. (1994), 'Group Versus Group: How Alliance Networks Compete', *Harvard Business Review*, July–August, pp. 62–74.

Hirshman, A.O. (1977), 'A Generalised Linkage Approach to Development, with Reference to Staples', *Essays on Economic Development and Cultural Change in Honour of Bert F. Hoselitz*, supplement to vol. 25 of *Economic Development and Cultural Change*, pp. 67–98.

Kihlstrom, R.E. and J.J. Laffont (1979), 'A General Equilibrium Theory of Firm Formation Based on Risk Aversion', *Journal of Political Economy* 87, pp. 719–48.

Kirzner, I.M. (1973), *Competition and Entrepreneurship* (Chicago: University of Chicago Press).

Lazonick, W. (1991), *Business Organisation and the Myth of the Market Economy* (Cambridge: Cambridge University Press), vol. 2, no. 1, pp. 1–24.

Lazonick, W. (1993), 'Industry Clusters versus Global Webs: Organizational Capabilities in the American Economy', *Industrial and Corporate Change*, 2.

Loasby, B.J. (1991), *Equilibrium and Evolution* (Manchester: Manchester University Press).

Lombardini, S. (1989), 'Market and Institutions' in Shiraishi and Tsuru (eds), Chapter 2, pp. 27–49.

Marx, K. (1977), *Capital*, vol. I (London: Lawrence and Wishart).

Moss Kanter, R. (1994), 'Collaborative Advantage: The Art of Alliances', *Harvard Business Review*, July–August, pp. 96–108.

Nelson R. (1988), 'Institutions Supporting Political Change in the United States', Chapter 15 in Dosi et al. (eds), pp. 312–29.

Page, J. (1994), 'The East-Asian Miracle: Building a Basis for Growth', *Finance and Development*, March, pp. 2–5.

Pelikan, P. (1988), 'Can the Innovation System of Capitalism be Outperformed?', Chapter 18 in Dosi et al. (eds), pp. 370–98.

Porter, M.E. (1990), *The Competitive Advantage of Nations* (London and Basingstoke: Macmillan).

Richardson, G.B. (1972), 'The Organisation of Industry', *Economic Journal* vol. 82, pp. 883–96.

Rosenberg, N. (1992), 'Economic Experiments', *Industrial and Corporate Change* 1, pp. 181–203.

Schotter, A. (1989), 'Comment' (on Lombardini) in Shiraishi and Tsuru (eds) pp. 50–5.

Schumpeter, J.A. (1947), *Capitalism, Socialism and Democracy*, 2nd edn (London: George Allen and Unwin).

Schumpeter, J.A. (1961), *The Theory of Economic Development*, trans. R. Opie (Oxford: Oxford University Press).

Schumpeter, J.A. (1965), 'Economic Theory and Entrepreneurial History' in H.G.J. Aitken, op. cit.

Senior, N.W. (1928), *Industrial Efficiency and Social Economy*, ed. S. Leon Levy, 2 vols (London: P.S. King & Son).

Shiraishi, T. and S. Tsuru (eds) (1989), *Economic Institutions in a Dynamic Society: Search for a New Frontier* (Basingstoke: Macmillan for the IEA).

Smith, A. (1976) *An Inquiry into the Nature and Causes of the Wealth of Nations*, 2 vols, R.H. Campbell, A.S. Skinner and W.B. Todd, eds (Oxford: Clarendon Press).

Teece, D. (1988), 'Technological Change and the Nature of the Firm', Chapter 19 in Dosi et al. (eds), pp. 256–281.

United Nations (1992), 'Entrepreneurship and the Development Challenges of the 1990s', Chapter 7 in *World Economic Survey* (New York: UN).

von Hayek, F.A. (1937), 'Economics and Knowledge', *Economica*, new series, 4, pp. 33–54.

World Bank (1991), 'The Climate for Enterprise', Chapter 4 in *World Development Report* (Oxford and New York: Oxford University Press).

World Bank (1993), *The East Asian Miracle: Economic Growth and Public Policy* (Oxford and New York: Oxford University Press).

5 Flexibility and Economic Progress[1]

Tony Killick

Selected Countries
017
A13

THE PRIMA FACIE CASE

We start with a paradox: that while its value – and the penalties imposed by its absence – are casually acknowledged in discussions of economic development, there is a near-total absence of explicit, analytical treatment of the flexibility of economies in the academic literature. At the same time, there appears a strong prima facie expectation that the flexibility of an economy will strongly influence its long-term economic performance, and that this attribute is of increasing importance.

First, consider the recent economic histories of three important regions: East Asia, centrally-planned East Europe and sub-Saharan Africa. The first of these has had an outstandingly successful record by almost any test; witness their popular label of 'miracle' economies (World Bank, 1993b). The economic records of the other two regions in the 1970s and 1980s were almost as unsuccessful as East Asia was successful, with declining living standards and chronic macroeconomic strains. The reasons for these contrasting experiences are many but a substantial part of the explanation can be plausibly attributed to the flexibility of the East Asian economies and the inflexibility of African and centrally-planned East European economies.

In the case of East Asia, flexibility is closely associated with success in taking advantage of opportunities in world markets for manufactured goods. Thus, in a study of the electronics industry, Mody (1990, p. 291) writes of firms in South Korea and Taiwan 'learning to manoeuvre in fast-changing markets by responding rapidly to new opportunities, taking greater risks, and meeting higher quality standards'. Indeed, this region has been characterised by the speed with which it has been able to accommodate rapid adjustment and structural change, and the apparently low social costs incurred in the process. A World Bank (1992, p. 3) study of experiences with structural adjustment programmes singles out Korea, Indonesia and Thailand as among the few countries in which the adjustment process was followed by a swift transition to a new growth path.

56

Chowdhury and Islam (1993, chapter 1) similarly trace the major structural changes that have occurred in the region. Many have commented on the apparently high degree of labour market flexibility in this region. And the World Bank 'miracles' study commended 'the pragmatic flexibility with which governments tried policy instruments in pursuit of economic objectives. Instruments that worked were retained. Instruments that failed or impeded other policy objectives were abandoned' (World Bank, 1993b, p. 86).

The starkest contrast is with Africa.[2] There, industrialisation, having exhausted most import-substitution possibilities, has ground to a halt. The share of primary products in total exports has remained stuck at over 90 per cent between 1965 and 1991,[3] despite trend declines in real world prices for traditional commodity exports, creating great balance-of-payments difficulties. Over the same period, the continent's share in world exports of manufactures, always minuscule, has diminished further. Africa's inability to take advantage of changing opportunities in trade is shown also in failures to diversify into the more dynamically-expanding regional markets, with Europe remaining overwhelmingly the most important destination for its exports and with little penetration of the newer markets. Relative inflexibility is also revealed by Africa's limited ability to benefit from advances in useful knowledge, with evidence from agriculture and industry that the technology gap is large and growing, and exceptionally weak institutional capacities in this area. A further indication is provided by comparative data on responses to devaluations, which again are to the disadvantage of sub-Saharan Africa.

The contribution by Alexander Neuber in the larger study (Killick, 1995, chapter 5) similarly argues the connection between economic deterioration in East European countries during the 1980s and the large systemic rigidities imposed by central planning. He shows these to have resulted in small supply elasticities, because of the material-balances approach to planning and chronic resulting shortages of inputs; little innovation, again because of the perverse incentive system and the absence of an efficient screening mechanism for innovations; highly imperfect informational flows, again related to the incentive structure; and much structural and institutional inertia, not least because of the soft budget constraint and the resulting absence of 'exit'.

That the flexibility or otherwise of an economy should have a powerful influence on its economic performance in the modern world is hardly surprising. All economies are constantly in a state of flux and there is an ever-present need to respond to – and take advantage of – changes in the economic environment. The imperative to do so has been intensified in recent decades as economic interdependence among nations has increased. An analogy suggests itself here with the concept of 'fitness' in Darwinian theory. We can view economic competition among nations as a kind of survival of the fittest, where fitness is determined by the speed with which economies can respond to shocks, and can move to take advantage of new technologies or markets, and adjust to the actions of others. The greater the ease, and the lower the costs, with which an economy can adjust, the more it is likely to prosper.

Changes in the economic environment can be classified into relatively unpredictable and short-term *shocks*, and longer-term *trends*. As regards the former, the most obvious are terms-of-trade shocks. The oil shocks of 1973–74 and 1979–80 are classic examples, bringing about large deteriorations in the commodity terms of trade of oil-importing countries, massive improvements in the terms of trade of major oil exporters, and large, if temporary, redistributions of world income. The vulnerability of commodity-exporting developing countries to other terms-of-trade shocks is also well known. In addition, they and others have had to contend with financial shocks, exemplified by the large, up–down–up, swings in Latin America's access to world savings over the last 20 years.

There are domestic shocks to cope with as well. In fact, natural disasters are a frequent source of economic crises in developing countries.[4] The vagaries of the weather are a potent factor in agriculturally-based economies, increasing the riskiness of farming and the dangers of famine.[5] We may also mention the frequency of organised violence and the large economic costs that often result from civil and international disturbances and wars. It may seem to strain the language to think of economies adapting to violence and yet we do talk of economies' resilience to the depredations of war. We should mention too the large-scale migrations that result from both violence and famine. The need to care for these large, sometimes sudden, influxes of people into regions often already poor can impose major economic strains.[6]

Economies also need to respond to various longer-term trends. Shifts in the composition of domestic and world demand are an example, illustrated by the large changes in the make-up of international trade in recent decades.[7] The accelerating pace of technological change is another, related, influence to which productive structures must respond, particularly in developing countries in constant danger of being left behind. Thus, the rapid development and application of microelectronic information technology has large implications for much of industrial activity, reducing information costs and introducing greater diversity, complexity and flexibility when applied to the control mechanisms of machinery and inventory management.[8] Their apparently superior capacity to adapt industrial structures to these technological developments is one of the principal ways in which East Asian countries have excelled.

The apparent slow-down of the industrial world to historically more normal rates of economic growth is a further apparent trend of large importance: it appears that the extraordinarily rapid growth among the Organisation for Economic Cooperation and Development (OECD) countries in the 1950s through to the 1970s has given way to slower growth since, with an associated rise in long-term unemployment.[9] More controversially, we can add global warming as a probable development to which national economies will need to respond, particularly those which remain agriculturally-based and already have large areas of marginal land. Other environmental problems also increasingly constrain sustainable development paths in ways that call for structural and policy responses.

It was in recognition of the importance of adaptation to shocks and trends (as well as to past policy mistakes) that there occurred in the 1980s the well-known proliferation of 'structural adjustment programmes' associated with the International Monetary Fund (IMF) and World Bank. In focusing on the determinants of the flexibility of economies we are thus implicitly agreeing on the importance of adjustment – but as a permanent necessity rather than a creature of the 1980s – and exploring the conditions which determine the success of adjustment efforts, and their costs.

CONCEPTUALISING FLEXIBILITY

We first take up the question of conceptualisation. Our unit is the national economy and Figure 5.1 attempts to summarise the dimensions of the flexibility of an economy.

Types and Agents of Change

Figure 5.1 distinguishes between responsive (or passive) and innovatory flexibility. Responsive flexibility refers to the reaction of economic agents to altered relative prices or other stimuli. The reactions of savers to changes in interest rates, or of exporters to a devaluation, or of governments to a natural disaster are examples. By contrast, innovatory flexibility refers to changes initiated by the exercise of entrepreneurship. Those who exercise this quality are the leaders, the visionaries, the shakers and movers of society. Individuals may display it by investing in training which anticipates the skills which will be in short supply in the future.

		short ◄—— Period of adjustment ——► long TYPE OF FLEXIBILITY	
		RESPONSIVE	INNOVATIVE
AGENTS (Ease of adjustment: easy ▲ ... hard ▼)	Individuals	1 *Elasticity of demand* *Elasticity of supply* *of labour*	4 *Investment in skills* *Entrepreneurship*
	Firms, other organisations	2 *Elasticity of supply* *Imitation/adaptation* *of products* *& processes*	5 *Investment, R&D,* *innovation*
	Institutions	3 *Transactions costs* *Policy management*	6 *Public investment* *(education, research,* *infrastructure)* *Socio-political innovation*
HYPOTHESISED DETERMINANTS		7 Information Market efficiency Openness Political autonomy Population age structure	8 Education Technological capability/ industrialisation Historical & social influences

FIGURE 5.1: *Dimensions of Economic Flexibility*

Corporate managements may display it through their spending on research and development and the resulting product or other innovations. Governments may display it through the introduction of agencies or policies which will give the economy a competitive edge in the future, say by the creation of advanced educational or transportation infrastructures. The active industrial policies of the South Korean government during the 1970s, designed to create a future comparative advantage in such industries as shipbuilding and motor manufacturing, is an example of innovatory flexibility by a government.

Figure 5.1 also indicates a time dimension to these classes of flexibility. Responsive flexibility is exemplified by the demand and supply elasticities familiar in standard microeconomics reactions to changes in relative prices. As such, it can be seen as short- to medium-term, although time is needed for elasticities to take on their maximum values. In contrast, innovatory flexibility typically involves investments and longer gestation lags. It may also involve the creation of new, or substantially altered, agencies – generally a protracted process.

On its vertical axis Figure 5.1 identifies three types of agents of change: individuals, organisations and institutions, arranged in ascending order of the ease with which, in general, they are able to adapt. Individuals come out on top. Inflexibility among the economies of Africa or in the centrally-planned economies of East Europe cannot be attributed to unresponsiveness on the part of their populations. The responsiveness of Africans as consumers and producers has been dramatically demonstrated by their resourcefulness in the economic decline and hardship that all too many of them have experienced. Thus in Zaire the economy has been systematically pillaged by a kleptocratic regime but its citizens have responded by creating, as a means of survival, a 'second' or parallel economy estimated to be twice as large as the officially-recorded one (MacGaffey, 1991). Fuel stolen from the copper industry keeps food supplies open to the towns. Roadside workshops keep vehicles on the road against all the odds. The profits of the second economy are used to finance the provision of public goods that the state fails to provide: health facilities, schools, road maintenance.

In less extreme forms, the Zairean story could be writ large for much of Africa: its peoples have responded vigorously to crises and to opportunities for capturing the rents created by import restrictions, price controls and other market restrictions. In fact, the response has been so vigorous that in a few African countries the state is in crisis, with only a tenuous hold on economic life and forced by its scale and superior efficiency to tolerate a parallel economy which decimates the tax base.

There is a similar story to tell about Eastern Europe. In the central planning era there was the same emergence of a large parallel economy, of semi-legal activities responding to opportunities for gain from scarcity premia in ways which were highly responsive to supply and demand. Managers of state enterprises learned to escape some of the confines of the plan by informal barter deals, or the use of procurement scouts to find scarce inputs. They established 'networks of intimate cooperation' and elaborate systems of side payments. They entered into informal, shop-floor pacts with their labour forces quite outside the plan framework. In Eastern Europe as in Africa it was not people's willingness to respond that resulted in inflexibility but the constraints imposed upon them. Evidence from another part of the world is also on display, in the vigour with which the people of China have taken advantage of economic liberalisation there. Despite large historical, cultural and geographical differences, people everywhere seem to belong to the species *Homo economicus*, and to equate development with modernisation.

This is not to say that everyone is equally responsive. Adaptability is a capacity which diminishes with age. It is enhanced by education, an aspect we shall explore shortly. People respond to incentives, but subject to the constrains upon them. Theodore Schultz postulates that:

> there are economic incentives to reallocate resources, that people respond to these incentives to the best of their ability, and that the difference in their performance is a measure of the difference among people with respect to the particular type of ability that is required. (Schultz, 1975, p. 834)

Lack of education is one constraint. Exploring others brings us to the second and third types of agents of change in Figure 5.1: organisations and institutions. In distinguishing between these we follow North, seeing institutions as:

> formal rules, informal constraints (norms of behavior, conventions, and self-imposed codes of conduct), and the enforcement characteristics of both. ... If institutions are the rules of the game organizations are the players. Organizations consist of groups of individuals engaged in purposive activity. The constraints imposed by the institutional framework (together with the other standard constraints of economics) define the opportunity set and therefore the kind of organizations that will come into existence. (North, 1992, pp. 9–10)

So it is to institutions that we must look in order to understand the constraints upon individual (and organisational) responsiveness. In support of this, note that Morris and Adelman's 1988 study of comparative patterns of economic development concluded that institutions, and their adaptability, mattered most in explaining differential rates of diffusion of economic growth. Outdated laws, a reactionary or corrupted judiciary resulting in unpredictable enforcement of contracts and property rights, or a hidebound public administration, can be potent obstacles to responsiveness, frustrating entrepreneurs and others wishing to take advantage of new opportunities. The post-independence history of India provides a salutary illustration of this truth.

Thus, while individual responsiveness is necessary for adaptive national economies, it is not a sufficient condition. Institutions and policies can prevent individual responsiveness from translating into economy-wide flexibility, or perhaps can compensate for deficiencies at the micro level. The nature of governments is such an institutional factor of great importance. A government which is insecure, corrupt or repressive is unlikely to give much heed to economic performance, or to have the legitimacy necessary to carry through the policies needed to adapt the economy to changing circumstances. Special interest groups will obstruct the reform of policies from which they benefit.

However, change is not impossible even when the state is behoven to interest groups. There is evidence of a kind of cost–benefit logic at work, in which the economic deterioration resulting from anti-adaptation policies throws up a countervailing public discontent which will either impel the government to act or overthrow it for a more reform-minded alternative. When combined with strong leadership, public acceptance of the need for change can render politically feasible policy shifts that would formerly have been judged suicidal.

While considering political factors, we should also mention the delicate balance to be struck between flexibility and continuity in government policies. The ways in which the public reacts to – and anticipates – government actions, and the techniques that it develops for frustrating government intentions, are now well recognised as crucial for the effectiveness of policy interventions. Corruption and parallel markets are examples of the public frustrating government intentions. It is now a commonplace that to be effective policies must be credible; people must believe they will be implemented and will stick.[10] This is why unstable or inconsistent governments have difficulty in achieving improved economic performance.

I have suggested that institutions are the least adaptable of the three categories of agents of change identified in Figure 5.1. One reason for this is that almost invariably powerful groups grow up with vested interests in maintaining the status quo. As North states:

> The process of change [of institutions] is overwhelmingly incremental. … The reason is that the economies of scope, complementarities, and network externalities that arise from a given matrix of formal rules, informal constraints, and enforcement characteristics will typically bias costs and benefits in favour of choices consistent with the existing framework. Therefore … institutional change will occur at those margins considered most pliable in the context of the bargaining power of interested parties. (North, 1992, p. 11)

Moreover, there is considerable scope for tension in the adaptation of institutions, resulting from the relative ease with which changes in formal rules may be legislated once a coalition for change has been assembled, as contrasted with the more obscure and osmotic ways in which informal constraints – reflecting value systems and social mores – alter over time.

However, as North acknowledges, there are situations in which revolutionary change becomes possible, of which Eastern Europe in the late 1980s was an example.

Forms of Flexibility

Reverting again to Figure 5.1, entries in the cells numbered 1 to 6 flag ways in which the forms of flexibility manifest themselves. Explanation of these, and their determinants, throws additional light on the concept but would take us beyond the boundaries of a journal article (see Killick, 1995, chapter 1). Most of them are self-explanatory. For example, price elasticities of demand and supply are familiar manifestations of some aspects of flexibility, just as firms' investments in R&D tell us a lot about their likely capacities for innovation.

Cell 3 perhaps requires more explanation. First, the reference to transactions costs.[11] This is a catch-all expression referring to the costs of providing various services necessary for efficient transactions in a market economy: the provision and exchange of information and other actions necessary to bring buyers and sellers together; the measurement and inspection of goods; the preparation and enforcement of contracts; and so on. In pre-modern economies transactions costs are reduced by face-to-face dealings and limited specialisation, and enforcement achieved through customary practice and social pressures, although they are raised by poor information.

As an economy begins to modernise, we can speculate that transactions costs tend to rise relative to economic activity, unless there is a parallel development of institutions to offset this tendency. Specialisation increases, more transactions occur impersonally through the intermediation of markets, the necessary network of middlemen becomes denser, there is more standardisation, more quality control, information needs multiply, custom becomes an increasingly inadequate means of enforcement. If rising transactions costs are not to frustrate economic development, institutions, particularly of the more formal type, need to develop to keep these costs to a minimum: 'Efficient markets are a consequence of institutions that provide low-cost measurement and enforcement of contract ... Essential to efficiency over time are institutions that provide economic and political flexibility to adapt to new opportunities' (North, 1992, p. 9). This implies sufficient flows of information for agents to know about the opportunities open to them and to be able to make rational decisions about them. The invention of money and other financial instruments is a powerful example of institutional innovations that reduce transactions costs.

The entry 'policy management' in cell 3 of Figure 5.1 covers a sub-set of the kind of institutional responsiveness discussed above, referring to the ability of the state to modify existing policies and introduce new ones, in the light of emerging needs. The management of fiscal and monetary policy so as to reconcile competing inflation, balance of payments, employment and growth objectives is one example. Another is actions to mitigate the effects of terms-of-trade shocks, but there are a host of other ways in which governments need constantly to review their policies – on trade, taxation and public spending – in the light of changing external and internal conditions. The readiness and wisdom with which the state undertakes such policy management will have much to do with the creation of an environment conducive to adaptation on the part of other economic agents. State institutions in East Asia have already been cited for a high-quality responsiveness which has contributed much to the apparent flexibility of the economies of that region.

Problems of Definition

By now it is evident that the notion of flexibility cannot be reduced to some brief, precise definition, let alone be quantified. Against this, we have made progress in identifying the characteristics of a flexible economy. Broadly expressed, we can define a flexible economy as one in which individuals, organisations and institutions efficiently adjust their goals and resource allocations in the light of changing constraints and opportunities. Note that ends as well as means are adapted. Objectives can be made more ambitious as old constraints give way, say to technological advances. Or objectives may be trimmed back as new constraints emerge, for example when a non-renewable resource becomes exhausted. Goals need to be constantly redefined in the context of changing conditions and values.

The key expression in the definition is the *efficient* adjustment of ends and means, but what does that mean? Part of the answer must refer to the speed with which agents are able to effect changes. An inflexible economy is one in which adjustment is slow. However, speed is not enough, for it will often be that rapid change can only be achieved by imposing large costs upon the population. Thus, a flexible economy is one in which there are both relatively low-cost and speedy reallocations of resources, leading to changing factor proportions, technologies and outputs in response to disequilibria. On the demand side, this implies responsiveness by purchasers to changing relative prices, and comparative ease of substitution in the disposition of income as between consumption and saving.

It must be admitted that in the matter of definition we have made only limited progress and this continuing elusiveness is an obstacle to taking the subject forward. However, it would be wrong to infer that the concept should therefore remain in a condition of neglect. Usage often comes before definition. Various concepts familiar in mainstream economics have established their usefulness despite fuzziness and unmeasurability: the examples of 'luxury goods', 'expectations', and 'the social welfare function' come to mind.

It may be that it would be a mistake to search for a general operational definition. It is likely to be more fruitful to seek partial definitions of flexibility which are useful in the contexts in which they are deployed. For example, one aspect of the adaptability of an economy that has already been reasonably well researched concerns the operation of labour markets. The notion of labour market flexibility has been given differing meanings, but they revolve round the idea of the capacity to adapt to change (Meulders and Wilkin, 1987, p. 5). Klau and Mittelstädt (1986, p. 10) identify four aspects: (i) real labour cost flexibility at the economy-wide level; (ii) adaptability of relative labour costs across occupations and enterprises; (iii) labour mobility; (iv) the flexibility of working time and work schedules.

The notion of labour market flexibility shares with our more overarching interest the qualities of being multi-faceted and difficult to distil into a precise definition. Economists nonetheless find the concept useful and have been able to develop quantified indicators of the degree of labour market flexibility to assess the extent to which various markets possess this quality, how this changes over time and how policy changes may improve upon it. (See also p. 76 on 'Eurosclerosis'.)

In the wider study on which this chapter reports, Peter Smith and Alistair Ulph develop a model which enables them to capture the notion of flexibility quite precisely, in the context of firms' technology choices (in Killick, 1995, chapter 8). They also provide numerical indicators of economy-wide flexibility, from which they derive a composite index. Their indicators include the investment ratio, years of schooling, exchange-rate flexibility, the size of the industrial sector and dependence on commodity exports. They compare the composite index values with their assessments of country responses to oil shocks, concluding that the general index is able to discriminate reasonably well between those countries which adjusted flexibly to the shocks and those which did not.

There is much scope for further work along these lines. One potentially useful approach to giving the notion of flexibility more operational content might be to concentrate on the identification and measurement of the avoidable transactions, or adjustment, costs which we have identified with inflexibility. Meanwhile we should not be unduly daunted by the definitional problem, although the two-way causality between flexibility and economic development requires sophistication in testing and caution in the interpretation of results.

DETERMINANTS OF NATIONAL ECONOMIC FLEXIBILITY

Cells 7 and 8 of Figure 5.1 set out suggested determinants of the flexibility of national economies – hypotheses that were broadly supported by the empirical studies reported in Killick (1995). The hypotheses are sketched in the following paragraphs, beginning with the determinants of responsive flexibility.

Information

Flexibility will be constrained by ignorance about changes in circumstance to which the economy – and policies – must adapt.[12] The flexible economy needs good intelligence: about changing conditions in world trade and finance; about the workings of the domestic economy; about the ways in which policy instruments impact upon the economy; about scientific matters, for example as they bear upon technological progress; and about how these and other variables interact with each other. Through information, the transactions costs of adaptation will be reduced and the likelihood of change enhanced.

Since transactions costs would be zero in a perfectly functioning market economy and imperfect information raises transactions costs, good low-cost information flows are a necessary condition for market efficiency. Stiglitz and his associates have urged the importance of this factor and have fruitfully applied the concept of imperfect information to the analysis of rural credit markets in developing countries.[13] Thus, Hoff and Stiglitz (1990) show how the high costs of obtaining information about potential borrowers – reflecting weak formal financial sector development in rural economies – lead to non-clearing and incomplete financial markets based on credit rationing. Because of their superior access to local-level knowledge, moneylenders and other informal financial intermediaries are better able to meet many of the population's demands for credit and other financial services.

Imperfect information, raising transactions costs, is a particularly large problem in developing country conditions. Indeed, for Klitgaard poor information flows are a defining characteristic of developing countries:[14]

one reason why market institutions work poorly in developing countries is that information about prices, quantities and quality is not readily available. One reason why government bureaucracies work poorly is that information about outputs and outcomes, about laudable achievements and illicit activities, is scarce. (Klitgaard 1991, p. 15)

Market Efficiency

Information is not enough, however, for it must also find reflection in people's incentives. Markets score heavily here, because of their ability to process huge amounts of information about conditions of supply and demand. Their decentralised nature, and their ability to translate information into price incentives and to coordinate a huge number of individual decisions through an interacting network, places them well in advance of what state planners can hope to achieve. Von Hayek (1945) put the point succinctly:[15]

> If we can agree that the economic problem of society is mainly one of rapid adaptation to changes in particular circumstances of time and place, it would seem to follow that the ultimate decisions must be left to the people who are familiar with these circumstances ... We cannot expect that this problem will be solved by first communicating all this knowledge to a central board which, after integrating all knowledge, issues its orders.

In short, a well-functioning market system is conducive to economic flexibility. We would therefore expect an economy dominated by the state, with heavy public participation in production, to be less flexible than one with a productive system based on private enterprise, and this appears to be born out by the stylised facts about centrally-planned Eastern Europe presented earlier.

However, the key word above is 'well-functioning', for all economies experience market failures, particularly in countries still at relatively early stages of development. Among the many conditions contributing to a well-functioning market system, the freedom of entry of new firms into existing markets is particularly important, encouraging the spread of successful ideas and safeguarding against industries becoming slow to take advantage of technological and other opportunities.

Openness

The suggestion here is that international trade is a potent medium for the transfer of information and the transmission of incentives to adapt. Through contractual arrangements and visible embodiment in new goods, merchandise trade provides a flow of information about technological advances, changing tastes and product development. Transnational corporations are similarly a common means by which such changes are conveyed from investing to recipient countries. Learning-by-exporting has, for example, been an important way in which the new economic giants of East Asia have raised their productivities and the quality of their output.[16] Competition from imports ensures that domestic producers must keep abreast or lose markets. More generally, a society which is thoroughly exposed to commerce with, and investments from, the rest of the world is more likely to be aware of the changes occurring around it, and more receptive to new ideas.

This line of approach thus provides a different perspective on the debate about trade policies: governments that provide undiscriminating protection, which penalise exports or which discourage foreign investment thereby reduce the likelihood that their economies will prove adequately adaptable in the face of changing circumstances.

Political Autonomy

The way political power is distributed may act as a barrier to adaptation. Existing policies – however ill-chosen – often have large inertial force because those who benefit are powerful enough to block change. This has often led the IMF and the World Bank to blame inadequate 'political will' for disappointing implementation of adjustment programmes. Unfortunately, the notion of political will is too superficial to take us far. It is necessary to dig beneath this surface to discover the forces acting upon governments and, in particular, the degree of autonomy which the agencies of state enjoy from interest group pressures when determining policies.

There is substantial agreement that relative state autonomy is a factor that has worked to the advantage of the East Asian 'miracle' economies. Thus, Jenkins (1991) identifies the high degree of autonomy of East Asian states, by comparison with those of Latin America, as the chief explanation of the superior development record of the former, while Shams (1989) sees the same factor as an important determinant of the region's implementation of adjustment programmes. The World Bank study of East Asia already cited sees 'technocratic insulation' as an institutional trait that has been crucial to the joint achievement of economic growth and improved income distribution in East Asia:

> technocratic insulation, the ability of economic technocrats to formulate and implement policies in keeping with politically formulated national goals with a minimum of lobbying for special favours from politicians and

interest groups. Without it, technocrats in the high performing Asian economies would have been unable to introduce and sustain rational economic policies, and some vital wealth-sharing mechanisms would have been neutralized soon after their inception. ... (World Bank, 1993b, p. 167)

Wade (1990) similarly identifies the insulation of decision makers from all but the strongest pressure groups and the existence of a powerful executive not beholden to the legislature as among the factors explaining the effectiveness of policy interventions among these countries.

Population Age Structure

The influences at work here are outlined below in the discussion of the development–flexibility connection.

Education

Turning now to the hypothesised influences on innovative flexibility, a population's access to education nominates itself as an important ingredient of this capacity. The educated person will understand more of his/her environment and the changing opportunities it offers and be more self-confident about taking advantage of them.[17] It is from the well-educated that an upwardly-mobile middle class with capitalistic values is most likely to be created, and it is from this group that most modernisation is likely to originate. It is the educated who serve as exemplars to the rest of the population, implicitly inviting them to shed the influences of ignorance and tradition. Moreover, those with scientific and technical educations will go far to determine the ability of a country to take advantage of modern technologies.

In a study of people's abilities to deal with disequilibria Theodore Schultz particularly stressed the value of education in enhancing the ability to adapt, by improving capacities to solve problems. He surveyed a large number of empirical studies bearing upon the influence of education in developing-country agriculture, concluding that there was enough evidence 'to give validity to the hypothesis that the ability to deal successfully with disequilibria is enhanced by education ...' (1975, p. 843).

Technological Capabilities

Even countries with no aspirations to become leaders in basic research or the development of new products nonetheless require a strong technological base if they are to be able to adapt foreign technologies to local needs (for some adaptation to local conditions is almost always needed) and to search in a selective manner for advances abroad which have potential for local application.[18] If they aspire to go beyond adaptation to a more innovatory mode – introducing more substantial improvements to existing products, or developing new products and processes – the depth of their technological capabilities will, of course, be even more crucial.

We can here follow Bell and Pavitt (1993, pp. 261–2) in thinking of technological capabilities as referring to 'the resources needed to generate and manage technical change, including skills, knowledge and experience, and institutional structures and linkages'. Among the inputs they identify as determining the accumulation of technological capabilities are the human and other resources necessary for researching, designing and testing; R&D at the firm level (because it is at the firm level that most productive technology is developed); 'tacit knowledge', that is, productive knowledge acquired through experience and embodied in people and institutions; and the external agglomeration economies secured from a growing volume of technology-based activities. Arguably, the emergence of manufacturing as a leading sector is a necessary condition for the development of an adequate technological capability, with its superior capacity to generate technological externalities.

Historical and Social Influences

To put the matter summarily, we here hypothesise the superiority, for the fostering of flexibility, of value systems and social structures which encourage the idea that human beings are able to improve their own lot, which value education, promote individual (or household) self-improvement, incorporate upward mobility based on merit, and which are outward- rather than inward-looking, embracing cultural diversity and open to external influences.

Tradition and religion nominate themselves as liable to be among the more important institutions. A flexible economy requires a population willing to take action to maximise whatever material benefits may be derived from changing conditions. This points in favour of an individualistic (or family-based) welfare-maximising approach, and mobility in pursuit of this objective, since collective action is apt both to be slower and more uncertain. These attributes may clash with traditional values, however, which often place more stress on the value of collective well-being and erect obstacles to mobility. On the other hand, traditional values may have a positive influence, for the beneficial effects of the political autonomy which has marked the political systems of East Asian countries must be understood as a social phenomenon, reflecting the values and institutions particular to that region.

Religion may have a like effect. Perhaps the key question here is what a religion teaches concerning human beings' relationship to their environment. Some faiths see human fate as predetermined by God's will, and acceptance of poverty as a mere prelude to a better life in the next. Such faiths are not likely to encourage enterprising self-help in response to a changing environment. Others may exert a more positive influence. Confucianism tends nowadays to be ranked alongside the Protestant Ethic as a medal winner.

Path dependence should be added here, i.e. the proposition that the route whereby the present has been reached influences the nature of the present. A study of regional government in Italy by Putnam (et al., 1993) has recently attracted attention as illustrating the deep historical roots of contemporary contrasts between the regions of that country. Killick (1995, chapter 6) similarly finds it necessary to dig below economic explanations to trace present sources of weakness in Africa back to the nature of pre-colonial society and the failures of colonialism to modernise this. Others have come to similar conclusions about the importance of historical influences on the responsiveness of policy processes. Thus, Ranis and Mahmood on the results of a survey of cross-country differences in development experiences:

> In summary, our findings suggest that the determinants of the long-run pattern of policy evolution are intimately linked to systems' initial conditions. These conditions, given partly by nature and partly by the legacy of history, affect not only their initial level of income and welfare, but also their policy responsiveness and flexibility over time, i.e. the extent to which policy is likely to be accommodative or obstructive of some basic time-phased evolutionary change. (Ranis and Mahmood 1992, p. 223)

Implicit in that quotation is the view, shared here, that an economy's flexibility and its development are intimately connected. It may be useful, therefore, to consider possible regularities in this connection.

THE FLEXIBILITY–DEVELOPMENT CONNECTION

Our starting point here is the structuralist view that underdeveloped economies are inflexible. Our suggested determinants of flexibility support this view and imply a roughly ∩-shaped, or inverted-U, relationship. Such a model is illustrated in Figure 5.2.[19] This postulates that at any given level of development both flexibility-raising and flexibility-reducing forces will be at work. The net effect of these is likely to leave the least developed economies with rigid economies, but there are net accretions to flexibility up to Y_1, beyond which it diminishes again.

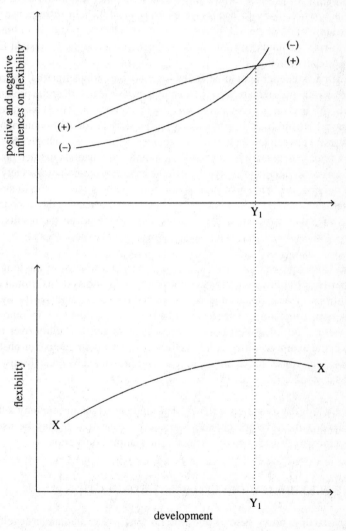

FIGURE 5.2: *The Flexibility–Development Connection*

What might be the basis for such a model? Consider first the reasons why flexibility may be enhanced by development. For reasons already mentioned, the data base and information flows can be expected to be poor at early stages of development. These can be expected to improve as the economy develops because it will be feasible to devote larger resources to the collection and dissemination of information, channels of communication will become better developed and a larger part of economic activity will take place within organised units more amenable to data-gathering.

Further, the hold of any traditional values and modes that impede adaptability will be gradually weakened as development proceeds, education levels improve and modernising attitudes come to dominate. The economy will become more industrialised, bringing greater potential for the rapid response of output to changing price relativities, and for the mobility of resources, because skills and some other assets will be less specific than in primary production.

There are also likely to be agglomeration economies arising from the growing size of the industrial sector, which influence the country's technological capacity. Thus Freeman argues that:

> it is the national system of innovation which is decisive, not the particular range of products. Universities, research institutions, technological infrastructure, industrial training systems, information systems, design centres and other scientific and technical institutions provide the essential foundation which alone make possible the adaptation to structural change in the economy associated with changes in techno-economic paradigm. (Freeman, 1989, p. 97)

For these and related reasons, indigenous technological capacities will increase and deepen with development, a transformation further accelerated by the externalities arising from the accumulation of experience and knowledge.

Partly because the domestic market will be enlarged by development, competition among domestic producers will grow, increasing the pressures upon them to be responsive. Dualism will diminish, for this is largely a feature of early-stage developing economies, and markets will become more complete. In other respects, too, we would expect market efficiency to improve, and factors to become more mobile. The larger size of developed economies can be an advantage in other ways. Being less reliant on commodity exports, they will not be so vulnerable to shocks transmitted from the rest of the world. And their more diversified structures of demand

and production will facilitate the movement of resources, and perhaps demand, between products.[20] At the same time, the advantage of a simple economic structure – that transactions costs tend to be low – may not be realised in underdeveloped economies because weak institutions may leave such costs higher than necessary.

For these reasons, we hypothesise that the less developed an economy, the less flexible it will be – a view consistent with our earlier characterisation of the condition of African economies. There is a vicious circle at work: inflexibility retards development and underdevelopment retards flexibility. Indeed, in some cases this may understate the case. A substantial proportion of least developed economies not only experience the rigidities just mentioned but have suffered serious economic and social deteriorations: declining incomes and living standards, decaying infrastructures, a worsening quality of health and education services, a shrinking tax base leading to inflationary pressures and adding to already acute balance-of-payments problems. In some such countries, there has been a simultaneous decay in the capabilities of the state, with economic life increasingly conducted through unregulated parallel markets, extensive corruption, a serious erosion of senior personnel and morale in the public services, and widespread alienation of peoples from their governments. Where such conditions prevail, the difficulties of successful adaptation are greatly increased.

However, it would not be justified to describe the flexibility–development connection as comprising a low-level trap. The association of inflexibility with underdevelopment is not likely to dominate outcomes. We shall shortly introduce some qualifications to the hypothesis of a ∩-shaped relationship and, in any case, there are things that the governments of even the poorest, most run-down countries can do to increase the adaptability of their economies, shifting upwards the X–X schedule of Figure 5.2. That is what structural adjustment programmes seek to do. What is suggested, however, is that, other things being equal, progress along the X–X schedule will be slower in the early stages and will gather pace as the economy modernises. The least developed face an uphill task and adjust more slowly than more developed economies.

What now of the upper turning point, when flexibility begins to diminish? The argument here is particularly associated with Olson's *The Rise and Decline of Nations* (1982, especially chapter 3). This postulates that, as an economy matures, society becomes more articulated into special-interest organisations and that these grow in relative influence. Many will be 'distributional' coalitions, such as trade unions and producer cartels, primarily concerned to enhance the share of their memberships in national income, rather than with the expansion of aggregate income or with the national interest. Hence Olson sees distributional coalitions as reducing factor mobilities and slowing down a society's capacity to adopt new technologies and reallocate resources in response to changing conditions (pp. 61–5).

Giersch (1986) argues a related case, to the effect that the economies of Western Europe are becoming increasingly rigid.[21] Like Olson, he relates this to the increased strength of special interest groups, especially of industrialists and organised labour, introducing major labour market rigidities (for example, through large severance-pay obligations) and undermining governments' abilities to achieve change through consensus. He writes of 'Eurosclerosis', linking his argument to governments' post-World War II commitments to full employment and arguing that Keynesian demand-management policies in pursuit of this turned into 'promises to protect'. He sees the resulting growth in protectionism acting as a brake on structural change and on the adoption of technological advances.

We should also recall the suggestion that transactions costs tend to rise as economies become more complex, unless cost-reducing institutions develop fast enough to offset this tendency. The arguments about distributional coalitions and Eurosclerosis could be reinterpreted along these lines, as part of a broader hypothesis that there is some tendency for transactions costs to outstrip institutional innovations at more advanced levels of economic development.

Demographic dimensions can be added to these arguments. The more mature industrialised economies are characterised by populations which are growing only slowly, if at all, and are therefore ageing.[22] An ageing population may reduce flexibility in a number of ways. First, it necessitates a shift in the provision of public services away from education (which can be thought of as an investment in human capital and technological capabilities) in favour of welfare provisions for the elderly (which do nothing to enhance future productivities). Moreover, when there is a rapid pace of technological progress, an ageing labour force will be less adept than a youthful one at absorbing these changes. Older workers are apt to be more resistant to retraining and, in any case, the profitability of investments in retraining diminishes sharply with the age of trainees. Similarly, an ageing labour force can be expected to be less mobile than a younger one, reducing an economy's ability to let old industries go and succeed in new ones, or will increase the 'adjustment costs' of doing so.[23]

An economy's maturity may also work to reduce adaptability through its effect on the age-structure of the stock of physical capital and the technologies embodied in it. A mature economy will be relatively capital-intensive. The volume of new investment in any one period will be small relative to the existing capital stock, and that stock can therefore be changed only rather slowly. It is for such reasons that it is reckoned to have been an advantage for the German and Japanese economies that much of their capital stock was destroyed during World War II, leaving them subsequently with a more modern capital base than most of their European and North American competitors.

To the case for a ∩-shaped development–flexibility relationship some caveats must now be entered. Some of the reasons why rigidities may increase with maturity are symmetrical, working to the advantage of the 'immature'. Thus, developing countries have youthful populations, which, by inversion of the earlier arguments, should give them positive advantages. Similarly, with the capital stock. It should also be said that most of the suggestions in this section are speculative, with little hard evidence in either direction. Both the shape and the stability of the ∩-curve are hence in question. Furthermore, some of the arguments appear rather ephemeral. For example, Giersch's arguments about Eurosclerosis, although made only a few years ago, already seem dated in some important respects, for the Conservative Revolution of recent years has diminished the power of trade unions and appears to have increased the flexibility of Europe's labour and capital markets.

It is not, in any case, suggested that the degree of flexibility is an invariable function of the stage of development. A major economic crisis can make radical changes acceptable which previously would have been politically impossible, as in the former communist countries of Eastern Europe at the beginning of the 1990s. Government actions that enhance exposure to international competition are among actions that can raise flexibility. So can other types of policy intervention, just as central planning repressed it. In short, the X–X curve can be induced to shift. Indeed, it may be that the development–flexibility relationship cannot be reduced to simple geometry at all. What is clear, however, is that there are a number of channels through which these variables influence each other. There is much scope for empirical research here, even though causality will be difficult to untangle.

CONCLUSION

Having commenced by arguing the case for the importance of flexibility as a determinant of the performance of national economies, it is appropriate to conclude by pointing out that flexibility should not be taken as desirable without qualification.

First, if we could imagine complete economic flexibility, with no restraints on labour and other factor movements, the outcome would be marked by enormous uncertainties, not to say chaos. Indeed, there is a trade-off between flexibility and confidence in the future. Since a sense of security is very important to most people, the desirability of diminishing this in the name of enhancing flexibility should not be taken for granted. Adaptation involves losses of income, reduced living standards, increased unemployment, the frustration of personal potentialities, even worsened morbidity and mortality: the social costs of adjustment.

A more technical point about costs concerns the tension between the flexibility of policy makers and the credibility of their decisions – what was earlier called the delicate balance to be struck between flexibility and continuity in policies. Policy adaptability requires a capacity to combine responsiveness with continuity of purpose. The modern theory of economic policy places much weight on the attribute of 'pre-commitment': a government's ability to persuade the public that its policy signals can be depended upon as a basis for investment and other decisions about the future by making credible commitments which restrict its future freedom to change these signals. What is needed in some circumstances is the capacity for 'strategic inflexibility' – the power to appear inflexible when that is called for. Thus, Chang's paper on the East Asian case in the larger study (Killick, 1995, chapter 7) develops the theme of 'flexible rigidities'. He sees trade-offs between short-run and long-run flexibility, arguing that in East Asia policy interventions created short-run rigidities in order to achieve greater long-term flexibility. A stable policy environment was created in the short term to encourage long-term planning and investments in specific assets necessary for the creation of flexible economic structures. However, this is a tricky balance to achieve. As Williamson (1991, p. 35) has observed about Eastern Europe: '... the stability value of socialism turned out to be an immobility burden in the end'. We can add that rapid-fire policy response is not necessarily optimal. There can often be merit in deferring action when there are major uncertainties: delay may permit a better-informed response later.

What these considerations tell us, then, is that we should not elevate flexibility as a goal to be pursued above all others and at all times. Because it has costs, its desirability should not be taken as axiomatic; and it needs to be traded off against other desiderata. Its value is an instrumental one, promoting long-term economic progress, but it is only one of the factors that have such value. Nevertheless, this chapter may persuade readers that the past neglect of the idea of flexibility should be rectified.

NOTES

1. Reprinted with permission from *World Development*, vol. 23, no. 5, pp. 721–34, 'Flexibility and Economic Progress', 1995, Elsevier Science Ltd, Pergamon Imprint, Oxford, England. This chapter draws upon a larger, multi-authored study (Killick, 1995) which was principally financed by the Ford Foundation. Its support is gratefully acknowledged, as is my large intellectual debt to my fellow contributors, from whom I have borrowed heavily in what follows. However, the view presented here is a personal one and the usual disclaimers apply. I am also grateful for the helpful comments of two anonymous referees.

2. See Killick (1995, chapter 6) for a fuller presentation of evidence of inflexibility and for supporting references.

3. Source: World Bank, *World Development Report, 1991* and *1993*, Table 16, which shows a share of 92 per cent in both 1965 and 1991.

4. Thus, a study of country experiences with IMF programmes found that natural disasters had been an important, perhaps dominant, factor in decisions to turn to the IMF for help in 6 out of 17 countries studied (see Killick and Malik, 1992, p. 604).

5. Bangladesh is the most spectacular example of a country prone to weather shocks, recording in 1960–81 17 major floods and 37 cyclones, and with many further disasters since.

6. Further weight is added to the importance of shocks for economic performance by an interesting study of long-term growth trends by Easterly et al. (1993), which points out that growth models seek to explain economic performance by reference to country attributes. These attributes are only slow-changing, however, whereas there are large observed variations in country growth rates over time. The authors argue that these facts can only be reconciled by the influence of exogenous shocks: 'Shocks, especially those to terms of trade, play a much larger role in explaining variance in growth rates than previously acknowledged' (p. 1). To this they might have added, 'and the ability to respond to these shocks'.

7. Thus, the share of primary products in total world merchandise exports fell from 57 per cent in 1950 to 26 per cent in 1991, with manufactures growing from 43 per cent to 74 per cent (Kenwood and Lougheed, 1993, Table 28; World Bank, 1993c, Table 15).

8. Indeed, some see this as rendering obsolete much industrial organisation based on techniques of mass production, giving way to much smaller-scale units based on 'flexible specialisation' (Piore and Sabel, 1984).

9. Thus, the OECD economies recorded an average growth rate of 4.2 per cent in 1962–79, against 2.4 per cent in 1979–92, although there are admittedly considerable movements around these averages (World Bank, 1993a, Table 6.2).

10. See Lächler (1988) for an exploration of this theme, applied to the question of anti-inflation policies in 'Southern Cone' Latin American countries.

11. The influence of North (1990 and 1992) on the following must be acknowledged.

12. Thus, Mody (1990, p. 311) attributes much of the proven ability of Taiwan's electronics industry to respond successfully to the use in that

country of various public productivity, research standardisation and marketing institutions to gather and disseminate information to private
history.

13. See the September 1990 special issue of the *World Bank Economic Review*
     on imperfect information and rural credit markets.

14. See also Stiglitz's essay in Chenery and Srinivasan (1988, volume 1,
     chapter 5) and the references cited there.

15. I have borrowed this highly apposite quote from Alexander Neuber's contri-
     bution to the larger project (Killick, 1995)

16. Thus, a major World Bank study (1993b, pp. 318–20) of the 'East Asian
     Miracle' argues the great importance of that region's manufactured exports
     for overcoming imperfect information by permitting the acquisition of the
     knowledge necessary for high productivity through the purchase of new
     equipment, direct foreign investment, the licensing of existing foreign tech-
     nologies, information from customers and in other ways.

17. An interesting recent piece of evidence pointing to a connection between
     education and responsiveness is reported in Bernheim and Scholz (1993).
     They found that in the US tax incentives to encourage saving are less effect-
     ive for those without a college education because, though both those with
     and without college education responded in some degree, the elasticity of
     the college-educated to changes in the rate of return was roughly seven
     times larger.

18. See Rosenberg (1982) and Fransman (1986) for valuable surveys of the lit-
     erature on innovation and technological change. Both these writers – and
     many others – stress the potentially high costs of the search process and that
     adaptation to local conditions is an almost invariable rule in the introduction
     of foreign technologies into the domestic productive system.

19. I should like to acknowledge the helpful suggestions of Moshe Syrquin in
     improving this presentation.

20. Thus the United Nations *World Economic Survey* (1985, p. 15) commented
     that the larger and more diversified economies with large production capaci-
     ties were better able to adjust to external shocks, taking advantage of under-
     utilised manufacturing capacity and an ability to switch from home to
     foreign markets in order to expand their exports.

21. Note, however, that his argument does not really fit into the hypothesis of a
     ∩-shaped relationship, for he compares Europe not so much with countries
     at an earlier stage of development as with the US and Japan.

22. For a good survey of these issues see Richter (1992) from whom I have bor-
     rowed freely.

23. These arguments can be related to those of one of the few economists to
     have written about the flexibility of economies. Cornwall (1977) sees such
     flexibility as a major influence on long-run growth, although he defines this,
     curiously, as the rate of growth of factor supplies (p. 39). He argues
     (pp. 181–2) that expanding capital stocks and labour forces are means of
     overcoming market imperfections and rigidities because they facilitate the
     reallocation of resources into new lines of production, and allow firms to
     take advantage of new technologies and the possibilities of increasing
     returns to scale.

REFERENCES

Bell, Martin and Keith Pavitt (1993), 'Accumulating technological capability in developing countries', in *Proceedings of World Bank Annual Conference on Development Economics, 1992* (Washington, DC: World Bank).

Bernheim, Douglas and John Scholz (1993), 'Private saving and public policy', Working Paper No. 4215 (Cambridge, MA: National Bureau of Economic Research).

Chenery, Hollis and T.N. Srinivasan (eds) (1988), *Handbook of Development Economics* vol. I (Amsterdam: North-Holland).

Chowdhury, Anis and Iyanatul Islam (1993), *The Newly Industrialising Economies of East Asia* (London: Routledge).

Cornwall, John (1977), *Modern Capitalism: Its Growth and Transformation* (London: Martin Robertson).

Easterly, William, Michael Kremer, Lant Pritchett and Lawrence Summers (1993) (processed), 'Good policy or good luck? Country growth performance and temporary shocks' (Washington, DC: World Bank).

Easterly, William and Ross Levine (1993) (processed), 'Is Africa different? Evidence from growth regressions' (Washington, DC: World Bank, April).

Fransman, Martin (1986), *Technology and Economic Development* (Brighton: Wheatsheaf Books).

Freeman, C. (1989), 'New technology and catching up', *European Journal of Development Research*, vol. 1, no. 1, June 1989.

Giersch, Herbert (1986), *Liberalisation for Faster Economic Growth* (London: Institute of Economic Affairs).

Hoff, Karla and Joseph E. Stiglitz (1990), 'Introduction: imperfect information and rural credit markets – puzzles and policy perspectives', *World Bank Economic Review*, vol. 4, no. 3, September.

Jenkins, Rhys (1991), 'The political economy of industrialisation: a comparison of Latin American and East Asian Newly Industrialising Countries', *Development and Change* vol. 22, no. 2, April.

Kenwood, A.G. and A.L. Lougheed (1993), *The Growth of the International Economy, 1820–1993* (London and New York: Routledge (3rd edition)).

Killick, Tony (ed.) (1995), *The Flexible Economy: Causes and Consequences of the Adaptability of National Economies* (London: Routledge and Overseas Development Institute).

Killick, Tony and Moazzam Malik (1992), 'Country experiences with IMF programmes', *World Economy* vol. 15, no. 5, September.

Klau, Friedrich and Axel Mittelstädt (1986), 'Labour market flexibility', *OECD Economic Studies* no. 6, Spring.

Klitgaard, Robert (1991), *Adjusting to Reality* (San Francisco, CA: ICS Press).

Lächler, Ulrich (1988), 'Credibility and the dynamics of disinflation in open economies', *Journal of Development Economics* vol. 28, no. 3, May.

MacGaffey, Janet et al. (1991), *The Real Economy of Zaire* (London: James Currey).

Meulders, Danièle and Luc Wilkin (1987), 'Labour market flexibility: critical introduction to the analysis of a concept', *Labour and Society* vol. 12, no. 1, January.

Mody, Ashoka (1990), 'Institutions and dynamic comparative advantage: the electronics industry in South Korea and Taiwan', *Cambridge Journal of Economics* vol. 14, no. 3, September.

Morris, Cynthia Taft and Irma Adelman (1988), *Comparative Patterns of Economic Development, 1850–1914* (Baltimore and London: Johns Hopkins University Press).

North, Douglass C. (1990), *Institutions, Institutional Change, and Economic Performance* (Cambridge: Cambridge University Press).

North, Douglass C. (1992), 'Transactions costs, institutions, and economic performance', Occasional Paper No. 30 (San Francisco, CA: International Center for Economic Growth).

Olson, Mancur (1982), *The Rise and Decline of Nations: Economic Growth, Stagflation, and Social Rigidities* (New Haven, CT: Yale University Press).

Piore, M.J. and C.F. Sabel (1984), *The Second Industrial Divide: Possibilities for Prosperity* (New York: Basic Books).

Putnam, R.D. with R. Leonardi and R.Y. Nanetti (1993), *Making Democracy Work: Civic Traditions in Modern Italy* (Princeton, NJ: Princeton University Press).

Ranis, Gustav and Syed A. Mahmood (1992), *The Political Economy of Development Policy Change* (Cambridge, MA and Oxford: Blackwell).

Richter, Josef (1992), 'Economic aspects of aging: review of the literature' in George J. Stolnitz (ed.), *Demographic Causes and Economic Consequences of Population Aging* (New York: United Nations).

Rosenberg, Nathan (1982), *Inside the Black Box: Technology and Economics* (Cambridge: Cambridge University Press).

Schultz, Theodore W. (1975), 'The value of the ability to deal with disequilibria', *Journal of Economic Literature* vol. XIII, no. 3, September.

Shams, Rasul (1989), 'Adjustment constraints in developing countries – a comparative study', *Intereconomics* vol. 24, no. 2, March/April.

United Nations (1985), *World Economic Survey 1985* (New York and Geneva: United Nations).

Von Hayek, Friedrich (1945), 'The use of knowledge in society', *American Economic Review* vol. 35, no. 4, pp. 519–30.

Wade, Robert (1990), *Governing the Market: Economic Theory and the Role of Government in East Asian Industrialization* (Princeton, NJ: Princeton University Press).

Williamson, Oliver (1991), 'Institutional aspects of economic reform: the transactions costs economics perspective', Mimeo (University of Berkeley).

World Bank (1991), *World Development Report, 1991* (Washington, DC: World Bank).

World Bank (1992), *The Third Report on Adjustment Lending: Private and Public Resources for Growth* (Washington, DC: World Bank).

World Bank (1993a), *Global Economic Prospects and the Developing Countries, 1993* (Washington, DC: World Bank).

World Bank (1993b), *The East Asian Miracle: Economic Growth and Public Policy* (New York: Oxford University Press).

World Bank (1993c), *World Development Report, 1993* (Washington, DC: World Bank).

Part II:
Social Responses

6 Is the Idea of Development Eurocentric?

Nigel Dower

COMMON CRITICISM OF WESTERN DOMINANCE

One of the most remarkable books to have come out in the last few years on development is *The Development Dictionary*, edited by Wolfgang Sachs, remarkable both for the vigour with which all the authors attack the core concept of development, and also, given their attitude, for its being called a dictionary! 'The idea of development stands like a ruin in the intellectual landscape', says Sachs in the Introduction (Sachs 1992). In the name of development the rest of the world is undergoing submission to the global economy and a kind of homogenisation of cultures as the western model of development based on economic growth, science, techno- logy and bureaucratic systems is taken to be the norm for everywhere. It is an immensely powerful ruin – indeed the Foucault-like subtitle of the book is 'A Guide to Knowledge as Power' – but a ruin in the sense that its impact is ruinous for the peoples of the world. Whatever human flourish- ing is, modern development processes are generally not helping it to occur and indeed impeding and undermining it. This is both because the elemen- tary necessities of life are not achieved and because the authentic and diverse ways of life are undermined.

Such thinking has many intellectual sources of course. Postmodernism and relativism stress the diversity of cultures threatened by development and the lack of a common reference point informed by reason. Marxist and Realist analysis of economic and international power will see the dis- course as a tool for dominant interests. More modestly, if one sees devel- opment as much more than economic growth, the implied comparison between North and South as developed and not-developed may be deeply questioned along with the assumption that the North provides the goal or model for the South. And at the most pragmatic level one can simply observe how often, even in terms of the standard goals of development aid, things go wrong.

85

Is then the idea of development essentially Eurocentric? By Eurocentric I mean:

(a)   The idea came from European thinking;[1]
(b)   It has spread to most of the rest of the world (and this in a way includes China), and would not be accepted and adopted as public policy in other parts of the world but for this transmission by the colonial/imperial powers and more recently Northern dominance in the economic and information systems of the world;
(c)   It is a bad thing that it has so spread, either because of the process of its imposition by 'power', or because of its results in that it displaces what is more valuable elsewhere, or both.

Since it will be relevant to some moves later on, let me distinguish between a weaker claim and a stronger claim. 'Eurocentric[d]' includes (a) and (b) but excludes (c) – hence 'd' for descriptive. 'Eurocentric[e]' includes (c) as well as (a) and (b), namely the evaluation that it is a bad thing – hence 'e' for evaluative.

I shall argue that the idea of development is both Eurocentric and not Eurocentric, depending upon what one means by 'idea'. At its root the idea or concept of development is not Eurocentric – in either the 'e' sense or the 'd' sense. What, however, is often called, more loosely, the 'idea' of development is commonly Eurocentric[d], and quite often Eurocentric[e]. Indeed I accept that many of the criticisms made of development are in order. Like many I am very worried about the destruction of cultures, the disvaluing of local or indigenous knowledge, the dominance of growth (even growth with equity) in development thinking. But to reject the idea of development because of this is to throw out the baby with the bathwater, and is in effect to reject the idea of development because of what is often done in the name of development.

I should add, to forestall any misunderstanding, that I am here talking about development as a process of socio-economic change which is an object of public policy. This sense is of course itself something that has grown out of (indeed is a development from) other senses of the term 'development'. That acorns develop into oak trees, that children develop into adults, that situations develop into crises, that towns develop into cities, that a derelict field can develop into an ornate garden, that prehominids developed into hominids, that feudal societies developed into capitalist societies – all this can be accepted. Some changes we call developments involve immanent teleology (as in biological processes), some changes are according to human purpose, individual or collective, some are processes of natural or social evolution (maybe goal-directed or law-governed or neither), some changes just happen and are either of neutral significance or simply bad news. The issue in this chapter is not about whether any of these uses are Eurocentric – they clearly are not – but the use of the term in a distinct, modern way, where the area of discourse is clear enough, but what we say about it is by no means clear or agreed.[2]

I used to think it was simply a matter of recognising that at its core development, as used in planning or programme contexts, is an evaluative concept – a process of socio-economic change which ought to happen – and so what is at issue between conventional advocates of growth, western technology, and so on, and those who go in for alternative technology, such as eco-friendly practices, is simply that each thinks different things ought to be done – either because their goals are different or because they believe that different means will achieve commonly agreed goals (like reduction of extreme poverty), or both. This rather bald statement of the evaluative character of development needs clarification, which I will turn to shortly.

I now think it is a more complex and in a sense a deeper issue. Development is not, as I shall argue in the last part of this chapter, an optional concept or a 'take-it-or-leave-it' concept. It is not merely that we do bring values and normative priorities – often different from each other – to bear on public policy decisions. There is a sense in which we must do so, once we have acquired the awareness that how things go in the policy arena is subject, however chaotically, indirectly or strangely as it often is, to collective choice. Not all societies were or are involved in a process we could call development (and there is no implication here that they ought to be or to have been). But once a certain way of thinking about social change and about the possibilities of combined or collective choices making a difference has become accepted, the idea of development has taken hold.[3] In this sense, to be elaborated later, development is far from being a European invention but a fundamental category of human experience and agency (though not an a priori category). A Latin American once said to a friend of mine, 'we don't want to be developed by you, we want to be liberated from you'. Here the point is taken, but the liberation movements of Latin America are about development in the fundamental sense which I intend, if anything is. The words 'development', 'dessarollo' or whatever else may not be used, but the idea is there all the same. But here I anticipate the goal I wish to reach. Let me go back to the beginning and consider more cautiously the opening statement that the idea of development is Eurocentric.

RESPONSE 1: ROBUSTLY ACCEPT THE EQUATION, BUT ARGUE THAT THE MODEL IS GOOD FOR ALL THE WORLD

Of course one response to the opening indictment, and perhaps the most common, which we might call the robust response, is to reject the criticism contained in it, and to claim that development is Eurocentric[d] but not Eurocentric[e]. One might accept that the idea of development is indeed European in origin and that for a variety of reasons it has spread to the rest of the world, but argue that this indeed is both good for the rest of the world and what in fact the rest of the world wants. All people want to be free from extreme poverty and also to have material comforts and affluence (except perhaps for a small minority of ascetics in any culture), and the western methods – economic, technological, political, bureaucratic – are simply what is needed to enable people to achieve these common goals. Even before 1989, the same picture held: what the communist countries offered was essentially the same package, with some variations of how modern economic and political systems are to be run. Development, so understood, represents indeed the 'end of history' in both senses – goal and completion.[4]

I do not accept this robust response, for reasons already indicated earlier. I do not intend to pursue this issue here as it takes me away from my main concern. Writers like Chambers (1983) and more recently Orskov (1993) have stressed the importance of indigenous culture, technology and wisdom. Riddell, in *Foreign Aid Reconsidered* (Riddell, 1987), while by no means condemnatory of aid in a sweeping way as Hayter (1981) once was, produced a more even balance sheet, but it still shows an awful lot wrong with development programmes as conceived of by western experts. I think we do have to take seriously too the thought that what motivates the development of developing countries by western trade and aid, has as much if not more to do with our own economic prospects as anything else. Development, it would seem, is a weapon, whatever else it is, in a power game.

My other reason for rejecting the equation 'development equals western-style economic growth', is simply that we foreclose on the options if we attempt to define it thus. The view that development is western-style economic growth is just one view of what development is, admittedly a very popular and dominant view, but still one view amongst others. Disagreement cannot be ruled out by definitional fiat. So I am also rejecting the claim that the idea of development is Eurocentric[d] as well, insofar as the chief motive for calling development Eurocentric[d] is the equation with economic growth and so on. Strictly, though, as the later argument shows, this is too quick, since it might be that the range of disagreements were within a common definition which was Eurocentric[d] because they were all variations on a European theme.

RESPONSE 2: DISTINGUISH BETWEEN CONCEPTIONS/CONCEPT OF DEVELOPMENT

We can give a little more precision to the last point if we can distinguish more clearly between the 'one' and the 'many', the one idea of development and the many accounts of what it is. Two pieces of conceptual apparatus can be introduced. John Rawls in his seminal work *A Theory of Justice* introduces a distinction between the concept of social justice and the many conceptions of social justice (Rawls, 1971). Here the idea is that we can all agree on the basic concept (roughly: the distribution of benefits and burdens of social cooperation) but we present different conceptions, incorporating different theories, and so on, of social justice, which we would not expect others to agree with us about. Whether or not this distinction is entirely successful with regard to social justice, I believe it to be heuristically useful in the case of development. Thus, broadly one might say that the concept of development is a process of socio-economic change subject to human control. Each person will have different views about what kind of change they want/think ought to happen, so each will present a rival conception of development.

A second conceptual tool I bring in here comes from Martha Nussbaum's article 'Non-Relative Virtues – an Aristotelian Approach' (Nussbaum, 1993). Although her focus is on virtues, it has a relevance (which she herself is aware of) to development issues – indeed, although she is well known as a classical scholar, she has collaborated recently with Amartya Sen in thinking philosophically about development. In that article she distinguished between what she calls a 'thin' account of virtue – a disposition to behave in a certain settled but chosen way in respect of an area of basic human experience, for example attitudes towards one's own death or towards possessions – and a 'thick' account, namely a particular theory about what that settled behaviour is which constitutes a virtue.[5] So again, we could make the point that there is a thin account of development and many thick accounts of development.

We can therefore now move to accept the criticism of much that is done in the name of development, but reject the claim that the idea of development is Eurocentric. A certain conception or, more accurately, a certain cluster of conceptions is indeed Eurocentric, both in the factual sense 'd' and in the evaluative judgement 'e' implicit in that. One of the thick accounts, using Nussbaum's terminology, is Eurocentric. But the idea of development is not, if by 'idea' we mean the concept or thin account, that is an account of what development is which all parties could agree on.

Let us try this suggestion out for size. What would this thin account be? Very cautiously we might say: it is a process of socio-economic change. Since the subject matter is clearly society and development must involve change, that at least seems basic. Isn't there more to be said? Such change does not just happen, something we simply witness, good, bad or indifferent. Development is the concept it is because the change is brought about by human agency, usually collective agency, or the agency of one or some in the interests of a larger group.

What, however, if one group is pursuing development which they think is good but which I, the thinker, judge to be bad? Do I call it development? I might say, 'it is what they think of as development', I might refer to it as 'development' (that is, in inverted commas), or qualify it as 'poor' or 'inappropriate' development. All these moves signal the making of an exception to a normal assumption (the default state one might say) when using the term development in a prescriptive context, that is, a context of deciding or recommending action. This normal assumption is that the idea of development incorporates the thinker's own value assessment as to what kind of change ought to happen. So we could say, as I have argued elsewhere, that the concept or thin account of development (that is, in planning/prescriptive contexts which provide the life-blood of the concept) is a process of socio-economic change which ought to happen (Dower, 1989). We can all agree that that is what we mean, but then disagree on the filling or thick account.

Whether or not my 'evaluative definition' of development is accepted, the general point does not perhaps entirely depend on its acceptance. This is that there may be many rival accounts of what development is. The dominant western model is one of them – pervasive as it is.

PROBLEM RESTATED: THE POSSIBILITY THAT AT A DEEPER LEVEL THE VERY IDEA/CONCEPT OF DEVELOPMENT IS WESTERN/CULTURALLY SPECIFIC.

The distinction between concept and conceptions, between the 'one' and the 'many' is, I think, right and provides the basis of the answer to the question of my paper: No, the idea of development is not Eurocentric, in either the descriptive sense or the evaluative sense. But in a sense this move is too quick, and too easy. There is in fact a deeper issue here, which needs more exploring. Perhaps the very idea of development is culturally specific and rooted in European thought, in Enlightenment thinking, in ideas of 'progress' and so on.

After all it was the rare if not unique combination of western science/technology which gave men (sic, I fear) the power to control nature[6] and thus to make sustained material progress possible, combined with the more generally liberating powers of reason which in its secular mode gave men the confidence or permission (as it were) to use that technological power to pursue heaven on earth. Is not development in the twentieth century basically the outgrowth of all that? Science and technology existed before (for example, China), but other religious world views did not liberate energies to transform the material world. Conversely ideas of material progress may have existed elsewhere without the material means or knowledge to do much about it.

SOME ASSUMPTIONS ABOUT DEVELOPMENT

Even if we grant that the model of development as western-style economic growth is too restrictive to be the concept, that is, what we mean by development, it may still be the case that there is rather more built into the idea of development than appears on the surface. Keeping an open mind therefore on the possibility that the idea of development is after all culture-specific to its European origins, I want to consider a range of features which, for a very large number of us, would indeed seem to be at the very core of what we mean by development (even if we are not happy with conventional economic growth assumptions).

Let us consider the following:

(a) It is a process of change on a social scale which is from a worse to a better state (or: which ought to happen).
(b) This change is subject to human control.
(c) There is a rational basis for social order.
(d) All human beings are intrinsically important as individuals.
(e) Human beings are autonomous agents with a need to exercise their autonomy.
(f) Consent/common good lies at the basis of social order.
(g) Centrality of the state as the embodiment of consent/channel of common good is accepted.
(h) Centrality or adequacy of the secular in the account of social change (for example, western ethical theories).

First let me elaborate a little what I mean by these features. It should be pointed out in passing that I present these as plausible candidates for the idea of development. A reader whose conception of development includes all these features (and no doubt many more) must ask: are these part of the core concept or what anyone would understand? If on the other hand thinkers, like myself,[7] are doubtful whether all these features do belong to their conception, then a fortiori they do not for them belong to the concept either (and should not therefore for anyone else who recognises these thinkers as having a bona fide understanding of development).

(a) A Process of Change from a Worse to a Better State

This has already been mentioned, but I am here making more explicit the evaluative/prescriptive character of the idea. Most people tend to think of development in terms of state of affairs at T1 (Time period 1) – so much extreme poverty, average nutritional levels as such and such, so much sub-standard housing, a level of Gross National Product (GNP) – and a state of affairs at T2 when there is less extreme poverty, higher levels of nutrition, less sub-standard housing, higher GNP, and so on. The latter states are, it is claimed, better than the former states, and this is the reason why the process ought to happen, or rather, to anticipate feature (b), ought to be made to happen. The rationale here is: more (quantitatively) of features accepted as good (or less of features accepted as bad).

But there may well be other kinds of reasons why a process of change ought to happen. Briefly, the state of affairs at T2 may be qualitatively better than at T1 – an improved social or legal structure, a new economic regime, democracy or equality compared with a lack of it before (consider South Africa's recent transition). Or, alternatively, part of what makes the process of change something that ought to happen may be the very quality of the process of change itself (that is, not merely measured by comparing time-slices) – initiative and vitality, participation, exercise of freedom.

(b) Change Subject to Human Control

Although value language ('good', 'bad', even 'ought') can be used in contexts where action is not envisaged or even thought appropriate or possible, the reason why development is thought of as under (a) above is precisely because it is a process of change which is at least to some extent subject to human control. How much control is possible or appropriate and what methods of direction are possible or appropriate are matters of great debate (though it is generally assumed as under (g) that the state has

a lot to do with it). We may not have the arrogant confidence of the nine-
teenth century in its belief in the inevitability of progress, but we do
believe in its possibility and indeed in some contexts its probability.

It does seem to be part of the core that, if development for a social unit is
a process that ought to happen, then either individuals are generally
involved in making decisions collectively about it, or some individuals,
agencies or institutions act on behalf of the unit as a whole. It is not enough
that a process of change take place as a by-product of each agent pursuing
his or her private goals. If Adam Smith had been right about the hidden
hand ensuring the public good while we are all beavering away at our
private goods, the idea of development would not have been necessary![8]

(c) A Rational Basis for Social Order

The reason why development processes are to some extent subject to
control, influence or direction, is because society is seen as a social order
based on reason, or at least informed by reason. Before the sociologists
reading this get too upset, let me tone down my suggestion. Indeed, as
with the previous feature (with which it is linked in this respect), the
manner and extent of reason's role in social order is a matter of great
debate. The minimal idea is this: human social order and structure do not
merely exist in some blind, unknown, or inevitable form. It is not merely a
herd instinct that makes us into the societies we form. Even if we stress
the roles of tradition and custom (often misleadingly cast into the role of
the antithesis of reason), they have the roles they do partly because those
who maintain them recognise them as contributing to human well-being
both instrumentally (as a means to peace, stability, predictable behaviour,
and so on) and intrinsically (being part of a tradition is part of one's good),
and also understand those traditions and customs in terms of their meanings which our reason enables us to grasp.

More generally, most thinkers will recognise that whatever other factors
inform or constrain the form of society we have, society serves (and
shapes) human goals, and that many aspects of social activity – law, politics, economics, and so on – are, or at least should be, focused on human
well-being.

The point I want to extract from these rather basic observations is
simply this: to the extent that the maintenance of social order, its structures, institutions and so on, is seen as directed to the achieving of human
well-being (and thus rationally justified), to the same extent there is the
possibility that those same structures and institutions could be modified
with regard to the same objective – the achieving of human well-being –

and thus, because change is needed, the furthering of it. Unless we acknowledge that there is reason for the way things are, we will not see why there may be reason for changing the way things are. Therefore, development discourse makes no sense unless one supposes the fairly powerful role of reason in society more generally.

(d) The Intrinsic Importance of all Individuals

Another feature which seems to be deep within the idea of development is the intrinsic and equal importance of all human beings. Whether we look at the discourse of human rights and its idea of basic rights attaching to all human beings as such, or at the utilitarian starting point that 'all are to count as one and no one more than one', or at Kant's conception of all human beings as rational ends worthy of respect, the common core of modern ethical thought, echoed quite clearly in the idea of development, is this insistence that individual human beings have intrinsic and equal value. The emphasis in development programmes on poverty alleviation (perhaps less than it should be) acknowledges this: the lives of poor people matter.

How, of course, this fundamental 'ideal' or starting point translates into practice is another matter. In a radically imperfect world of limited resources, conflicts of interests, injustice and selfishness, some very uneven, selective and limited efforts are made in the name of development. But that it is about, in the last analysis, the good of people generally and equally would seem central to the idea.

(e) The Exercise of Autonomy

By the exercise of autonomy I mean two things: first, human beings are agents who do things in and with their lives; and second, they have a will which they exercise not just in private agency, but in participation in the public life of their society, whether through reflection, voicing opinions, discussion, decision making or seeking/taking on public roles. It is with less confidence that I suggest that these ideas are embedded in the idea of development, but I am inclined to think that, though they are not often alluded to, and sometimes ignored or forgotten in the practice of development, they are there and show themselves in the following features.

First development is a dynamic process in which agents act in certain ways to improve things, for themselves if not for others. Poor people are not merely passive experiencers of deprivation, their effective agency is often undermined and development empowers them to act and take control. However much development agencies plan changes to improve the lives of poor people, planning needs to involve the active participation by and cooperation of poor people in what is planned. That this objective is all too often ignored, with fatal results, is all too clear. But the point is that our recognition of these failings stems internally from what development, as a normative standard, requires.

Second, combining (d) and (e) together, and leading into (f), the will of ordinary people is meant somehow to be reflected in the development process – whether this is shown in democratic processes (varied as these maybe) or more weakly in some form of assent or consent. People have a view about what is done to, for or around them in society and by government, and their status as autonomous thinkers needs to be acknowledged.

(f) Consent/Common Good at the Basis of Social Order

These features, which are separate and could be put in separate sections, are really extensions of what is implicit in (d) and (e), and make explicit social and political assumptions about the idea of development.

It would be going too far to suggest that there is general agreement, even within western thought, about the democratic nature of development, but the more basic idea of consent is perhaps acceptable. Even non-democratic regimes attempt to represent what they do in the name of 'development' as acceptable to people generally. (That often they either fail, if they mean it, or do not mean it, is also be to acknowledged.)

One of the main reasons why this is assumed is that the development process is directed to the 'common good'. The common good does not mean the resultant 'good of all', as some may suffer that others prosper (that is, trade-offs/compromises), or some may be ignored because others are targeted for benefit (that is, allocation dilemmas), but it does involve the weaker idea of the good of all, in the sense indicated under (d), that the good of everyone counts on the moral baseline. A policy which said openly, 'this is for the sectional interests of my group, we do not care what happens to others, either now or in the future', just would not be a development policy, since it would either be ignoring the moral status of the others or, worse, treating them merely as means to their own ends. (Again, much development is exploitative in practice, but it falls short of the inner logic of the concept and its normative requirements).

(g) Centrality of the State

The nation-state has always in the modern era of development discourse had a central role in that thinking, so much so that it is plausible to think of development as national development or the development of a country, conceived of as a unit under a single government. The reasons for this are not hard to find. First, as a matter of fact states, because of their bureaucratic apparatus, their coercive power (behind regulations) and structures for implementing the common good, have had a centrally controlling role in how development, economic or otherwise, goes. Second, the structures of legitimisation in political theory support this dominant role. Development is about the common good (in respect of change), political power properly acquired has the right to pursue the public good in ways other institutions do not, so development is rightly the province of the nation-state and its government. Third, the nation-state is not merely the key instrument and legitimate instrument for the pursuit of public goals (including change), it is also the focus of loyalty and identity for its citizens, so that 'national development' has a kind of intrinsic value as well.

All this is consistent with many variations. It is not denied that one can talk of regional development, or the development of a city on the one hand, or of international development on the other. But the former is contained within the framework of power/legitimacy of the nation-state's development, and the latter is either a by-product of or a background condition for national developments generally.[9] Nor it is assumed that all agree on what the role of the state should be or what the extent of its involvement should be. Recent thinking has moved away from the heavy-handed interventionist state, but it is still conducted within the assumption that the state has a pre-eminent role. (Consider how much the standing of government is affected by economic performance even for economic libertarians!)

(h) Centrality or Adequacy of the Secular

Finally, in this by no means complete list of features which are potentially part of the idea of development, let me identify the essentially secular nature of development. The point is not that the process of change is a process occurring in this life but rather that the central criteria by which development is measured are secular criteria – less poverty, more wealth, greater liberties (including religious freedom as a social freedom, rather than an inner freedom defined in spiritual terms). The centrality of such secular criteria does not divide the non-religious from the religious. Both share these assumptions. A religious person may see his religion as separate from the domain of the social/political, or else have his own private religious reasons and motivations for supporting development defined as a secular process.

It is worth noting that the recent increase of interest in 'development ethics' very much centres round the framework of utilitarianism, human rights, Kantianism, Aristotelianism, Contractarianism – all secular ethical theories (though none inconsistent with acceptance by religious thinkers, working from further premises).[10]

RESPONSES TO THESE FEATURES

Are all these features from (a) to (h) parts of the very idea/concept of development? Or are they or many of them only parts of a specific conception of development?

Granted that emphasis on economic growth is not part of the concept of development, are any or all of these features different in being part of the very idea? It would take too long to consider them all separately (though the exercise would be useful), so let me briefly outline the structure of my argument (which there is insufficient space to give in detail) for saying that most of them (except the first two, which I come back to later on) are not part of the concept of development.

There are really two questions to be asked here: first, are any or all these features Eurocentric? Second, are any or all these features part of the 'idea' of development or are there some countries involved in development (and so conceiving themselves) which do not share some of these features? My answer briefly is: no, they are not Eurocentric, and no, many of the features are not part of the idea of development either. It is important at this point to see that denying that features are Eurocentric does not entail that they are universal or part of the concept of development. Certain features may well be shared by European culture and the cultures of some other societies without being universally shared. And if other countries which do not share them are nevertheless involved in intentional social change, then prima facie they are also involved in development and so development cannot be defined in terms of these features.

Thus, though it is important to make the point that to the extent that some non-European societies do genuinely agree with the idea of development as having these features, this agreement does not entail Eurocentrism or the claim of unjustified imposition in respect of these countries, this line of thought still fails to recognise the extent to which some societies do see themselves involved in development as they understand it, without sharing all these assumptions, for example about the centrality of the state or of the secular. For instance it is clear that there are some Islamic conceptions of development which are essentially theocratic in character. Many, even in the West, question the central role of the state. (Consider the new libertarian party in the US as an extreme example.) Not all theories of social or political order would necessarily accept the claims of individualism, autonomy, consent or the common good, certainly not in the 'liberal' way these are often taken to mean – though, as I indicate later, some concern for the public good or the good of the whole community does seem necessary as the basis of any ethical judgement about what kind of change ought to happen.

It would seem therefore to follow that many of these features are not part of the idea of development, but are rather widely shared features of different conceptions of development. It is still open to others to advocate alternative conceptions of development, including various minority views in the North (including my own). Does this then leave us with a very thin account of development (as something all using it can agree upon), namely (a) and (b) above – a process or socio-economic change which ought to happen – along with (c) as a precondition for any argued case for change? Still, this would show that the idea of development was not Eurocentric, even if dominant conceptions of it are (and some of their features can be criticised as such).

This result is in some ways rather a disappointing one. Is that all we can say about the concept? But at the same time it is an exciting result. The concept is an essentially contestable one. How we define it declares our values, how we want our society to go (within the realms of the possible).

Why is it worth fighting about? Why are so many different conceptions offered? Why is there reluctance to give the concept up, as Sachs and his fellow dictionary-writers seem to be recommending (though they offer no alternative)? In the remaining part of this chapter I want to sketch the outline of an argument showing why. We do not give it up, because we cannot! (As I noted earlier, we can give up the word – though most people as a matter of fact don't – but not the idea.)

DEVELOPMENT AS A SOCIAL IMPERATIVE

Though it is not necessary that people living in society should conceive of themselves as living in a society undergoing development, development is nevertheless a kind of social imperative, or a requirement of collective practical reasoning, for any society that recognises that:

(a)   it has some kind of collective responsibility for the way things go in the society as a whole;
(b)   things are not going as well as they could; and therefore,
(c)   there is reason to try and bring about change.

This formulation needs some expansion. (a) is meant to capture the thought that people in a society recognise that the general conditions of existence – the state of the natural environment and the forms of social existence – are not simply a fact of ineluctable fate or despotic power, but depend to some extent upon what people do. This does not imply democracy but at least a recognition that if rulers are to rule for the common good rather than their own good (as Aristotle (1988 Bk III) noted as the proper form of rule), then it matters to people what that is and how it is promoted. There will however be great variations in what the 'common good' means: the root idea here is simply that there is an ethical perspective about what ought to happen in the society as a whole. In (b) the phrase 'as well as they could' is significant. It is not the recognition that things are going badly (compared with how they might go in an ideal world), but that change for the better is within the realm of the practicable.

So far I have left it rather vague in what respects things may not be going as well as they could. We tend to think primarily of things like people being in extreme poverty, or economic hardship more generally, but we could just as easily think of things like the quality of social life (its moral rules, laws, liberties, institutions), the state of knowledge or culture, the prevalence of certain religious beliefs, and so on.

It is tempting to think that these ways in which change may be identified as desirable are not merely arbitrary but have a definite structure to them, and so one might identify spheres of social reality subject to development thinking. There are parallels with the idea of virtue (and indeed personal development). Here I am following some ideas in Nussbaum's paper mentioned earlier. She notes (1) whatever view a person or society has about the content of the virtues (thick account), they have to have some view; (2) there are various spheres of human experience which are the subject matter of the virtues (thin account) – death, pleasure, material goods, and so on (Nussbaum, 1993).

Likewise, I want to suggest, with development. That is, we should accept the necessity of 'development' as a social imperative, when change is both possible and desirable, in respect to basic spheres of social reality. What then are these spheres of social reality?

(a) Basic elements of well-being.
(b) A healthy and resources-full physical environment, or Nature.
(c) A properly functioning social environment, or Culture.
(d) Commitment to continuity.

Although much more needs to be said about these features, the following brief remarks may suffice for the present purpose.

(a) Basic Elements of Well-Being

As a basis, there is a view of well-being/flourishing, and commitment to promoting the conditions for this for its members, that is, conditions for survival, comfort and satisfying activities. Each society will have its own view on the elements of well-being – so to some extent these will be diverse. In some 'pluralistic' societies, diversity will be internal to its conception of well-being.[11]

As conditions of (and generally elements in) well-being the following are to be accepted. (Again there will be some diversity, not over whether they are accepted but over the practical embodiment of them.)

(b) A Healthy and Resources-Full Physical Environment, or Nature

This serves two purposes: first, as supplier of materials resources for survival, comfort and satisfying activities; and second, as a background condition or 'oikos' in which meaningful activities – aesthetic, spiritual and recreational – can take place.

(c) A Properly Functioning Social Environment, or Culture

This has (at least) four aspects: first, peace, order and security for members, as a basic precondition for most human activities; second, justice, both in respect to who has what power in society (political legitimacy) and in respect to the methods of allocating resources (including land) and protecting rights; third, general behaviour in accordance with a moral code, both for regulating interpersonal conduct and as enhancing personal well-being; and fourth, culture more generally, in terms of a dynamic world view and value system, including both myths, theology, and so on (including the possibility of pluralist world views), and art, crafts, technology, systems of knowledge and so on.

(d) Commitment to Continuity

There is some kind of commitment to the continuation into the future of the above values, both by the transmission of values and world views in education, and in appropriate forms of action for the future (for example, tree planting).

'Development' arises once there is recognition that things are not going as well as they could in any of these spheres of social reality, therefore change is desirable. As is often noted, there is an important connection between development and the pursuit of peace, justice and care for the environment – these it will be noticed are important features in the above structure of social concerns. But the connection is a complex one. Development does not enter into the initial structure of social concerns as such. It does not correspond to the 'well-being' part, but rather to all the parts in principle, and in practice to those parts in which there is perceived to be a significant need for change. Perhaps in an ideal society where all these features were fully achieved, there would be no need for the dynamic of development (in a sense the society would be in a state of full development or utopia), but in the real world this is not the case, and the dynamic of development can arise in any or all of the areas where things can go badly and there is a will for change.

The above account is incomplete. In any case, it only provides necessary conditions for development thinking to arise, not sufficient conditions for it to occur appropriately. Individuals or groups may very well seek to change societies in the above respects without pursuing development. They may simply be seeking or exercising power for themselves or a sectional group. Alternatively change may be sought by a group (for example, Muslim fundamentalists in a secular Arab state or economic libertarians in a welfare state) which they believe to be good for their society but is not. Similarly free-market capitalists may seek change in a traditional society which is better without such changes.

It is tempting to build in something like 'change based on proper sounding of a democratic consensus', but democratic consensus is neither necessary nor sufficient to guarantee appropriate development. Nevertheless, it is when people as a whole are in a position to take responsibility for the overall good of their society and recognise that significant changes are both possible and desirable, that the idea of development as an object of prescriptive interest takes root, and once rooted is difficult to eradicate.

NOTES

1. Here as elsewhere I include North America, though of course if one looks for the roots far enough back, it would be Europe itself.
2. It so happens that I belong to two organisations, the World Development Movement and the International Development Ethics Association; one a political pressure group, the other an academic/practitioners group concerned with development ethics. Both are highly critical of much development thinking, but both have 'development' in their titles, and both see fit to defend what they take to be the right interpretation of development.
3. Without making evaluative comparisons, consider how once the age of innocence in a child is lost and the power of moral choice is acquired, choice is inescapable from then on.

4.   Since development is itself, as noted earlier, a highly teleological concept at least in some contexts, one way, almost Hegelian, of applying this might be to say that the (unconscious) goal of human development through history is to reach a point of understanding how to organise human existence according to the modern and 'final' ideal of 'development'.

5.   These 'thick' accounts may vary from society to society, though Nussbaum herself argues against a radically relativist view.

6.   This power to control nature is of course limited, and the belief in it one of the causes of the current environmental crisis.

7.   My own conception of development, which is not part of what I am trying to present here, would not include all these features, at least as they are currently formulated and without other emphases.

8.   This is of course an overstatement but the fact remains that if we were fully informed rational economic agents, the state's role would be minimal.

9.   See Dower 1996b for a contrary view on international development.

10.   See, for example, Aman 1991 as an example of this secular debate.

11.   From the point of view of a development theorist, the recognition of the centrality of a conception of well-being neither entails that he offers a universal account of it for all development, nor entails that he cannot criticise some accounts of human well-being. That debate is simply a different one. For a more extended discussion of the universalism/diversity issue in the context of 'world ethics' see, for example, Dower 1996a.

REFERENCES

Aman, K. (ed.) (1991), *Ethical Principles for Development: Needs, Capabilities or Rights?* (The Institute for Critical Thinking, Montclair State University).

Aristotle (1988), *Politics*, ed. (Cambridge University Press).

Chambers, R. (1983), *Rural Development – Putting the Last First* (Longman).

Dower, N. (1989), *What is Development? A Philosopher's Answer* (University of Glasgow Centre for Development Studies).

Dower, N. (1996a), 'Europe and the Globalisation of Ethics', in P. Dukes and M. Hepworth (eds), *Frontiers of European Culture* (Edwin Mellen).

Dower, N. (1996b), 'The Idea of International Development: some Ethical Issues', in M. Wright (ed.), *Normative Issues in International Relations* (Avebury Press).

Hayter, T. (1981), *The Creation of World Poverty* (Pluto Press).

Nussbaum, M. (1993), 'Non-Relative Virtues – an Aristotelian Approach', in A. Sen and M. Nussbaum (eds), *The Quality of Life* (Oxford: Clarendon Press).

Orskov, R. (1993), *Reality in Rural Development Aid – with Emphasis on Livestock* (Rowett Research Services Ltd).

Rawls, J. (1971), *A Theory of Justice* (Harvard University Press).

Riddell, R. (1987), *Foreign Aid Reconsidered* (James Currey).

Sachs, W. (ed.) (1992), *The Development Dictionary – a Guide to Knowledge as Power* (Zed Books).

7 Life Chances, Lifeworlds and a Rural Future

Jan Kees van Donge

This chapter presents a modest piece of field work (a survey among primary school leavers in the Mgeta division, Uluguru mountains, Tanzania) which raises important questions about rational behaviour. The assumption of rationality in actors' behaviour may be a hidden orthodoxy in much development discourse. For example, in the past decade there has been a resurgence in belief in the market; participatory procedures and bottom-up approaches are advocated in development planning, and there is a shift of attention from 'scientific' knowledge to local knowledge. These influential keywords all assume that local actors act with insight in their own situation in terms of strategic interests or goals which they want to realise. Such rationality may be distorted or hidden, but crucial to these approaches is a belief in an inherent rationality. There is often an implication that the role of development studies is to uncover such rationality which may be distorted by, for example, intervention in markets, oppressive social structures or a top-down development discourse.

The survey was not prompted however by the practice of development efforts, but arose from coping with problems raised vis-à-vis development theory in a research situation. The questionnaire was administered at the end of research which was carried out intermittently over a period of four years (1985–89). A clear image had emerged of the pattern of social change and the development trajectory of the area (which is described below) but I did not feel that I was coming close to the meaning of social life, and that had been a central object of the research. I felt at that point a persistent failure to penetrate social life in the area.

Inspired by changing insights in development theory, the guiding idea had been to search for the social construction of actors' lifeworlds in order to elucidate the particular outcome of social change in the area.[1] For example, Long (1977) argued (at a time when these approaches were hegemonic) that neither modernisation theory nor dependency theory explained adequately the diverse and heterogeneous outcomes of social change. An actor-oriented approach, which sees social change as constructed by actors in social practices, was needed to break this impasse.

Similarly, Booth (1985) in a seminal article criticised neo-Marxist development theory as tautological and teleological, thereby leaving no room
for the heterogeneity of the many possible outcomes of development.
According to him, lack of attention to cultural factors is one of the reasons
for the failure of this theory to provide an explanation for development. In
a recent summing up of the state of the art in development studies, Booth
(1992) writes that actor-oriented approaches are 'a fascinating challenge to
sociological explanation in development studies and beyond' (p. 22).

It seemed promising therefore to study the social interpretations of
reality or lifeworlds through hermeneutic interpretation and discourse
analysis (Bauman, 1978) in order to understand how actors structure social
behaviour so that particular outcomes of development occur. The discourse I found in Mgeta, however, was fragmentary, contradictory and
often hard to interpret. I could not discover meaning in much conversation, like for example, elaborate greetings and the exchange of platitudes.
If there was meaning, then statements showed mostly only rudimentary
interpretation of social situations. Statements about land conflicts, for
example, did not amount to much more than exclaiming loudly *shida ya
ardhi* (land is a problem), and probing did not lead to more sophisticated
arguments.

Survey techniques are less suitable than the recording of spontaneous
discourse for the purpose of uncovering the meaning in social action. The
use of a questionnaire structures much more the responses which will be
elicited, and the answers may more easily be an ideological presentation.
Probing open questioning did not produce results however, and a survey
offered the possibility of reaching many more respondents. School leavers
appeared to be a strategic target group, given the issues in the research.
Eliciting their views on the future seemed to be a way to discover the
social interpretations of reality which structure social behaviour into particular forms.

Mgeta faces serious agricultural decline to which the dominant response
is migration to urban areas. The expectation was therefore that the
responses would show a positive valuation of migration to urban areas and
trade and a negative one of a future in agriculture. The actual response
showed the reverse and revealed, therefore, values which were highly discordant with social practice. Instead of clarifying lifeworlds which structure social action, the responses reinforced the impression of a
fragmentary, contradictory social interpretation of reality which had only
one common thread: a devaluation of the actual social practices in the
area. The questionnaire thus undoubtedly revealed a 'taken for granted'
lifeworld, but failed to show a logical and direct connection between

thought and action. Discourse analysis assumes that the use of language is pragmatic in nature and that was not apparent here.

This does not belittle the need for attention to human agency and the way actors structure social behaviour. For example, Vandergeest and Buttel (1988) argued for a return to the Weberian heritage in development theory which allots a central place to meaning (*Verstehen*): 'development sociologists must take into account why people do what they do in terms of subjective meaning attached to what they do, rather than explain all action by appealing to economic and other formal laws and models of society' (p. 690). This chapter does not cast doubt on the general thrust of this argument, but it should not be immediately assumed that actors are rational, acting in accordance with their interpretation of the world. Actors can be rational, but they are not necessarily so. Rationality should be a matter of empirical verification in which ontological judgements are secondary. 'Why people do what they do' can be a more complicated question than the analytical tool of searching for the rationality in behaviour assumes. This does not imply an ethical or value judgement on rationality or irrationality. The stance adopted merely opens up fields of study which an assumed rationality may close off.

The survey responses unquestionably revealed an ideological representation, and it may be objected that the findings presented here do not capture the 'real' interpretations which guide everyday practices, especially as this is such a danger in survey research. The questionnaire was administered in the presence of teachers in a classroom situation through the medium of Kiswahili to primary school pupils just before they left school in 1989.[2] The danger undoubtedly exists that an officially sanctioned ideological presentation was produced. Government policy in Tanzania in the past decades has stressed the values of self-reliance, agriculture and rural development as opposed to trade and urban migration. Nyerere affirmed these values strongly in his 'Education for self reliance' (1967).[3] Since it was possible that only one of multiple competing lifeworlds had been captured in the research, a follow up visit, which used a much more qualitative approach outside the classroom, was made to probe the situation further. The follow up research did not alter the significant finding that a particular dominant ideology, discordant with social practice, was professed with great unanimity and has therefore to be taken into account as a social force. The later research buttressed the original findings and suggested that, where alternative interpretations of ideology do exist, they may only be adhered to in private and lack a social dimension.

This chapter will first outline the observed realities of social practice in Mgeta which will then be compared with the responses to the questionnaire. In the conclusion, the wider implications of the questions raised in this research for theorising about development and development practice will be discussed.

LIFE CHANCES IN MGETA

Mountainous areas rising steeply from surrounding plains (like the Uluguru) are a striking feature of Tanzanian geography. Such areas have a high rainfall, high population density and intensive agriculture relative to the surrounding plains. Population growth has usually led however to great pressure on land there. In the Uluguru, and especially in Mgeta, this problem is particularly severe because land is not very fertile and is becoming increasingly exhausted. The slopes are very steep and erosion is therefore a spectacular problem.

Land is taken into cultivation regardless of the consequences for erosion and exhaustion. The main crop is maize. This is a difficult crop in the higher altitudes and takes up to nine months to mature there as the climate is too cold and misty. In the whole division, maize yields are declining rapidly due to exhaustion of the soil. This extensive maize farming is usually legitimised as an attempt at self-sufficiency. At the same time it is commonly admitted that this aim is unattainable. Agronomists have argued that the agronomy of the area should be restructured. One could imagine, for example, a future where people would limit acreages and leave steep slopes fallow, build permanent terraces, rotate crops, find new valuable crops to generate cash. Such a restructuring was already a theme in the Uluguru Land Usage Scheme, implemented in the 1950s and similar opinions have been voiced since then, but such advice has not yet been followed.[4] Agriculture as a source of cash has, however, become important: people grow vegetables for the urban markets, especially Dar es Salaam. Vegetable cultivation, however, requires well-watered plots and these are increasingly scarce. A future in agriculture is therefore problematic.

Due to pressure on land, emigration has been the major response to the growing need for cash. There is a huge migration of Waluguru to urban areas, especially to Dar es Salaam, where many are to be found in markets selling vegetables. The vegetable trade between towns and Mgeta is another major source of income. The need for cash to buy food is compelling. In Mgeta, farming is, as stated above, a reserve activity: it has to be supplemented with other income unless one belongs to the minority who own the scarce plots suited to vegetable growing. Therefore people in Mgeta have either to trade or to rely on remittances from urban areas if they want to stay on the land. Trade is pervasive in Mgeta, but this has not resulted in a clear differentiation between rich and poor. Trade is an insecure way of making a living (van Donge, 1992a, 1992b).

Education is of minor importance as a response to the declining resource base of the mountains. The area is dotted with primary schools which are well attended, but very few pupils (varying from none to two or three in each school) pass the final primary examination in an average year. The quality of primary education is probably also declining.[5] In a survey in the Mgeta division, household heads had no more than primary education, and only rarely did their children attend higher education.[6]

In this respect, Mgeta is strikingly different from, for example, the Usambara mountains or Kilimanjaro where a clamour for education has been a major response to declining life chances in the rural economy (Samoff, 1979; Kerner, 1985; Sender and Smith, 1990; Cooksey et al., 1990).[7] Unlike in Usambara and on Kilimanjaro therefore, access to education is not a major force in class formation in Mgeta. Places in government secondary schools are allocated on a quota per district basis to improve the chances of disadvantaged regions. Nevertheless, there is a big differential participation in secondary education among different areas and ethnic groups in Tanzania. A comparison of the proportion of Waluguru in secondary school as compared with the proportion in the total Tanzanian population, dating from 1983, shows that the Waluguru groupings are under represented in secondary schools (a ratio of 0.48) (Cooksey et al., 1990). This is probably flattered by the fact that many Uluguru children may get access to education by attending urban schools, which have higher pass rates. A newly elected MP in 1985 gained considerable popularity when he started, with the support of the Catholic Mission, the first secondary school within the Mgeta division. Local pupils are given preference for admission, but, even so, many pupils admitted have an urban background and stay with local relatives. The chance to build an alternative source of wealth through investment in education is thus very limited in Mgeta.

THE OPTIONS AS PERCEIVED BY PRIMARY SCHOOL LEAVERS

People in Mgeta can straddle many economic activities in their life. Farming and trade; migration and holding on to a living on the land, are elements which are found in various combinations in people's lives. The discrete options presented to school leavers in the questionnaire (farming, continued education, wage labour in town, trading in town and trading between Mgeta and Dar es Salaam) are necessarily an abstraction. The definite responses to a ranking of these options indicate, however, that these questions most likely refer to a particular way of thinking. An acquaintance over four years with how people in Mgeta talk about their lives led to the formulation of these questions in the first instance. Social change in Mgeta has led more to a general spread of poverty without significant accumulation than to a differentiation between rich and poor. Primary school leavers are therefore, in that respect, to a large extent a homogeneous mass, and differences in wealth in their background do not constitute a reason for different life expectations.

The options given may seem simple, but (as will be shown below) responses showed a limited awareness of the options in life. This may be partly due to the age of respondents. They were young: their age varied from 11 to 17; most of them were in the age group 13–15 (87 per cent). Their life experience could, however, have brought them into contact with a considerable variation in human experience, because they were aware of urban life towards the end of primary school. Only a small minority (12 per cent) had never left Mgeta, while almost half of them (46.7 per cent) had often travelled outside the area. They rarely mentioned destinations other than the towns of Morogoro and Dar es Salaam as the place last visited (11.5 per cent). Contacts with the smaller town Morogoro were, however, more frequent (58.8 per cent) than contacts with Dar es Salaam (29.8 per cent). Most of these recent visits lasted more than a month (53.1 per cent) and sometimes even more than a year (12.3 per cent). Their urban experience tends to be limited, however, to a particular segment of society. Many of the people with whom these school leavers had stayed made their living from trade (43.3 per cent), and the other livelihoods reported (44 per cent) seldom demanded much education.

The respondents were asked to rank according to preference the following five options for their future: continuing with education, farming, wage labour in town, trading between Mgeta and Dar es Salaam, and trading in urban areas. Table 7.1 shows the scores to the preferences indicating overwhelming preference for farming, with trading in vegetables between Mgeta and Dar es Salaam obviously least preferred. Not only were trading careers less preferred than farming or continued education, but it is striking that wage labour in town was also more preferred than trade.

Table 7.2 shows the mean ranking of preference as compared with the mean ranking of estimated remuneration as well as the respondents' expressed career expectations. Trading may be less preferred than wage labour in town, but it was considered more remunerative. The monetary rewards of alternative futures may compensate for less prestige in career

Table 7.1: *Frequencies (%) of Preferences for Future Careers among Primary School Children in Mgeta*

	First	Second	Third	Fourth	Fifth
Farming	41.9	37.8	8.8	8.8	2.7
Further education	50.0	13.7	8.2	11.6	16.4
Wage labour in town	9.7	17.2	29.0	22.1	22.1
Trade in town	–	21.5	31.9	35.4	11.1
Trade Dar–Mgeta	0.7	12.2	24.3	19.6	43.2

TABLE 7.2: *Preferences and Expectations for Future Careers among Primary School Children in Mgeta*

Career	Mean ranking of preference	Variance	Mean ranking of remuneration	Expectation %
Farming	1.926	1.103	2.24	44.0
Continued education	2.308	2.449	1.86	32.7
Urban wage labour	3.297	1.585	3.28	14.7
Trade in town	3.361	0.890		4.0
Trade Mgeta			2.99	
– Dar-es-Salaam	3.926	1.226		4.0

choice, and the school leavers were therefore asked to rank the four options in this respect. Education was here also mostly ranked first, and farming was mentioned as the second preference.

A preference of career options does not, of course, indicate expectations in life; dreams have to be confronted with reality.[8] The response to career expectation showed a slightly different pattern than that in career options. Most pupils expected to become farmers (44 per cent as compared with 41.9 per cent first preference); a large group expected to continue education (32.7 per cent as compared with 50 per cent first preference); few expected to work for wages in town (14.7 per cent as compared with 9.7 per cent first preference), but even fewer expected to make their living as traders (8 per cent as compared with 0.7 per cent first preference). One cannot conclude, therefore, that expectations are strikingly more realistic than preferences.

The pervasive nature of negative feelings towards trade and positive ones towards agriculture and education are overwhelming in the response. A prestige ranking of various professions showed a similar pattern. Table 7.3 indicates clearly how the prestige ranking corresponds to the ranking of career choices. Farmer and teacher were ranked highest and the three trading occupations were rated the lowest. The variance in these scores was also relatively small which indicates much consensus relative to other rankings. The other occupations (medical assistant, village secretary, priest) showed much more ambiguous responses. Not only were they ranked in the middle, but the scores showed also a higher variance in ranking. The variance was extreme in the case of priest. This divergence in opinions corresponds to the impression one gets in daily life in Mgeta.[9]

The indeterminate nature in these scores is, however, probably above all an indication of a blurred image. Teacher, medical assistant, village secretary and priest are professions which require education and which are visible in daily life in Mgeta. Yet, these positions may be outside the active lifeworlds as experienced. As mentioned above, this indicates a limited awareness of options in life. It is thus not surprising that teaching is more consistently rated, despite requiring education, as it is the profession most visible to school children.

There are two possible sources of bias which may explain these scores. The questionnaire was administered to those pupils who were in class, and

TABLE 7.3: *Prestige Ranking of Professions by School Leavers in Mgeta*

Professions	% distribution of ranking[*]								Mean	Variance
	1	2	3	4	5	6	7	8		
Farming	40	16	17	11	12	2	1	1	2.503	2.590
Teaching	33	30	15	11	5	3	3	1	2.513	2.681
Medical Asst.	4	17	17	23	16	10	6	6	4.140	3.289
Priest	17	14	16	13	7	6	12	16	4.216	6.075
Village Secr.	3	10	18	16	17	12	11	12	4.767	3.932
Trade/Mgeta–Dar	1	7	9	8	16	20	12	27	5.741	3.851
Shop/Mgeta	1	5	5	10	12	28	23	16	5.811	2.916
Market/Dar	1	2	4	10	17	17	32	16	6.034	2.447

[*]Percentages do not add up to one hundred due to rounding off to the nearest number.

one could expect those who value education negatively to be absent. However, the preference for further education is not surprising as education tends to confer prestige everywhere. The over-representation of girls may be another source of bias. More girls (88) than boys (62) answered the questionnaire. There are two possible explanations for this. The respondents were in the age groups when young people start to explore links with urban life. More males than female migrate, and this may be one explanation for the female surplus in the sample. Many young boys enter the vegetable trade between Mgeta and Dar es Salaam and will then be absent from school. Girls tend not to enter this trade (van Donge, 1992a, 1992b). It is therefore not surprising that girls rated trade lower in career choice than boys. There may thus be a dependent relation between sex and career choice, albeit a weak one. There was definitely no ground for assuming dependence between sex and prestige ranking of professions.[10] The responses in general revealed, therefore, feelings which are felt independent of sex.

These preferences and expectations document thus a striking prevalence of particular sentiments among this group. Farming is a much more valued existence than either wage labour or trade. The claim is that, for preference, one does not enter trade. Trade is even less preferred than wage labour, although it is considered more remunerative. These ideological notions are thus in marked discord with social practice: social life in Mgeta is permeated by migration to urban areas and trade; people leave agriculture which is in serious decline.

SCHOOL LEAVERS' PERCEPTION OF THEIR SITUATION

A pilot study administered the above-mentioned questions in one school only. This gave a first indication of the prevalence of these strong feelings, which contradict so obviously social practices in Mgeta. Further questions on farming, education and trade were added to the questionnaire to probe this issue. These were in the form of statements referring to actual social practice, many of which had been picked up in casual conversation. Respondents were asked to express agreement or disagreement on a four point scale or could opt for neutrality. The scores are summarised in Table 7.4.[11]

The most consistent finding was a positive valuation of education. This may not be surprising among children who are in school, but it is striking that this value was expressed independent of future career opportunities. A massive 90 per cent agreed that education is a good thing because it helps

TABLE 7.4: *Distribution of Degree of Agreement (%) with Statements on Education, Agriculture and Trade among School Leavers in Mgeta*

	Very true	True	Do not know	Not true	A lie
Education					
– One should work hard in school as education is useful in business and agriculture.	45.3	44.7	–	8.0	2.0
– Education is meaningless because it does not help you to get work.	3.4	9.5	5.4	56.8	25.0
– Very few people get places in higher education and it is therefore a waste to go to school.	9.6	13.7	14.4	41.1	21.2
– If you get educated you will get jobs with small salaries therefore it is better to do business.	6.7	26.8	4.0	39.6	22.8
Agriculture					
– People here in Mgeta cannot depend upon agriculture for a living because there is not enough land and especially land suitable for vegetable cultivation is scarce.	14.2	30.4	7.4	41.9	6.1
– It is easier to trade and earn money to buy food than to grown one's own food here in Mgeta.	7.3	12.7	3.3	68.0	8.7
– People here in Mgeta could earn much money from agriculture if they did not spend so much time on petty trade.	26.4	39.9	12.2	17.6	4.1
– Income from vegetable cultivation in business.	14.3	37.4	15.6	29.3	3.4
Trade					
– Trade is easier than farming.	10.1	21.6	12.2	48.0	8.1
– Here in Mgeta many people try to enter trade, but many fail.	37.2	43.4	14.5	2.8	2.1
– Traders become rich because they exploit peasants.	32.0	33.3	5.4	18.4	10.9

in business and agriculture, and there were no abstentions. This item attracted the highest number of extreme scores, which were virtually all in support (strong agreement: 45.3 per cent). A majority expressed positive feelings towards education in the other items referring specifically to education. A large majority (81.8 per cent) disagreed with the statement that education is meaningless as it does not help you to get a job, while few expressed no opinion (5.4 per cent). Strength of feeling was substantial, but not overwhelming (25 per cent strong disagreement).

School was highly valued not only irrespective of employment opportunities but also independent of the chance of further education. The undeniable fact is that very few of these pupils have a chance of further education, despite the fact that so many said that they want it. A sizeable majority (62.3 per cent) disagreed that schooling is a waste of time as so few people get places in higher education. Relatively many respondents were neutral (14.4 per cent) and there was also considerable, though not dominant, strength of feeling (21.2 per cent strong disagreement).

Further education tends to be geared to work in the formal sector. Wages and salaries are usually extremely low in this sector in Tanzania, and one would therefore expect more preference for a future in the informal sector. Yet, a majority (62.4 per cent) expressed disagreement with the statement that 'If you manage to get higher education you will get work with a low salary and therefore it is better to go for a life in business'. In this case also there were few abstentions (4 per cent) and again a fair number of extreme opinions in support of education (22.8 per cent).

There is thus in this population a dominant strand of positive feeling towards education, which is not directly related to the possibility of further education or job opportunities. Education has a value in itself. However, when statements associate the effect of education with pessimistic estimations of life despite education (does not give more money, no job, no places in higher schooling), opinions are somewhat less homogeneous: more respondents have no opinion and the strength of support in one particular direction is less pronounced.

The statements with respect to agriculture did not reveal such unambiguous feelings as those on education. Majorities were smaller, strength of feeling was less and relatively large proportions expressed no opinion. The statements aimed to elucidate the fact that pupils have high expectations of agriculture, while it is common wisdom that agriculture is in serious decline in Mgeta. It is commonplace in daily conversation in Mgeta to remark that 'People in Mgeta cannot depend on agriculture to make a living, because there is not enough land and few plots are suitable for vegetables which provide cash.' The statement did not, however, produce a clear consensus among the respondents. It is amazing, given the widely felt land shortage, that slightly more pupils disagreed than agreed (48 per cent as against 44.6 per cent).

In Mgeta, farming can hardly be considered independent of trade, because many people in the area engage in trading to raise the necessary cash to buy, for example, food/maize. A large majority (76.7 per cent), however, disagreed with the statement that it is easier/better to trade and buy food/maize instead of growing it oneself. A somewhat smaller majority (66.3 per cent) agreed with the statement that people in Mgeta could earn more money if they concentrated on agriculture instead of spending so much time on petty trade.

These last two statements were framed as a clash of interest between agriculture and trading, but it is of course not necessarily so. Another statement suggested such complementarity: one needs income from vegetable plots to be successful in trading. However, this truism common in the community found a less unambivalent response than might have been expected: 51.7 per cent agreed, 32.7 per cent disagreed and 15.6 per cent had no opinion.

Despite the tendency, mentioned above, to compare farming unfavourably with trade, only a small majority (56.1 per cent) disagreed with the statement that trade is easier than farming. This should be seen in conjunction with a near consensus on the statement that many people in Mgeta try to enter trade, but many fail: 80.6 per cent agreed, and feeling was strong: 37.2 per cent agreed very much. If trade is not seen as an easy option one could reasonably expect respect for successful trading, but that is not necessarily the case: 65.3 per cent agreed with the statement that traders become rich because they exploit farmers. Few were neutral on this question (5.4 per cent) and many expressed strong agreement (32 per cent).

If we look at the statements which get the most unequivocal response then three elements may be distinguished: (a) education has a high value, but it is not primarily seen as a means of upward mobility; (b) farming tends to be highly valued, especially in opposition to trade and the dependency on the outside world this entails; (c) trade is considered a hazardous existence and it tends to be seen as an activity at the expense of farmers.

A NON-CAPITALIST SPIRIT

Successful indoctrination is one obvious explanation for the type of response to the questionnaire. 'Education for self reliance' was part of Tanzania's *Ujamaa* ideology propagating anti-capitalist values and idealising rural life. If that is the case, then such values may lose meaning when confronted with the world outside school. In that world, the move to urban areas is dominant; for many people, trade is necessary to survive and (except for some) a living cannot be made from agriculture. It may also be that the questionnaire had structured responses to a large degree. A different picture might emerge in open, unstructured interviews with people who had left school a considerable time ago.

Such interviews were held, during a return visit to Tanzania in 1991, with people who had left primary school between three and ten years previously. Twenty interviews were held, half of those with people in Mgeta and the other half with people from Mgeta in Dar es Salaam. The response to open questions was poor in contrast to the response to the structured statements which had been administered to the school leavers in 1989. The same pattern emerged in this session as mentioned above: farming was idealised and trade was valued little, if not despised.

Follow up questions were asked in these interviews, but these did not elucidate the contradiction between social thought and social practice. Farming was invariably accorded a higher preference and esteem than any other profession. Migrants in Dar es Salaam did not interpret their migration as turning away from farming, but expected to be farming one day. The response to an open question as to what they expected to be doing 20 years from now inevitably elicited farming as a response in both Mgeta and Dar es Salaam. Further questioning as to what kind of farming invariably led to their mentioning the same crops as are now grown in Mgeta. Nobody mentioned farming outside Mgeta as an option. The agronomic problems of Mgeta (shortage of land, declining fertility and erosion) were never spontaneously mentioned. A great belief in the power of science (*utalaam*) to be disseminated by government was the response to confrontation with such problems. The content of such a scientific approach to farming was vague, except for one element: the use of artificial fertiliser. Conservation, more intensive care of the land and a search for new crops were conspicuously absent in such replies.

Responses to questions on trade were similarly stereotyped and universal, but in a negative way. All respondents, even if they were traders themselves, agreed with the statement that traders exploit farmers. The antagonism between farmers and traders was often vehemently stated, and many complaints were voiced about the unreliability of traders who would take goods on credit and then not pay. To an outside observer, this would suggest the possibility of respect for a successful trader who is at the same time dependable and trustworthy. Such sentiments were not even voiced after probing. The idea of a trader being successful through skill simply did not exist.

These responses thus do not represent an aversion to the form which involvement in wider networks has taken for people in Mgeta, but a generalised negative response to such involvement per se. The spirit manifested is therefore a non-capitalist spirit and not an anti-capitalist one demanding reform. Tanzania's socialist policies never aroused enthusiasm in Mgeta, and socialist sentiments are simply not heard.[12]

A guiding idea in these qualitative interviews was to probe for the existence of an achievement orientation.[13] Two questions were essential for that: first, whom they considered a successful person in life; and, second, what they expected to be doing in 20 years' time. The answer to the second question was unambiguous: farming. The first question drew less response. Respondents simply did not state role models of successful people. It is likely that there was no elaborately constructed lifeworld as to what can and should be achieved. The statements from the questionnaire on the other hand, as stated above, elicited lively responses and must have tapped important issues. The spirit evoked may best be called a non-capitalist spirit. Living off the land is eulogised; participation in wider exchange networks involving trade is abhorred and standards of achievement through competition are not developed. This mentality is above all evoked for public display. It was virtually impossible to speak to people alone during these interviews, most of which took the form of group sessions. The result was a great deal of playing to the audience during which there was actual resentment if the ideological representation of independent life on the land was questioned.

Such display buttressed thus the socially formed perceptions of economic life. If people face the discrepancy with actual social behaviour, they have to retreat into a private world. The following incident illustrated this:

The discussion on farming, trade and education was rambling along the familiar themes in a household composed of a mother, her daughters and the male household head. The latter suddenly stood up and started a long monologue. He boasted of the family's educational achievements which were unusual in Mgeta. Several of the children were teachers and junior civil servants. He claimed it all stemmed from one thing: the power of the hoe. His hard work on the land, combined with following advice from the agricultural adviser, was the reason for success. He denied any fundamental problems in agriculture in Mgeta like land scarcity, erosion or declining soil fertility.

My research assistant afterwards expressed surprise about his behaviour. The man is usually taciturn, and my assistant mentioned beer as the explanation for his eloquence. He also presented a very different explanation for the educational success in that family. The successful children were born previous to the man's relationship with these children's mother. They had been educated by a maternal grandfather who was a relatively successful shopkeeper. The successfully educated children had associated more with that household than with their mother's. They even refused to stay with their mother on holidays. The maternal grandfather died a considerable time ago. The man's bitterness about relations with his wife's father lingered on after the father's death. The family was embroiled in many conflicts in which the new husband was a main protagonist, and he was instigating a dispute about the well-built house which was left to his wife's sister. The wife's sister's children are also (by Mgeta standards) unusually successful in education. They are among the very few who pass the primary school examination; one is in secondary school and one is a middle-ranking civil servant (my research assistant).

The presentation of himself as a successful man who had educated children was thus not true. His strong affirmation of the values of agriculture stemmed more from a position of weakness than of strength. The position of males in Mgeta is often weak. During the interview, he sat apart from the others, suggesting marginality in the group. This is not unusual in Mgeta. It not only expresses the separate social spheres of male and female, but also reflects the marginal position males can have in the strongly matrilineal Luguru society. This is reinforced by uxorilocality: in this case also, the man had moved to his wife's place (van Donge, 1992a). He represented therefore a much more general phenomenon. It is virtually impossible in Mgeta to build and maintain a household depending on the land, and it is thus not attractive to males to form a family there. His response to this situation was a denial of facts as a form of regression. Again this is socially reaffirmed. It is rare in Mgeta to penetrate the private worlds which may hold different interpretations. It happened in this case because my research assistant was part of the social situation.

This incident reveals how the values as expressed in responses to the questionnaire function. The value of education is above doubt and needs no defence or dispute. The values of farming, making a living on the land, need to be asserted forcefully. The hidden meaning in this public display affirming the value of work on the land was to deny the legitimacy of gain through trade. The mentality expressed was obviously at odds with the realities of life in Mgeta, but was pervasive wherever we talked about these issues. It seems therefore unlikely that such sentiments are merely the result of indoctrinations through primary school.

CONCLUSION

The research findings presented here raise further issues. First, the content of this ideological representation (idealising an independent existence on the land) may not be typical only for Mgeta, but point to wider patterns in the culture of peasant societies in Africa. For example, research in Southern Malawi showed a similar preoccupation with maize cultivation as found in Mgeta: 'Very few are able to reach the next harvest without shortages, but this ideal informs everyone's action and rationale'; maize, 'more than an income generating activity in the dry language of analysts is a way of life' (Peters, 1988). Hyden (1980) considers opinions idealising an independent existence on the land as values belonging to a peasant mode of production. Sub-Saharan Africa, as exemplified by Tanzania, is, in his view, characterised by an uncaptured peasantry which can withdraw from state and market in autarchic households. These peasant values are contradictory to the spirit of accumulation and economic transformation typical for capitalism and the same can be said about the values revealed by this research. Implicit in Hyden's analysis, however, is the belief that social practice results from rational calculation, given particular socially-induced utility preferences. Such values are a logical interpretation of a factual situation. That is not the case in Mgeta however (nor in Southern Malawi) because withdrawal from wider networks is impossible. Households cannot even attain food security. His description of peasant culture probably captures, however, a widespread ideal which is not necessarily borne out by social practice.

On a more general level, the questions raised here may suggest more fruitful directions to be taken in the examination of the relationship between culture and development. A simplistic relationship between action and culture is easily assumed: for example, 'culture is conceptualized as the socially-established framework of meaning which orients social action' (Vandergeest and Buttel 1988, p. 690).[14] There is undoubtedly an established framework of meaning in Mgeta, but it does not orient social action. It is irrelevant to social action or, if there is a relationship, then it is an indirect one. For example, it must make a difference to be a successful trader in an environment where trade is prestigious as compared with one where trade is despised. The discrepancy between social thought and social practice as found in Mgeta relates to important strands of thinking in the social sciences which are neglected in development theory. It fits, for instance, Merton's definition of anomie: 'when the cultural and social structure are malintegrated, the first calling for behaviour and attitudes which the second precludes' (Merton 1956, p. 163). He refers then to the American prescription to all to be successful, while success in a competitive situation is accessible to only a few. He discerns various possible reactions to this, ranging from aggression to withdrawal.

The dominant response in Mgeta to the impossibility of adhering to the socially-induced ideal seems to be ritualism: the socially-approved norms must be endorsed but they do not structure behaviour. The social induction of beliefs, irrespective of their cognitive validity, is also a major theme of research in social psychology. Mere group pressures can be significant in the maintenance of beliefs (Krech et al., 1962). Festinger's research into cognitive dissonance also showed that people do not automatically construct beliefs on the basis of rational perception. If facts do not fit established modes of thought, people do not automatically change their ways of thinking: they can deny such facts or maintain contradictory beliefs (Festinger et al., 1956). The Mgeta research reveals clear examples of cognitive dissonance. The dominant feeling in Mgeta appears to be an aversion to involvement in wider exchange while this latter is an undeniable fact of life. Self-sufficiency in food is a value which is endorsed strongly, but at the same time people acknowledge that it is becoming less and less possible because of land shortage, soil exhaustion and so on.

Further research into psychological factors might be a fruitful line of enquiry to explain such findings as presented here. The lifeworlds captured in this research may be seen as repressing socially relevant, but painful, facts. Confrontation with such facts (that is, declining soil fertility, erosion, land scarcity) often leads to the call for a *deus ex machina*: solutions are expected to come from outside (from government) and science plays a messianic role in this. The eulogisation of agriculture lessens the pain of facing economic decline. Such a line of enquiry would not write off actions as being the whims of individuals, and this is important because it is striking how the ideological representations are socially endorsed and function socially.

The implications of opening up fields of enquiry in this direction may be significant for development practice. The obstacles to public discussion of the real problems of erosion, land exhaustion, monocropping and so on are evident from this material. An obvious conclusion from this research is that primary school leavers in Mgeta are mentally poorly equipped to face threatening poverty in a life of petty trade or marginal farming. Nyerere's 'Education for self reliance' has not lost its actuality as a call to prepare children for the economic conditions in which they will find themselves. A call to revitalise rural life seems eminently sensible in Mgeta, especially if an alternative to a life at the margin in urban areas is thereby presented.[15]

The research in Mgeta raises the question of how to give rural life and agriculture an adequate meaning instead of a merely ritualistic one. An ideological embrace of rural life as exposed here will not give rise to different practices. The relationship between social practice and life-worlds appears to be less linear than proponents of educational reform suggest.

Educational reform which leads to changes in social practices requires, therefore, more study of actual life changes and lifeworlds. Such a study could result in a much more ambiguous appreciation of rural life which discerns the problems in living off the land in an area like Mgeta. Social research can enlighten the way social practices are created, and the inherent rationality of the purposeful actor should not be presupposed.

Similar observations can be made on the use of the fashionable key-words of market, participation, local knowledge referred to at the beginning of this paper. These words have of course sympathetic political implications, but their use can lead to imputing a rationality into social life which is not there. The result of this can simply be a reification of politically desirable images (idealising the local actor) instead of the provision of insights into social life. The role of social science in development practice may be more fruitfully seen as demystifying social life rather than uncovering inherent rationality.

NOTES

1.   The concept of a lifeworld has entered sociology through the work of the phenomenologist, Alfred Schutz. Berger and Luckmann (1966) used it as the core of a theoretical framework and defined it as an ontological community which structures social action. The concept is also prominent in the sociology of Habermas, who defines it as follows: 'In their interpretative accomplishments the members of a communication community demarcate the one objective world and their intersubjectively shared world from the subjective world of individuals and other collectivities' (Habermas, 1980, p. 70). Berger and Luckmann's definition is more direct and unambiguous. Habermas lumps the 'one objective world' and the intersubjectively shared world together in his definition. The analysis of lifeworlds in this chapter implies, however, an analysis of 'an intersubjectively shared world' which is an interpretation by actors of phenomena which are accessible to observation and in that sense part of an objective world. The focus is on the relationship between the objective world and the lifeworld. Neither does this chapter share Habermas' normative commitment to search for (true) communicative rationality in which reason is freed. Empirical research can, in my opinion, clarify the way in which the world is socially interpreted, but cannot find a true interpretation binding on the actors involved.

2. A total of 158 pupils, drawn from five schools distributed throughout the division, answered a questionnaire in class. Only eight questionnaires had to be discarded as the pupils were obviously not literate enough to answer the questions. The findings of this survey deserve attention as they raise important issues in the interpretation of rural change in Tanzania, but they are presented with the following reservation. The respondents are not necessarily representative of their age group in Mgeta, because those who were in class are not necessarily all those who should have been in class. The schools were chosen randomly, but one cannot say whether the young people who attend school are representative of the youth in Mgeta.

3. 'Tanzania will continue to have a predominantly rural economy for a long time to come. And as it is in the rural areas that people live and work, so it is rural life that has to be improved.' Therefore education 'must also prepare young people for the work they will be called upon to do in the society which exists in Tanzania – a rural society where improvement will depend largely upon the efforts of the people in agriculture and village development' (Nyerere, 1967, pp. 20–1).

4. This was already an essential element of the Uluguru Land Usage Scheme (ULUS) which the colonial government tried to implement in the area in the 1950s. It had to be abandoned in the face of popular resistance (Fosbrooke and Young, 1960, and interview with Mr H. Tomkins Russell, extension worker for ULUS in Mgeta, Honiton, September 1990). Missionaries who worked in the area expressed similar views. The same agronomic themes crop up in the work of the Franco-Tanzanian horticultural project which is presently active in the area.

5. The area is staunchly Catholic and is a fertile recruiting field for the priesthood. The quality of primary school leavers who wanted to enter minor seminary declined so much however that the Catholic Church started an intermediary school for remedial teaching and further selection.

6. The household survey covered nine neighbourhoods randomly selected in various parts of Mgeta division (for further details see van Donge, 1992a, p. 78). Only one head in the 201 households had more than primary education, and he was absent working in the diplomatic service in a junior position. Children were or had been following post-primary education in only a few cases (14 households). If children were continuing education then usually a number of children in one household progressed beyond primary school. Such children as a rule attained modest positions like teacher, clerk, machine operator. Only one household could boast of a university student, doing medicine in Dar es Salaam. Typically, he was supported by educated brothers and sisters who were working in junior capacities in one of the international hotels in Dar es Salaam.

7. For example, differential responses between areas to further education have been explained as resulting from a rational interpretation of scarcities. Kerner (1985) compared the advantageous educational position of Chagga girls on Kilimanjaro with the position of young girls in Tabora, where girls are seen primarily as farm/household labour and procreators. She explains the difference as the result of the land shortage in Kilimanjaro, which orients both male and female children towards the urban job market and commercial activities rather than farming. Education for girls then makes

sense as an insurance for old age, especially as girls tend to remit more and will think about their mothers who have a marginal position in the patriarchal Chagga society. Her explanations postulate, therefore, a direct causality between the interpretation of the socio-economic situation and behaviour of school leavers. Such determinism does not make sense, however, in a comparison between the Wachagga and the Waluguru. Both areas suffer from land scarcity, and massive outward migration is the major response. Unlike the Wachagga, however, the Waluguru have not responded with massive investment in education and neither is there such a pronounced gender difference in access to higher education among the Waluguru as in Kilimanjaro (Cooksey et al., 1990). From the perspective of a rational interpretation of scarcities, both areas should show the same pattern, but they do not. The value of the material presented here may be that it points to ways of overcoming the limits of such economistic interpretations.

8.   Heijnen (1968) and Kaayk (1976) found in Mwanza such a realistic appreciation of possibilities: peasant farming was considered a desirable option given the market position in which school leavers found themselves.

9.   There is much criticism of the behaviour of priests. Apart from common human weaknesses, they tend to stay for very short periods in these rural communities. Catholicism continues, however, to have a virtual monopoly in Mgeta.

10. The statistical analysis is set out below:

Cross-tabulation by sex	Chi square	D.F.	Significance
Choice of farming	10.69589	4	0.0302
Respect for farming	11.69835	7	0.1109
Choice trade Dar–Mgeta	20.28154	4	0.0004
Respect trade Dar–Mgeta	2.21271	7	0.816
Choice trade in town	17.35040	3	0.0006
Respect trade Dar market	2.31647	7	0.404

11. Three statements have been left out of consideration in this chapter because they appeared not to add anything to the subject matter discussed. The responses to these statements do not, however, contradict in any way the pattern described.

12. For example, there are cooperatives in Mgeta, but these are dominated by traders who thus get access to equipment such as lorries on favourable terms from the government. I have found no trace of an egalitarian movement channelling in other directions this resentment against profits made at their expense.

13. The idea was to administer similar questions to those of Levine (1966) in Nigeria. He analysed dreams among different ethnic groups in Nigeria as to achievement orientation. There was, however, an absolute unwillingness to discuss dream content. Levine studied secondary school pupils as well, and one can expect that these have more elaborate social interpretations.

14. The quotation from Vandergeest and Buttle (1988) is particularly apt to point to the problem, but a similar linear assumption is made in other influential theoretical thinking. Bates, for example, distinguishes three fundamental principles in the 'collective choice school of political economy', one of which is the premise of rational choice. He allows for imperfect

information, because people may choose to be ignorant. He maintains however: 'It requires only that choice makers order alternative courses of action in terms of the consequences for the values they seek to obtain and that they choose that alternative which they expect to yield the most favourable outcome' (Bates, 1983, p. 135). The research findings in this paper debate precisely this assumption. The sociology of Giddens allows a central role for the knowledgeable and capable actor in his theory: for example, 'The purposive content of everyday action consists *in the continual successful "monitoring" by the actor of his own activity* [his italics], it is indicative of a casual mastery of day to day events that men normally take for granted' (Giddens, 1987, p. 82). Such successful reflexive monitoring may exist, but not necessarily so. It is thus more a matter for empirical verification than an assumption beyond questioning.

15.   The ideas laid down in 'Education for self reliance' are current in much wider debates on education in Africa. See also, for example, Sheffield (1967); Dumont (1968). Such ideas have a long history: for instance, 'The Phelps-Stokes commission expressed the view, that the low esteem for agriculture resulted from the type of education given' (Kaayk, 1976, p. 91). Mrs Phelps-Stokes was an American lady who left money for a study of education in Africa in the early 1920s.

REFERENCES

Bates, R. (1983), *Essays in the Political Economy of Rural Africa* (Cambridge: Cambridge University Press).

Bauman, Z. (1978), *Hermeneutics and Social Science: Approaches to Understanding* (London: Hutchinson).

Berger, P.L. and Thomas Luckmann (1966), *The Social Construction of Reality: A Treatise in the Sociology of Knowledge* (Harmondsworth: Penguin).

Booth, D. (1985), 'Marxism and development sociology: interpreting the impasse', *World Development* 13 (7).

Booth, D. (1992), 'Social Development Research: an agenda for the 1990s', *The European Journal of Development Research* 4 (1).

Cooksey, B., G. Malekela and D. Ndabi (1990), *Girls Educational Opportunities and Performance in Tanzania* (Dar es Salaam: TADREG).

Dumont, R. (1968), *A False Start in Africa* (London: Sphere Publications).

Festinger, L., H.W. Riecken and S. Schachter (1956), *When Prophecy Fails* (Minneapolis: University of Minnesota Press).

Fosbrooke, H. and R. Young (1960), *Land and Politics among the Luguru* (London: Routledge and Kegan Paul).

Giddens A. (1987), *New Rules of Sociological Method* (London: Hutchinson).

Heijnen, J.D. (1986), *Development and Education in the Mwanza District (Tanzania): A Case Study of Migration and Peasant Farming* (Rotterdam: Bronder offset).

Hyden, G. (1980), *Beyond Ujamaa in Tanzania: Underdevelopment and an Uncaptured Peasantry* (London: Heinemann Educational Books).

Kaayk, J. (1976), *Education, Estrangement and Adjustment: A Study among Pupils and School Leavers in Bukumbi, a Rural Community in Tanzania* (The Hague: Mouton).

Kerner, D.O. (1985), 'Reading at home is like dancing in the church: a comparison of educational opportunities in two Tanzanian regions'. Paper presented at the American Anthropological Association Annual Meeting, Washington, D.C.

Krech, D., R.S. Crutchfield and E.L. Ballachey (1962), *Individual in Society: A Textbook of Social Psychology* (New York: McGraw-Hill).

Levine, R.A. (1966), *Dreams and Deeds: Achievement Motivation in Nigeria.* (Chicago and London: University of Chicago Press).

Long, N. (1977), *An Introduction to the Sociology of Rural Development* (London: Tavistock Publications).

Merton, R.K. (1956), *Social Theory and Social Structure* (London: The Free Press of Glencoe/Collier-Macmillan).

Nyerere, J.K. (1967), 'Education for self-reliance', reprinted in H. Hinzen and V.H. Hundsdorfer (eds) (1979), *Education for Liberation and Development: The Tanzanian Experience* (London: Evans Brothers).

Peters, P. (1988), 'The links between production and consumption and the achievement of food security among smallholder farmers in Zomba South', in *Report of the Workshop on Household Food Security and Nutrition*, 28–31 August, Centre for Social Research: Zomba.

Samoff, J. (1979), 'Education, class formation and the structure of power', *The Journal of Modern African Studies* 29 (4).

Sender, J. and S. Smith (1990), *Poverty, Class and Gender in Rural Africa: A Tanzanian Case Study* (London: Routledge).

Sheffield J.R. (ed.) (1967), *Education, Employment and Rural Development* (Nairobi: East African Publishing House).

Vandergeest, P. and F.H. Buttel (1988), 'Marx, Weber and development sociology: beyond the impasse', *World Development* 16 (6).

van Donge, J.K. (1992a), 'Agricultural decline in Tanzania: the case of the Uluguru mountains', *African Affairs* (91) 362, pp. 73–94.

van Donge, J.K. (1992b), 'Waluguru traders in Dar es Salaam', *African Affairs* (91) 363, pp. 181–205.

8 Flexible Work and Female Labour: The Global Integration of Chilean Fruit Production

Stephanie Barrientos

INTRODUCTION[1]

Chile is often presented as a model of the economic success which can be achieved through neoliberal export-led growth, based on non-traditional primary produce. This is because of its high rates of economic growth since the late 1980s. A key element in this success has been the rapid expansion of fruit exports to the North, and today Chile is a major player in the global market for fresh fruit.[2] A crucial prerequisite for this export success has been the annual mobilisation of a large temporary female labour force in fruit production within the central region of the country. At the base of Chile's fruit exports, therefore, is the productive capacity and flexibility of women workers, yet their contribution to the Chilean export model has been given little attention in the literature.

The aim of this chapter is to examine this temporary female labour force, and why it has played such an important role in the global integration of Chilean fruit production. I start by examining the background to the rapid expansion of fruit export production and employment. I then go on to consider the role played by women's employment in fruit production, exploring the relative flexibility and employment patterns of women workers in fruit. It is argued that female workers are concentrated into the most flexible employment within fruit relative to male workers, and that this has been central both to export specialisation in the central region and to meeting the requirements of Northern supermarkets. With the transition to democracy a large flexible female labour force is likely to remain the basis of fruit production, given the continued commitment to the neo-liberal model and global integration.

125

GLOBAL INTEGRATION AND AGRARIAN TRANSFORMATION

The global fruit market of the North is dominated by large supermarket chains, meeting increased consumer demand for year-long fresh fruit supplies. Overall, Chile accounts for 14 per cent of total world exports of fresh temperate fruit, but as an off-season supplier it is isolated from competition with Northern producers. Chile provides 45 per cent of total southern hemisphere exports of temperate fruit, with its grapes accounting for 83.6 per cent and nectarines and peaches 93.4 per cent of their respective product exports (Table 8.1).

The comparative advantage of Chilean fruit has resulted from a combination of factors. The industry is located in the centre of the country with the majority of fruit exports coming from the regions around Santiago and Valparaiso, particularly Regions V, VI and the Metropolitan Region. As can be seen from Table 8.2, these three regions contain the majority of fruit production, and accounted for approximately 75 per cent of Chile's fruit exports in 1992–3. This area benefits from a stable temperate climate, fertile land and plentiful water supplies from the Andes. It also enjoys a relatively good infrastructure, with close proximity to the main ports and airport. Modern irrigation systems, computerised production and packing methods, use of refrigerated storage and transportation, and especially the advance in containerised shipping have all combined to allow the expansion of global fruit exports.

TABLE 8.1: *World Fruit Exports (Thousands of Metric Tonnes, 1990–91 Season)*

	Apples	Pears	Grapes	Nectarines & Peaches
Chile	318.0	90.2	471.9	66.4
TSH	1027.9	370.4	564.4	71.1
Chile as % TSH	30.9%	24.4%	83.6%	93.4%
TNH	2658.0	557.5	1078.9	747.1
Total World	3685.8	927.9	1643.3	818.2
Chile as % World	8.6%	9.7%	28.7%	8.1%

TSH = Total Southern Hemisphere
TNH = Total Northern Hemisphere
SOURCE: Asociación de Exportadores, 1992; U.N. Food and Agriculture Organisation, Trade Yearbook, 1991.

Important to Chile's comparative advantage is also the employment of a large temporary flexible labour force, with relatively low labour costs. Precise data for temporary employment in the fruit sector in Chile are not available, and are difficult to estimate. Estimates by specialists working in the field range between 255,000 and 700,000 temporary fruit workers.[3] Despite these problems, Table 8.2 contains a rough estimate of temporary workers for 1992–93, based on the total number of hectares planted and in production per region, and the estimate of Venegas (1993) of one permanent worker per 3.7 hectares planted and two temporary workers per hectare in production. The total of 287,440 temporary workers employed arrived at by this method is at the lower end of existing estimates, but excludes ancillary workers, such as those in transport. Table 8.2 gives a profile of the regional distribution of permanent and temporary workers, showing that approximately 78 per cent of fruit employment was concentrated in the three key central regions.

Over half the temporary labour force is female, the so-called 'temporeras', who play a key role in the specialised production of fruit for export. Women temporary workers are primarily employed in packing, and female employment tends to be concentrated in the peak months of the season between December and March each year (Venegas, 1992a; Díaz, 1991). Agriculture is by nature seasonal and thus involves temporary employment, but as will be shown, women are concentrated into the most flexible labour functions required by export production.

The background to the explosion in fruit exports and expansion of flexible female employment was the creation of a large rural surplus wage labour force after 1973. This came about through the liberalisation of land and labour markets under the dictatorship.[4] The military government's policy facilitated the rapid expansion of capitalist farming by entrepreneurs, who were able to buy medium-sized farms or 'parcelas', particularly in those regions dominated by fruit production. The military pursued a strategy of export-led growth which included the expansion of fruit production, and which had originally been advocated in the Fruit Plan of 1968 (Encheñique, 1990). Capital was attracted to the profitable non-traditional export sector, and there was a process of modernisation, which allowed the introduction of modern techniques of production and infrastructure. This enabled entrepreneurial medium-sized producers to lock into the agro-export industry.

Large numbers of peasants were expelled from the land into rural shanty towns and cities after 1973. In the absence of traditional forms of hacienda employment, this rural population could only turn to its wage labour as a means of subsistence. Substantial levels of rural poverty forced

TABLE 8.2: *Fruit Production, Estimated Employment and Exports by Region 1992–93*

Region	Total Area Planted with Fruit (hectares)	Total Area in Production (hectares)[a]	Estimated Permanent Workers Employed[b]	Estimated Temporary Workers Employed[c]	Fruit Exported No. of Boxes (thousands)	% of Total Exports
III	6 170	5 150	1 668	10 300	3 269.4	2.35
IV	8 390	6 890	2 268	13 780	12 423.3	8.91
V	34 060	27 370	9 205	54 740	26 643.2	19.12
METROPOL.	47 650	37 700	12 878	75 400	40 536.7	29.09
VI	59 600	47 000	16 108	94 000	36 916.5	26.49
VII	26 510	19 610	7 165	39 220	14 312.6	10.27
TOTAL	182 380	143 720	49 292	287 440	(139 365.8)[d]	(100.00)[d]

[a] Area in Production = Area Planted − Area in formation

[b] Based on estimation of Venegas (1993) of 1 permanent worker per 3.7 hectares of total area planted

[c] Based on estimate of Venegas (1993) of 2 temporary workers employed in harvesting and packing per 1 hectare in production, excluding ancillary workers (transport etc.)

[d] Total exported includes 5264.2 boxes (3.78%) from other regions

SOURCE: INE Estadisticas Agropecuarias 1992–93; own estimates; Asociación de Exportadores 1993–94.

many poor agrarian families to adopt survival strategies in which all able members took up waged work whenever possible. This included women who had not traditionally been formally employed in their own right under the hacienda (Bradshaw, 1990; Lago, 1992). This rapidly expanded the semi-urbanised rural labour force, and together with small-scale peasants needing to supplement their meagre incomes, became the basis of a large, cheap, temporary and flexible labour force, dependent on wage labour for survival (Gómez and Echneñique, 1988; Díaz, 1991; Kay, 1993).

At a national level, the military government had a strategy of labour market deregulation, implemented politically through the repression of worker organisation, legally through modification of the labour code, and informally through failure to enforce existing legislation. At the political level, the vicious repression after 1973 of rural trade unions, which had previously protected the primarily male agricultural workforce, facilitated the reduction of agricultural wages and conditions of employment (Kay and Silva, 1992). Producers often also used the employment of women who had not previously been organised by trade unions, as a vehicle for avoiding traditional labour organisation and implementing new working practices based on temporary employment typified in fruit production (Venegas 1992b).

Labour legislation introduced between 1979 and 1987 formalised the move to a more flexible and deregulated labour market; restricted temporary workers' employment rights; and limited legal trade-union activity, shifting from collective bargaining to individual negotiation between employer and employee (Ruiz-Tagle, 1991; Jarvis, 1992). However, all temporary workers were still legally meant to be employed under labour contracts entitling the worker to certain minimum rights and deductions for pension and other benefits. But legal regulations give the employer a high degree of flexibility in the hiring and laying off of labour, and the same temporary contract can be regularly renewed over long periods of time (some male fruit workers are semi-permanently employed on 'temporary' contracts). Many seasonal workers work for the same employer for years, but only ever on a limited temporary contract. Despite the transition to democracy, the legal framework continues to facilitate this highly flexible employment.

In addition to deregulation, lack of enforcement allows employers to avoid implementation of the remaining minimal regulations. This tendency is highest among the smaller and medium-sized fruit producers, and less pronounced among the larger and transnational producers, who tend to adhere to the labour code. Case studies have found between 40 and 50 per cent of temporary workers have no contract of employment at all (Díaz, 1991; Venegas 1992a).[5] Both changes in labour market regulation and lack of enforcement have thus facilitated the rapid growth in temporary employment in agriculture generally, with temporary workers increasing from 41 per cent of the rural labour force in 1964–65 to 75 per cent in 1987 (Gómez and Echeñique, 1988). This trend has been even greater in fruit production, however, where approximately 85 per cent of the labour force is temporary.

Agricultural production inherently involves seasonal work, and fruit production is relatively labour-intensive, creating the basis for temporary employment. In a diversified agrarian system, employment can be spread over a range of products which can be harvested over a more staggered period of time. The high degree of concentration on fruit production (monocultivation) in the central regions has greatly reduced diversification, and concentrated labour requirements,[6] which, because of the volume of output for export, necessitates a massive surge of labour in the peak period. Further, fruit exportation to international supermarkets is a high precision business. Successful exportation involves attaining consistent 'high quality' (based mainly on colour, shape and size), meeting very tight deadlines for production (hormones play a key role in bringing fruit on at the right time) and the very rapid harvesting and processing of large quantities of fruit in order that it does not deteriorate.

Employment patterns within the sector are also determined by the relationship between the producers and exporters. A large number of heterogeneous domestic producers, approximately 8000, lock into rigid production schedules dictated by a small number of large export firms, with only 20 firms controlling 80 per cent of total exports (*Eurofruit*, various issues, 1994–95). The export firms supply the producers with technical advice, credit, transport and packing facilities. Still, for many of the small and medium-sized independent producers, business can be precarious, and they are at the mercy of the larger exporters (Korovkin, 1992). International competition and volatility of markets can easily have an adverse effect on them, but flexibility of female employment helps to constrain labour costs, providing an important cushion for fruit producers in the global fruit market.

FLEXIBLE LABOUR AND THE INTEGRATION OF FEMALE TEMPORARY WORKERS INTO FRUIT PRODUCTION

There is a clear segmentation by gender in fruit labour. During the winter, the vast majority of permanent or semi-permanent employment is male, and women are only integrated into the labour market with the surge in temporary employment during the spring and summer months. Female employment is concentrated particularly in the production of table grapes and in packing. A study in the Aconcagua Valley found that over 70 per cent of employment in packing was female (Rodriguez and Venegas, 1989).

The traditional reasons for the employment of women in fruit production partly relate, as has been found in studies of export production in many other countries, to employers' perceptions of the 'attributes' of female labour. First, fruit production does not require great physical effort; second, it is argued women have a 'natural' skill and dexterity ('nimble fingers') which allows them to manipulate the fruit delicately (especially in packing and grape production where presentation is important); third, women have a more responsible attitude to work; and fourth, women are seen as more obedient to authority, questioning less the conditions under which they are employed. Interviews with Chilean fruit employers would appear to bear out that this is their perception of female labour (Díaz, 1991; Valdés, 1988), although the idea that the above are 'natural' as opposed to socially conditioned attributes has long been criticised in feminist work (Elson and Pearson, 1981). These factors are relevant to the producers' need to attain high quality of presentation of the fruit, but my focus is also on the way in which female labour has been concentrated into the most flexible labour functions, facilitating the global integration of Chilean fruit production.

Flexible labour generally relates to work which can include temporary, part-time, short-term contracts, homeworking, and self-employment (Hakim, 1987). In agriculture, seasonality itself is a major determinant of temporary employment. However, the flexibility of female labour in Chilean fruit production is much greater relative to male labour, both in terms of employment practice during the season and as a basis for the annual mobilisation of a large temporary labour force. There is a lot of debate over labour flexibility in developed countries, with no single definition commonly agreed (Atkinson, 1984; Meulders and Wilkin, 1987; Pollert 1988a, 1988b, 1991). I will follow the classification employed by Rubery (1989), examining flexibility from four aspects:

Numerical flexibility relates to the ability to adjust labour purchased to labour requirements. In the case of fruit, lack of legal regulation allows producers arbitrary power to increase and decrease the number of workers through the season and hours worked at different times of the season. Many workers are employed on temporary contracts with no specified time period, but simply until the job is completed. Women fruit workers are particularly subject to numerical flexibility because they are only drawn into production at the peak of the season, fulfilling functions which are only carried out at this time of the year.

An example of this is given in Figure 8.1, showing the annual profile of the number of workers employed by a sample of seven firms from Santa Maria in the Aconcagua Valley in Region V in 1984–85. This shows that in these firms female employment is mainly concentrated between October and March, first in the fields where women are employed particularly in the pruning of grapes, and then in packing. During this period 93 per cent of the female work-days are demanded, in contrast to 71 per cent of male work-days during the same period (Rodriguez, 1987). Venegas (1992b) estimated that in 1988 only 5 per cent of permanent work was carried out by women, but they constituted over 50 per cent of temporary fruit labour.

Women are also more subject to numerical flexibility than men in terms of the potential variation in the number of hours worked per day. Men are mainly concentrated in the fields, where natural daylight limits hours worked to 8–10 hours. In packing, where women are more concentrated, artificial light allows the extension of hours worked, which can vary between 8 and 16 hours per day. Numerical flexibility is further reinforced by the large number of employers operating without contracts of employment, and interviews suggest that more women workers have no contract than men. These employers observe no regulations covering the expansion and contraction of hours of work and numbers employed through the peak of the season, further minimising labour costs.

Functional flexibility relates to the ability to move workers from job to job within a firm. In fruit production this also involves switching from one type of fruit to another as the season progresses, and moving workers from field work to packing, especially in the production of grapes. Women are more exposed to functional flexibility than men as exemplified in Figure 8.1, where they are moved from pruning in the fields between October and December to packing from December to March. Male employment remains concentrated in the fields throughout, although a minority of women continued to be employed in harvesting during the peak (despite this being a supposedly 'male occupation').

Pay flexibility relates to the ability to change rates of pay. Both rates and methods of pay are variable in fruit production, but again women are subject to the most flexible pay arrangements. Pickers and field workers (largely male) are paid mainly on fixed daily rates, as are a few tasks within the packing sheds such as crane drivers and *mozos* (servants) who are mainly male. However, most jobs within packing are paid on a piece rate (with some employers giving an additional arbitrary bonus at the height of the

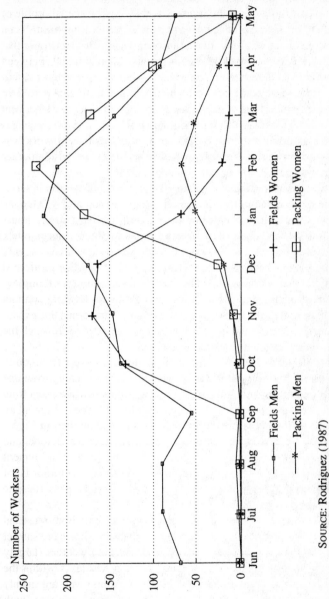

Number of Workers

SOURCE: Rodriguez (1987)
Data taken from sample of 7 employers' payrolls, Santa Maria, Region V 1984–5

—■— Fields Men   —+— Fields Women

—*— Packing Men   —□— Packing Women

FIGURE 8.1: *Number of Temporary Workers Hired per Month, Santa Maria, 1984–85*

season). Piece rates are paid by the box which passes quality control. They are the most flexible form of pay, maximising productivity, and extending working hours at the height of the season, because many workers only have the opportunity at this time of the year to earn reasonable incomes. Given that women are concentrated in these functions within the packing sheds, they form the majority of workers on this type of flexible pay. Pay is variable between regions, between producers and within the same firm at different points of the season. It tends to be higher in the north of the country (where there is a shortage of fruit labour), and also tends to be higher amongst the larger, relative to the medium and smaller, producers. The extent of the variability of pay by task and within task (and hence the difficulty of estimating average pay rates) is shown in Table 8.3, which gives an example of the varying rates for different tasks received by women temporary workers in a sample of packing houses in 1993–94. Total pay is also dependent on production levels and individual productivity. This allows a high potential variability in pay, but there is evidence that intense labour market pressure at the height of the season, and employers' need to retain experienced packers, means some firms will guarantee their workers a minimum daily rate when production levels are slack, thus reducing flexibility (Dominguez et al., 1994). Women workers on piece rates in the packing sheds who have high rates of individual productivity and work long hours are able to earn higher incomes than predominantly male workers on daily rates in the fields. The Comisión Nacional Campesina (CNC) estimated that the overall average income of temporary fruit workers in the 1993–94 season was Chilean $57,000 (US$ 134) per month approximately.[7]

Labour market flexibility relates to the ability to move between different firms and in and out of the industry. The large number of medium-sized

TABLE 8.3: *Estimates of Female Pay Rates in Fruit Packing 1993–94*

	Chilean $	US$
AVERAGE DAILY RATE	1 738	4.08
PIECE RATES (PER BOX)		
Selection	12–23	0.03–0.05
Cleaning	40–94	0.09–0.22
Packing	20–32	0.05–0.08

Number of Boxes Packed per day 10 to 70 depending on production levels and individual worker productivity.

SOURCE: F. Rojas, ODEPA, Ministerio de Agricultura
    Average data from five packing houses 1993/94 season.

producers allows a degree of labour movement between firms, but for women workers, proximity to the home often acts as a constraint on any movement, and many temporary workers report working for the same employer year after year. As seen above, female employment is more concentrated into the peak of the season than male employment. Concentration on fruit for export means a lack of alternative sources of employment outside the season, and case studies have found that women find it much harder to find any non-fruit work during the winter months. Venegas (1992a) found that on average, female temporary workers were unemployed 59 per cent more days than male temporary workers. For women, movement in and out of the industry effectively means movement between employment and unemployment, even though a large number want to work in the winter. Thus while the female labour market is flexible to the employer in that women workers can move fluidly in and out of the industry, it is not so flexible to the women for whom there is little alternative.

The other side of labour flexibility is also labour insecurity. Functional flexibility means women are often subject to the arbitrary dictates of employers and managers, with no form of redress. Wage flexibility means women are able to earn some of the highest incomes in the sector, but only by intense working and long hours without a break during the season, with no source of income during the winter months, leading to a high incidence of poverty amongst fruit workers.[8] Numerical flexibility means insecurity of work and earnings. Labour market flexibility means switching between periods of exceptionally long working hours, and prolonged periods out of work when women have no choice but to return to the home.

Flexibility also allows employers to reduce non-wage labour costs to themselves, by shifting these on to workers. Lack of proper health insurance, social insurance and pension rights, for example, are all borne by the 'flexible' workers, especially women if they are less likely to have contracts. In addition, lack of regulation and enforcement in the sector allows poor working conditions, lack of sanitation and high health risks from intense use of pesticides (including an increased incidence of malformed children being born), all costs borne by the workers. Many of the women fruit workers also endure the burden of the 'double day', continuing to bear the main domestic and childcare responsibilities in the household on top of a 16-hour working day. The peak of fruit production falls during the school holidays, and the absence of any adequate childcare facilities or social welfare provision is a major problem.

However, the integration of rural women into formal paid work has simultaneously given them a greater independence, making them an important contributor to the household income, undermining the traditional division of labour in which their role was seen as subordinate to men and confined to the home. Employment in fruit has provided both a point of social contact and interaction, as well as greater social recognition. Many of the women see temporary work in fruit as preferable to domestic labour, which is the main alternative, and do not want a return to the past.

Another factor in the extensive employment of women is also the concentration on *export* production in the central regions dominated by the fruit sector, and the qualitative, quantitative and seasonal labour force requirements it generates. At the height of the season there is a surge in labour demand, and women are bought into employment in very large numbers. This coincides with the demand for more 'delicate' labour associated with preparing the fruit for export. Thus women are not simply employed because of a labour shortage (there were periods in the recession in the mid-1980s when women members of families were employed but male members were not). The labour also has to be semi-skilled, and preferably experienced – as this reduces 'on the job' training costs for employers. Female labour meets these requirements partly because of its perceived 'natural' attributes, especially in pruning and packing; but also because of the experience gained by working in fruit year after year, often for the same employer, sometimes for ten years or more.

As we saw in Table 8.2, approximately 78 per cent of fruit employment is concentrated in the three regions around Santiago (Regions V, VI and the Metropolitan Region). In those regions, the surge in labour demand at the height of the fruit season puts immense pressure on the agricultural labour market. As a result, all women of working age are employable. The majority of women fruit workers are married or partnered with children, and employment is not limited to mainly young, single women as many studies of export production elsewhere have found (Arizpe and Aranda, 1981).[9] Despite this, the employment of a large agrarian female labour force is not sufficient to meet labour demand at the height of the season in these regions. As migration is not significant,[10] employers have to use all sources of labour including youth, students, plus urban and city informal sector and blue collar workers who are bused to and from their place of work on a daily basis (a form of 'reverse migration').[11]

Women workers thus form a backbone of semi-skilled labour, which returns to the home during the winter months, to be depended upon year after year. While the employment itself is 'temporary', women who have traditionally been tied to the home actually provide a permanent and reliable source of labour, which is essential to fulfilling the functions needed to guarantee the consistent high quality of exports demanded by Northern supermarkets annually. It is an exploitation of the traditional gender division of labour, and lack of alternative employment for women relative to men, which reinforces the stability of the women's supply of labour as the most flexible component in the fruit labour force.

CONCLUSION

With the transition to democracy since 1990, the government has been pursuing a dual policy of 'equity with growth', combining a strong commitment to the neoliberal export-led model, with a reduction in the high levels of poverty and social inequality bequeathed by the military dictatorship. A number of official organisations have taken up issues relating to the 'temporeras'. However, all these initiatives have focused on social welfare provision to the temporary workers (particularly the initiation of programmes relating to the provision of childcare during the height of the season), and apart from marginal changes, the government has failed to address fundamental issues relating to their pay or conditions of work. Temporary fruit workers still have no legal right to collective negotiation, which can only take place with the voluntary agreement of the employers, and strikes are illegal (Petras & Leiva, 1994).

This failure is a product of the dilemma of pursuing a strategy of 'growth with equity'. Were major reforms introduced which guaranteed significant improvements in the pay and conditions of the temporary workers, the international competitiveness of Chilean fruit, one of the central tenets in the export-led growth model, could be undermined. Central to the comparative advantage and global integration of fruit has been the highly flexible rural labour markets, with women concentrated into the most flexible functions. There have been amendments to the Labour Code, but these have been fairly cosmetic,[12] and the policy of fostering flexible labour markets has remained central, both under President Aylwin and his successor Eduardo Frei. In the interests of growth, therefore, improving equity is confined to social provision outside the productive sphere, and flexible female temporary workers are likely to remain a major component of the fruit labour market.

In conclusion, therefore, the creation of a large flexible female labour force has been central to maintaining the consistent high quality and stability of supply required to export to Northern supermarkets. Women have been concentrated into the most flexible forms of employment relative to male fruit workers. They are employed for the shortest period of time, and have played a pivotal role in providing a permanent source of temporary labour which could meet the surge in demand for experienced and semi-skilled labour at the peak of the season. They work the most flexible hours, receive the most flexible pay, and are less likely to have proper contracts or associated benefits. This helps producers to reduce non-wage costs and to cushion themselves in an increasingly volatile and competitive international market.

As such, the 'temporeras' have been at the cutting edge of Chile's integration into global fruit markets since 1982. For many rural women, this is the first time they have been integrated into the formal labour market, allowing them greater independence. However, the costs of the 'comparative advantage' of Chilean fruit have also been borne by these women workers. They have been subject to high insecurity, poor conditions, lack of insurance provision or legal protection and high unemployment in the winter months. In addition they experience the problems of the double day, health problems, lack of social or childcare provision, and poverty. For them, the 'fruits' of success have also had a bitter taste.

NOTES

1. The main sources of information for this paper are three important case studies carried out among temporary fruit workers (Díaz, 1991; Venegas, 1992a; PREALC, 1990), plus interviews with professionals and workers in the field during two visits to Chile in 1993 and 1994. I would particularly like to thank: Sylvia Venegas (SERNAM), Gonzalo Falabella (Corporación Mancomunal and Casa del Temporero), Rosa Parisi (CAFOD), Claudia Chacaltana and Julia Aravena (ICAR), Francisco Rojas (ODEPA, Ministry of Agriculture), Sergio Gómex (FLACSO), Mafalda Galdames and Francisca Rodriguez (CNC) and Soledad Valdés (PRODEMU). I would also like to thank Elide Balocchi for her assistance.

2. Between 1982 and 1992 the volume of exports of Chilean fruit increased by 256 per cent, with fruit accounting for 13 per cent of total Chilean exports in 1991 (Asociación de Exportadores, 1992). The average annual rate of growth of GDP for the period 1989–93 was 7 per cent, reaching an annual rate of 10 per cent in both 1989 and 1992 (Economist Intelligence Unit, 1994).

3. Venegas (1993) estimates 255,000, and Petras and Leiva (1994) cite 700,000 temporary fruit workers at the peak of the season, but there are no official data available. Estimates vary both because of the volatility of employment, and also according to whether associated temporary employment is included, such as transport workers.

4. The background to this was the agrarian reform, initiated by President Frei in 1964 and continued by Allende, heralding the end of the traditional agrarian system, followed after 1973 by the military government's counter-reform policy. See Kay and Silva, 1992; Hojman, 1990, 1993.

5. Many temporary workers do not push for contracts, either because of lack of knowledge, fear of the employer, or because they can see no point in having deductions of 20.6 per cent being made from their wage given their current level of poverty, and the uncertainty of receiving real benefits (Díaz, 1991; Venegas, 1992a and 1993).

6. The season starts earlier in the north of the country (where production has been extended into desert regions through the use of modern computerised drip irrigation systems), and then moves south. However, the whole production season is concentrated into six months of the year, between October and March.

7. In 1988 Chilean fruit workers' pay was an estimated 20 times less than their Californian equivalents (Díaz, 1991).

8. On average, over half the families in Venegas' study fell below the poverty line in 1988–89, defined by a minimum basket (Canasta mínima de satisfacción de necesidades básicas) needed to satisfy basic needs equivalent to $Chilean 9842.17 per person during this period (Venegas, 1992a).

9. In the case study of women temporary workers by Díaz, 41 per cent of the women were aged 20–29 years, 27 per cent were aged 30–39 years, and 23 per cent were aged 40 years and over (Díaz, 1991).

10. Migration is only significant in the north, where the season is earlier than the centre. Temporary fruit workers migrate north, returning to the central regions as the season progresses.

11. In the Aconcagua Valley (close to Santiago) it was found that 20 per cent of temporary workers came from peasant households, 52 per cent came from towns and villages, and 28 per cent from cities (Gómez and Echeñique, 1988).

12. The main changes to the Labour Code affecting the temporary workers relate to: (i) the signing of contracts within five days of commencement of work (which obviously has no effect on those without contracts); (ii) the provision of adequate and hygienic lodgings (affecting those migrant workers to the north); (iii) the provision of adequate and hygienic conditions for the consumption of food at work by temporary workers; and (iv) the provision of transport for workers living over 3 km away in the absence of public transport (Venegas, 1993).

REFERENCES

Arizpe, L. and J. Aranda (1981), 'The "Comparative Advantages" of Women's Disadvantages: Women Workers in the Strawberry Export Agribusiness in Mexico', *Signs* 7 (2), pp. 453–73.

Asociación de Exportadores de Chile, *Estadísticas de Exportaciones Hortofrutícolas*, 1991–92 and 1993–94, Santiago.

Atkinson, J. (1984), 'Manpower Strategies for Flexible Organisations', *Personnel Management* August, pp. 28–31.

Bradshaw, S. (1990), 'Women in Chilean Rural Society' in D. Hojman (ed.), *Neoliberal Agriculture in Rural Chile* (Basingstoke: Macmillan).

Díaz, E. (1991), *Investigación Participativa Acerca de las Trabajadoras Temporeras de la Fruta* (San Bernardo: Centro El Canela de Nos).

Dominguez, J.I., G. Vargas and M.I. Vial (1994), 'Productividad e Incentivos Laborales En Fruticultura' *Panorama Económico de la Agricultura* March–April, 93, pp. 3–8.

Echeñique, J. (1990), 'Las Dos Caras de la Agricultura y las Políticas Posibles', *Proposiciones* 18, pp. 145–58.

Economist Intelligence Unit (1994) *Chile, Country Report, 4th qtr*, London.

Elson, D. and R. Pearson (1981), 'Nimble Fingers Make Cheap Workers, An Analysis of Women's Employment in Third World Export Manufacturing', *Feminist Review* Spring, pp. 87–107.

Eurofruit, various issues, 1994–95.

Gómez, S. and J. Echeñique (1988), *La Agricultura Chilena, Las Dos Caras de la Modernización* (Santiago: FLACSO).

Hakim, C. (1987), 'Trends in the Flexible Workforce', *Employment Gazette* November, pp. 549–60.

Hojman, D. (ed.) (1990), *Neo-liberal Agriculture in Rural Chile* (Basingstoke: Macmillan).

Hojman, D. (ed.) (1993), *Change in the Chilean Countryside* (Basingstoke: Macmillan).

Jarvis, L. (1992), 'The Unravelling of Agrarian Reform', in C. Kay and P. Silva (eds), *Development and Change in the Chilean Countryside* (Amsterdam: CEDLA).

Kay, C. (1993), 'The Agrarian Policy of the Aylwin Government: Continuity or Change', in D. Hojman (ed.), *Change In the Chilean Countryside* (Basingstoke: Macmillan).

Kay, C. and P. Silva (eds) (1992), *Development and Change in the Chilean Countryside* (Amsterdam: CELDA).

Korovkin, T. (1992), 'Peasants, Grapes and Corporations: the Growth of Contract Farming in a Chilean Community', *Journal of Peasant Studies* 19 (2), pp. 228–54.

Lago, M.S. (1992), 'Rural Women and the Neo-liberal Model', in C. Kay and P. Silva (eds), *Development and Change in the Chilean Countryside* (Amsterdam: CELDA).

Meulders, D. and L. Wilkin (1987), 'Labour Market Flexiblity: Critical Introduction to the Analysis of a Concept', *Labour and Society* January, 12 (1), pp. 3–17.

Petras J. and F. Leiva, with H. Veltmeyer (1994), *Democracy and Poverty in Chile, The Limits to Electoral Politics* (Boulder, CO: Westview).

Pollert, A. (1988a), 'Dismantling Flexibility', *Capital and Class* May, 34, pp. 42–75.

Pollert, A. (1988b), 'The "Flexible Firm": Fixation or Fact?', *Work, Employment and Society* 2 (3), pp. 281–316.

Pollert, A. (ed.) (1991), *Farewell to Flexibility* (Oxford: Blackwell).

Programa Regional del Empleo para Americana Latina y el Caribe (PREALC) (1990), *Ciclos Ocupacionales y Disponibilidad de Mano de Obra Temporal en Dos Comunas de Valle de Aconcagua*, no. 344, Santiago.

Rodriguez, D. (1987), *Agricultural Modernisation and Labour Markets in Latin America: The Case of Fruit Production in Central Chile,* PhD Thesis, University of Texas at Austin.

Rodriguez, D. and S. Venegas (1989), *De Praderas A Parronales, Un Estudio sobre Estructura Agraria y Mercado Laboral en el Valle de Aconcagua* (Santiago: GEA).

Rubery, J. (1989), 'Labour Market Flexibility in Britain', in F. Green (ed.), *The Restructuring of the UK Economy* (Hemel Hempstead: Harvester Wheatsheaf).

Ruiz-Tangle, J. (1991), *Trabajo y Economía – en el retorno a la democracia* (Santiago: PET).

Valdés, X. (1988), 'Feminización del Mercado de Trabajo Agrícola: Las Temporeras', in *Mundo De Mujer – Continuidad y Cambio* (Santiago: Centro de Estudios de Mujer).

Venegas, S. (1992a), *Una Gota al Dia ... Un Chorro Al Año. El Impacto Social de la Expansión Frutícola* (Santiago: GEA).

Venegas, S. (1992b), *Mujer Rural: Campesinas y Temporeras* (Santiago: Ministerio de Agricultura, INDAP).

Venegas, S. (1993), 'Programas de apoyo a temporeros y temporeras en Chile', in S. Gómez and E. Klein (eds) *Los Pobres del Campo. El Trabajador Eventual,* Santiago, Organización Internacional del Trabajo.

9 Diversifying Health Sector Finance in Botswana: The Impact of an Emergent Private Sector[1]

Jacqueline Charlton

INTRODUCTION

Equality of access to health care is one of the most deep-rooted beliefs and one which is found in most societies, developed and developing. Debates concerning health policy reform tend therefore to be conducted within this framework. Even among the most ardent advocates of 'the market' such beliefs find resonance. For example, Margaret Thatcher, speaking in 1983, argued that 'the principle that adequate health care should be provided for all, regardless of their ability to pay, must be the foundation of all arrangements for financing health care'.

In respect of developing countries, such arguments are the basis for decisions concerning public funding of health services. As Cichon and Gillion (1993) have argued 'to be poor and in good health is one thing. To be poor and in bad health turns hardship into misery – a situation which is made worse if health care services are unavailable, unaffordable, restricted, delayed or of low quality.' Discussions about health care are therefore inseparable from discussion of redistributive policies within the state in general – of transfer payments from one group to another whether it be from richer to poorer groups or from urban to rural areas.

This chapter seeks to examine the financing of health services in Botswana where the problems of funding health care are not so much those of a total lack of resources, but rather reflect problems in the distribution of resources between rural and urban areas, between the affluent and the poor and between primary and tertiary levels of health care. Even in richer countries, the constraints on government spending on health are increasing as costs rise and expectations increase. New approaches are being sought to the problems of cost control and to improving the effectiveness of health investments.

The World Bank study 'Financing Health Services in Developing Countries' (World Bank, 1987) suggested a range of options for the reform of health finance. These included decentralisation of public health provision, the introduction of charges, encouraging the use of personal insurance to cover health risks and encouraging the development of a private sector in health care. All these elements can been seen to have formed part of Botswana's response to health sector change and reform in recent years. They are principles that are proving influential across the Southern African Development Community (SADC) region in general, most notably in Zimbabwe (World Bank, 1992), and are likely to prove persuasive in the development of health finance systems in the new South Africa.

PUBLIC SECTOR HEALTH FINANCE

Botswana has not faced the economic crises found in most of the rest of sub-Saharan Africa. A steady growth in the economy and a favourable donor disposition towards the country, given its democratic and economic stability (donor per capita assistance in 1991 is put at US$ 102.5 – significantly higher than the majority of countries in sub-Saharan Africa and only exceeded by Mauritania, Zambia, Namibia and Gabon), has allowed the government to develop its health services significantly since independence. As the economy has developed and incomes have risen (per capita income in Botswana reached US$ 2790 in 1992, equal to that of Malaysia and above that of South Africa), the performance of the health sector in achieving targets has been exemplary.

During the planning period of National Development Plan (NDP) 6 (MFDP, 1985) substantial improvements in the performance of the health sector were observable. The objective of access to health facilities, as envisaged in NDP 6, was achieved in the period to 1991: 85 per cent of the population were within 15 km of a health facility, with 73 per cent within 8 km. The maternal and child health programme was highly successful: the target for infant and child mortality, 50/1000, was well exceeded – 37/1000. This represents the best performance in any African country (excluding Mauritius – 19/1000). The target during NDP 7 (MFDP, 1991) will be 30/1000. It is perhaps worth noting the success of the government's feeding programmes during periods of drought. The 'Growth Monitoring and Nutrition Survey' guides government policy during drought periods. In 1984, 28 per cent of children were underweight. By 1988 when the drought ended this had fallen to 15 per cent. Immunisation programmes were slightly under the target of 75 per cent, although achieving 67 per cent. It is hoped to achieve 85 per cent immunisation by the end of the present planning period. Tuberculosis, in the past a major problem in Botswana, has been largely eliminated in the child population with an annual risk of infection in children of less than 1 per cent – developed country status. Ninety-nine per cent of children are now immunised against TB. There are still high rates of infection within the adult population reflecting the high rates experienced in the past in childhood.

The percentage of government recurrent expenditure allocated to health has remained fairly constant over the period 1980–93 (CSO, 1993).

	%	Pula (m)
1980	6.1	10.11
1989	4.9	57.33
1993	6.1	163.89

Although the percentage share of recurrent expenditure fell in 1989, it is worth noting that other expenditures on health-related policies, particularly those of nutrition and feeding, were put in place during the period of severe drought. During the same period inflation has shown rates fluctuating from 12.5 per cent in 1980 to 16.1 per cent in 1993. Overall health expenditure during the period therefore has fallen slightly in real terms, while maintaining its overall share of total government recurrent expenditure.

Expenditure on health over the period has averaged 3.3 per cent of total development expenditure. Total expenditure on health (development and recurrent budgets) therefore is currently running at approximately 4.2 per cent of total government expenditure and 5.1 per cent of Gross National

TABLE 9.1: *Comparative Health Expenditures (1991)*

	% Government Expenditures % on Health	% of GNP
Botswana	4.2	5.1
Singapore	4.6	5.7
Malaysia	6.8	5.0
Zimbabwe	7.6	6.2
Kenya	5.4	4.3

SOURCE: World Bank, 1993

Product (GNP). This is comparable with other countries of sub-Saharan Africa (4.5 per cent). Thus, sustained economic growth has ensured that Botswana has made notable progress towards improving health. Elsewhere the debt crisis which so adversely affected sub-Saharan Africa during the 1980s is mirrored in the declining indicators of health in relation to the region. Increasing infant mortality, poverty and nutrition indicators and the consequent rising incidence of disease are well documented for other African states. Botswana, however, was able to avoid this cycle of decline in relation to health and can therefore show considerable progress towards the achievement of health objectives.

ALLOCATION OF HEALTH RESOURCES

Government policy is based on a commitment to primary health care coupled with a system of referral hospitals. The government finances thirteen primary hospitals, six district hospitals, two national referral hospitals and one psychiatric hospital. The district and town councils have executive responsibility for the provision of primary health care for the people of their districts and have particular responsibility for the provision of mobile stops, health posts and clinics. Primary health care strategy is coordinated between the Ministry of Health and the Ministry of Local Government and Lands (District Councils) by the Primary Health Care Coordinating Committee within the Ministry of Health.

Health care in Botswana is also provided by the Mission hospitals who have their origins in the history of the country prior to independence. The country's three Mission hospitals are responsible for 415 beds and thus make an important contribution to health provision in the country. The Mission hospitals are well-integrated into the public health system. The Association of Medical Missions in Botswana has an executive coordinator based in the Ministry of Health whose role is to dovetail Mission services with national government policy. The Mission hospitals receive an annual grant in aid from the Ministry of Health of about 13 million Pula (Estimate for 1994/95 is 13.8m). Mission hospitals fulfil essentially the same role within the system as the District hospitals.

Thus, Government and Mission facilities provide the bulk of health care in Botswana and account for the major share of government resources. These two sectors are financed from recurrent and development expenditure budgets and provide access across the country at nominal cost for all citizens.

Government recurrent expenditure on health services illustrates the direction in which resources flow:

TABLE 9.2: *Recurrent Public Expenditure on Health Services*

	1993/94 (Pula m)	%	1994/95 (estimates) (Pula m)	%
Hospital Services	72.50	47.90	77.90	47.10
Primary Health Care	29.70	19.60	34.80	21.05
Missions	13.30	8.80	13.80	8.34
District Councils	35.82	23.70	39.58	23.90
Total	151.32		165.28	

SOURCE: Annual Statement of Accounts 1992; Statistical Bulletin 1993; Estimates of Expenditure from the Consolidated and Development Funds 1994; Ministry of Local Government and Lands 1994.

In addition Administration, Training and Research is 12.57m Pula which gives the total expenditure figure of 163.89m Pula.

There is therefore a significant increase in expenditure shown in the 1994/95 budget forecasts reinforcing the importance of cost control in relation to these items.

TABLE 9.3: *Public Development Expenditure on Health*

	1993/94 (Pula m)	1994/95 (estimates) (Pula m)
Hospital Services	22.4	21.7
Tertiary Hospitals	21.0	20.0
District Hospitals	1.4	1.7
Primary Health Care	10.2	14.8
District Councils	4.0	4.0
Technical Support*	10.0	17.7
Health Manpower	8.0	11.0
Total	54.6	69.2

SOURCE: Annual Statement of Accounts 1992; Statistical Bulletin 1993; Estimates of Expenditure from the Consolidated and Development Funds 1994; Ministry of Local Government and Lands 1994.
* Technical Support includes expenditure on pharmaceuticals and on medical equipment.

TABLE 9.4: *Income from Fees and Charges*

	1993/94 *(Pula)*	1994/95 *(Pula)*
Clinics (District Councils)	242 460	915 200
Hospitals	162 264	not available
Primary Health Care	125 484	not available

The rise in estimated income from charges for 1994/95 is the result of the increase in the nominal charge levied on patients for first consultations. This increased charge will bear most heavily on the poorest and the non-insured. However, as the charge is collected directly by the service provider and is ploughed back into services at that level, it is delivering the direct connection between collection and use of resources considered so important (World Bank, 1987). In addition, '[S]tudies indicate that user fees amounting to less than 1 per cent of annual household income have little impact on the utilisation of health services, even by the poor' (World Bank, 1993). Fees any higher than this could be a deterrent to use, so that if Botswana were to consider using direct user charging more widely, mechanisms for exempting the poorest would be essential. However, any formal 'sliding scale' system is difficult to operate and expensive to administer. Mission hospitals do commonly exercise discretion in respect of charging, governmental systems are less flexible.

Over the period of NDP 6 (1985–91) resources were committed on a large scale to infrastructural development, in particular the up-rating of the major referral hospital in Gaborone and the building of another major tertiary hospital in the second city, Francistown. The period of NDP 6 saw a massive overspend on tertiary hospital expenditure which represented a 45 per cent overrun on estimated expenditure. Although primary health care overran its budget, this was only by 5 per cent.

The 1970s had seen government expenditure concentrated on the development of rural health services as part of the general rural development programme. This in turn was part of the more general commitment to primary health care as the option most likely to rapidly impact on the health status of the population. However, the development of primary health care facilities and the successes of the programmes in themselves generated increased demand for referral services. This resulted initially in the development of the district hospitals. The impact of these enhanced district facilities was to increase demand considerably on the one tertiary level hospital in Gaborone. The government response to the increased demand was an investment programme to enhance the facilities at the Princess Marina Hospital in Gaborone and the initiation of the building of the new tertiary level hospital in Francistown. This hospital provides an additional 364 beds at a cost of 32.5m Pula.

The period of NDP 7, 1991–97, (MFDP, 1991) indicates a move away from infrastructural investment to increased investment in human resources (see below) and in primary health care. The focus for primary health care will be to address the needs of areas which are still inadequately provided for in terms of medical facilities, to improve the quality of existing programmes, to improve utilisation rates in order to ensure effectiveness and affordability, and to upgrade services to ensure a comprehensive coverage. In addition, secondary and tertiary facilities are to be upgraded where necessary to cope with additional referral needs.

The movement of resources away from the tertiary and hospital services is however far from easy as the infrastructure demands recurrent spending to support it. In fact, therefore, although there is a strong commitment to seeing the movement of resources to primary health care, to deliver this, given the direction which development has already taken, will present problems. As the World Development Report (1993) has pointed out, '[I]f governments spend too much on tertiary care, not only can they not adequately finance the most cost effective care, but they also cannot provide equitably what care they do offer because facilities will inevitably be geographically concentrated'.

STAFFING THE HEALTH SECTOR

Perhaps the major problem which has faced Botswana since independence has been its chronic shortage of trained and skilled human resources. Botswana's development has to a very large extent therefore depended on the recruitment of a high proportion of expatriate specialists in all sectors of the economy, not least in the health sector. Despite the excellent record of investment in health facilities and its successful performance in improving health in the country, Botswana continues to exhibit Third World status in terms of the number of doctors per 1000 of the population. By 1991, Botswana still had only 0.2 doctors per 1000 population compared with 0.37 per 1000 for Malaysia. However, it still exhibits the best ratio for doctors within sub-Saharan Africa comparing favourably with Nigeria (0.15 per 1000) or Zimbabwe (0.16 per 1000). Only South Africa with a ratio of 0.61 per 1000 is better, but clearly special factors are at work here, with the distribution of doctors heavily skewed towards one sector of the population.

The difficult situation in respect of human resources is well illustrated by the 1988 figures which show 199 doctors in Botswana of whom 171 are non-citizens. Training needs for doctors are therefore urgent – but equally are replicated by the urgent needs in other professional areas such as accountancy and veterinary medicine. NDP 7 indicates that the additional doctors needed by the year 2002 will be 111 – giving a total of 310. This figure will maintain the ratio of doctors per 1000 population at the current rate of 0.2 rather than move Botswana forward towards a better provision. Even this modest standstill target will be achieved only if expatriate doctors are in post. To localise posts would require the training of an additional 282 Batswana doctors between now and the year 2001 – an unrealistic target. The government is aware of the problem of shortfall in respect of doctors. A major factor in the shortfall is the lack of school leavers who qualify for entry to medical schools. As Botswana has no medical school of its own, it is dependent on education places in other countries. Although a small number of Batswana are currently completing medical training, these graduates will only scratch the surface of Botswana's medical needs. The NDP 6 target for doctor training was 40, but in fact only 13 were trained.

The ability of Botswana to attract foreign doctors and finance their salaries will be dependent on the performance of the economy or on the ability of Botswana to attract aid contract personnel from overseas. At present, Botswana draws doctors from a number of countries – most recently there has been an increase in the number of doctors from China. In 1993, the government introduced new legislation which had the effect of speeding up the process of work permit allocation – a clear commitment to meeting skilled human resource shortages in all categories by the import of skills.

Nurse education and training has been successful in localising the nursing profession in Botswana (probably only about 100 overseas nurses now work in the public sector) and in expanding the numbers and quality of nurses in the country. There are increasing numbers of graduate nurses trained at the University of Botswana and a general up-rating of nurse education to improve skills is currently taking place. However, the number of nurses required by the year 2002 is estimated at double the present number and substantial resources will therefore be required to train this cohort. Perhaps more significantly, the number of nurse managers in senior grades is falling short of projections quite considerably. Given a government commitment to improving management within the public health services this shortfall represents a significant hindrance to the delivery of objectives.

Other health professionals including dentists, physiotherapists, radiographers and laboratory technologists are in short supply and also heavily dependent on expatriate recruitment. The Health Education Programme which had been emphasised as a primary health care priority in NDP 6 had called for the training of health education officers and nutrition officers. However, with the expansion of services and staff wastage, by 1990 only eight of the 20 Districts had such an officer in post.

Thus, the human resource problems facing Botswana have led to a situation in which 'the existing health service infrastructure is underutilised and unable to produce health services of intended quality' (Ministry of Health, 1992). These shortages of skilled staff have a major impact on the primary and secondary levels of health provision. Trained doctors and nurses (and indeed paramedics and technicians) prefer to work in the higher level facilities. This undermines the principle of referral upwards only when justified. Patients themselves recognise the poorer quality of the lower-level services and present themselves for treatment at the tertiary level whenever possible.

As infrastructure has been developed, so the demand for trained health personnel to staff the facilities has increased. The Draft Health Manpower Plan for Botswana 1992–2005 (Ministry of Health, 1992) aims to increase numbers of nurses and paramedics so that the existing and projected health facilities and programmes will be fully utilised and of the desired quality by the year 2005. Despite the proposed training initiatives it is unlikely that the numbers of trained staff required to operate facilities and undertake further development will be provided on target. This will mean either that further inputs of expatriate labour must be financed, or that existing facilities will remain understaffed and therefore underutilised. The performance of the economy over the next ten years will be a major factor in determining the approach which will be adopted.

EQUITY, EFFICIENCY AND EFFECTIVENESS IN PUBLIC HEALTH SERVICES

The overall effect of manpower shortages and manpower deficiencies has meant that patient care, treatment and diagnostic capacity has not always been effective. In addition, population increases and growth both in demand for services and in expectations is stretching capacity considerably. As is evident in many countries, there has been an upward drift in demand for general hospital, and more particularly, tertiary-level care. Such escalation of expectation amongst consumers is apparent in many African countries. For example, in Kenya 'the Kenyatta National Hospital is overloaded with unreferred outpatients by-passing the primary level municipal facilities' (Bloom and Segall, 1993). In Botswana this has left primary hospitals and clinics underutilised while capacities at higher levels, as evidenced by bed occupancy rates, have been severely stretched. Bed occupancy rates at the two national referral hospitals are indicative of the intensifying problem: between 1989 and 1990 the rate in Gaborone rose from 115 per cent to 241 per cent, and for Francistown from 145 per cent to 372 per cent. These figures can be compared with 1991 data of 78 per cent for general hospitals, 67 per cent for primary hospitals, 16 per cent for clinics and 58 per cent for the private sector.

From 1990 the demand for beds in primary hospitals shows a very rapid fall. Demand seems to have transferred to higher-level hospitals as the expectations of patients have increased and as better and more facilities have become available at the higher levels. This clearly has important implications for the future.

Of course, the interests of equity mean that to 'adjust' 'inefficient' facilities in the system by withdrawing funding and closing them down, is not an option. The government is strongly committed to an equal pace of development across the country as a whole. Thus, accessibility to health care is a major pillar of policy and not one which would be sacrificed for reasons of managerial efficiency. However, there are other aspects to this problem which might more easily be addressed. If, as can be argued, there has been an upward drift in the demand for medical services, that is, people prefer the secondary or tertiary hospital to the primary clinic or hospital, the reasons for this need to be analysed.

One of the factors in this upward drift in expectations is the perceived 'quality' of the medical care available from the personnel working in the facilities. The evidence is strong that, as in many other parts of the developing world, well-trained and experienced staff – doctors and nurses – prefer to work in the secondary and preferably the tertiary hospitals. In other situations it might be argued that incentives to work in the remoter areas might be considered. However, in the case of Botswana, the overall staffing shortfall leaves this option unlikely to deliver results. It is probably the case therefore, that government policy under NDP 7 to ensure that referral hospitals are not first ports of call for health care, will be extremely difficult actually to enforce. If patients are to be encouraged to seek treatment at the most appropriate and therefore the most cost effect-

ive level, mechanisms to ensure this will need to be put in place.
Zimbabwe's approach has been the introduction of an additional fee for
patients who by-pass lower levels of health care, reporting instead to
tertiary-level hospitals. If applied in Botswana, this strategy could improve
the efficiency of the primary units and offload some of the burden from the
tertiary and secondary levels.

THE DEVELOPMENT OF THE PRIVATE SECTOR

Botswana is not unique in seeing the costs of public provision of medical
care for its population rising rapidly as a result both of increased costs of
drugs, technology and staff and as a result of rising expectations from
citizens of what the health services should provide. In 1993 the government tripled the charges for visits to hospitals and clinics to two Pula per
visit. Fees are paid directly to the clinic or hospital and in the case of
primary and secondary hospitals are retained by the district council as
revenue for use in the running of services (an important incentive to collect
fees efficiently). Patients who are admitted to hospital are not charged if
they accept treatment in the general wards. However, if they wish to be
transferred to a 'private' ward in a public hospital, they are charged 60 Pula
per day inclusive of all treatment, drugs and medical and nursing charges.

The government recognised in 1990 that the public health system was
under severe strain. Not only were manpower and hospital resources
unable to meet demand, but also the quality and effectiveness of health
care was being questioned. With this growing problem becoming increasingly significant the government took a number of steps which represented
a recognition that 'Government alone cannot meet the total demand for
health services' (MFDP, 1985). The Ministry of Health therefore carried
forward a number of policy initiatives 'aimed at redistributing some of the
responsibility for provision of health care to the private sector'.

Two strands can be seen in the policy. First, the government passed the
Private Hospitals and Nursing Homes Act in 1989. This legislation was
expected to allow the private sector 'to contribute to overall health service
provision without placing undue pressure on Government's recurrent
budget'. There seems no doubt that the government was somewhat
ambivalent about the passage of the Act. While recognising the need to
offload pressure from public sector facilities, there was a reluctance
wholeheartedly to endorse the setting up of a private hospital in the
country. This reflects the government's continuing concern that it should
continue to influence the pattern of development of medical services

across the whole country, and underlines the importance attached to ensuring that disparities between rich and poor are minimised.

The private hospital itself has faced problems in its first four years. The initial management team which operated the hospital proved unsuccessful. Investors, one thought to have lost 4m Pula in the hospital in the initial period, have been active in restructuring the financial and management systems. The hospital has now been taken over by a consortium of original investors plus a large hospital investment and management group from South Africa which now holds a controlling 51 per cent interest. The company operates 16 hospitals in South Africa and clearly has a sound business plan for developing and operating the Gaborone hospital. However, the market for the hospital will for the foreseeable future have to come from within the country. Given the strength of the Pula in relation to other regional currencies, patients are unlikely to be forthcoming. Also, given the ease of access to South African medical facilities, some patients in Botswana will still prefer to travel to South Africa for medical treatment which can be cheaper and more specialised.

When the private hospital was set up, there was an agreement between the hospital and the government of Botswana, that staff from the public health service would not be 'poached' by the private hospital. Given the chronic manpower shortages this was a crucial agreement. Largely, this policy would seem to have been adhered to. Certainly in respect of doctors and specialists it can be clearly seen that these are 'imported' – usually from either South Africa or Zimbabwe. The same applies to nursing staff. It could be argued therefore that the net effect of the hospital has been to increase the total supply of professional human resources within the country, while funding these from non-public sources.

The private hospital currently has 114 beds. However, demand to date has meant that only 88 of these are in operation and staffed. This gives an average occupancy rate for 1994 of 58.45 per cent on 88 beds or 45.12 per cent on 114 beds. At present, the growth per month (in- and out-patients) is running at 2 per cent – about 4000 patients per month. Certainly the costs to patients and the medical aid schemes are high. It is argued that it is still cheaper to have medical care in Johannesburg than to see the South African specialist in Gaborone. One estimate suggests that the cost of care in Botswana is double the cost in South Africa. Clearly, this disparity within a closely integrated regional market cannot continue indefinitely.

Alongside the change in policy regarding private medicine, the government took steps to enable more of those employed in the formal sector to access private medicine. Essentially, this was an attempt to offload some of the costs of health care from the government to the individual. At the

same time, it had the additional effect of making the private hospital more
viable by increasing the numbers of people who could afford to be treated
at the hospital. The measure adopted was probably long overdue. The government introduced the Botswana Public Officers Medical Aid Scheme
(BPOMAS). For the first time, public servants could become insured for
medical care. This placed the public servant in the same position as the
employee of a business enterprise or of a parastatal organisation and
overall has increased the numbers of individuals with medical insurance
by just under 10,000. While many of these will continue to consume
national health resources in the public hospitals, many will now make a
contribution to their care in 'private' wards in these hospitals, or will
undertake treatment at the private hospital.

THE MEDICAL AID SCHEMES

The mechanisms for financing private medical care in Botswana are
important in the context of assessments about the future development of this
sector. The expansion of personal insurance for health reflects the government's concern over the sustainability of resource inputs into the public
health sector given rising costs, rising demands and rising expectations.

There are now three medical aid schemes in Botswana, all of which are
established under the Friendly Societies Act, 1972. Each scheme caters
for a particular section of the employed population. Until recently, there
was only one scheme, which was open only to employees of the private
and parastatal sector. In 1990 two new schemes were established: one to
cover public servants and the second to compete with the original provider
for the cover of parastatal workers. All schemes are funded by contributions from individual members and from their employers. Although individuals do not receive income tax relief on their contributions, companies
do receive corporate tax relief. The percentage paid by employers varies.
However, in the majority of cases, and certainly in respect of public and
parastatal employees, the employer's contribution represents 50 per cent
of the cost of contributions. It is fair to say therefore that government does
'subsidise' health provision for those insured by medical aid schemes. As
some of this provision will be provided by the private sector, the government is thereby providing an implicit subsidy to this sector.

The Botswana Medical Aid Society (BMAS) was established in 1970 to
cater for the needs of the growing industrial and commercial formal sector
within the country. Only those who are employed by a constituent member
of the Society and their dependents may be insured under the scheme.

There are currently 1200 corporate members. The numbers of those insured under the scheme has shown a gradual rise over the last 25 years in line with the growth in size of the formal sector. By the end of 1994 it is estimated that there will be 11,600 individual members representing a total of about 40,000 people covered by the scheme. The definition of 'dependent' is rather wider than that allowed by many insurance schemes in developed countries. A member may cover his wife, any number of dependent children and both parents. Premiums rise as the number of dependents increases. Thus, by entering into formal sector employment, a member can immediately access preferential health care for the extended family. However, should members lose their jobs for any reason, any right to medical aid cover immediately ceases, that is, the Medical Aid Scheme is a corporate scheme. If, therefore, you are no longer employed by a corporate member, you cannot continue to be insured. Pensioners of corporate members however do continue to be insured.

There is a range of schemes offering different rates of coverage to the members at differential levels of annual subscription. These are classified as low, standard and high option schemes. Interestingly, the take-up of the low option scheme is diminishing as members opt for higher levels of cover. This illustrates a growing awareness of the levels of risk associated with ill-health and also of growing expectations concerning the quality and perhaps quantity of health services.

In the year ending December 1993, the Medical Aid Scheme made an operating profit of 935,678 Pula. An analysis of this surplus shows that subscription income rose by 10 million Pula between 1992 and 1993. This increase is only partly accounted for by an increase in the number of members. The major factor was a rise in subscription rates which had to be imposed after an operating loss of 3.1 million Pula was made in 1992. The major factor in this operating loss was the escalation in costs during the year. In particular, hospital benefits rose from 3.8 million Pula in 1992 to 6.3 million Pula in 1993. Maternity benefits showed a similar rise from 498,000 to 994,000 Pula.

BPOMAS was established by Presidential Directive No. 4, 1990. Although the Director of Public Service Management, when informing staff of the setting up of the scheme, emphasised that it is 'a result of requests received from public officers', this is only one part of the rationale. There seems no doubt that the setting up of the scheme is not so much a response to demands from the civil service union as a mechanism for 'ensuring that members contribute financially to their own health care' in order to offload some of the pressure from public health facilities to the private sector. It has also been suggested that another reason for introducing the scheme was to help combat civil service absenteeism. Private medicine allows a specific time to be allotted for an appointment. Thus, the excuse of civil servants that they required a day off to visit the doctor is now no longer valid!

Certainly, given that the scheme covers civil servants (but not at present industrial-class civil servants), local government officers, teachers and medical workers, its introduction has far-reaching consequences for the pattern of demand for health services in Botswana. Potentially, given that industrial-class civil servants will eventually become eligible for inclusion, almost 77,000 people become eligible for inclusion within the scheme – plus, of course, their dependents. In fact, the number likely to join is rather smaller than this. Many of those employed in public services will have partners working in the business or parastatal sectors who are already covered.

The scheme currently has just over 9000 members out of a possible estimated present market of 59,000 public servants. The administrators are keen to capture a greater number of members and are pursuing ways of offering incentives to new members. Certainly the scheme has not been without its problems. Three million Pula of reserves invested in 1990 was wiped out by 1993 and government intervention proved necessary. A more cautious investment policy is now pursued.

The third medical aid scheme, PULA, is administered by the same company who run BPOMAS. This scheme is very similar to BMAS in that it is directed at the same parastatal and company market. At present, corporate members of BMAS insist that their employees join the BMAS scheme. However, PULA is hoping that a more open market will develop in which employees may choose which scheme they will join. There are only 1600 members of this scheme at present. Competition between schemes over levels of benefits and contributions may well take place with families moving between schemes if advantages can be seen for this. The development of this market in medical aid might well lead to the more effective management of costs as the schemes struggle to keep contribution increases to a minimum.

THE MINE HOSPITALS

The fourth component of health provision in Botswana is that of the three mine hospitals. These three hospitals provide a total of 196 beds and treat employees of the mining companies. The rationale behind the setting up of such hospitals was largely as a device to attract staff to work in the mines.

As in the case of medical manpower, Botswana was and is deficient in engineering, and other professional and technical skills used in the mining industry. Foreign professionals would not come to work in the mines unless adequate health care was available for both themselves and their families. The mine hospitals therefore provide a first level of care for employees at which treatment can be undertaken prior to transferring patients elsewhere should this be necessary. The finance for the hospitals and their staff is provided by the mining companies. Some 13,300 people are employed within the mining industry, and thus the contribution of the mine hospitals to overall health care is substantial. Of the total numbers employed, some 7 per cent are expatriates who receive additional health cover for treatment privately or in other countries.

THE FIVE PARALLEL HEALTH SECTORS

Thus, Botswana has developed five parallel health sectors (including use of foreign hospitals) each serving particular sub-groups within the population:

1. The public health system.
2. The Mission hospitals (which are closely tied into the public health system).
3. The mine hospitals, whose medical facilities are directed at one sector of the employed workforce and their dependents.
4. A small local private sector which is accessible to all those in the country who are members of various health insurance schemes. Within this component, there are two groups of insured: those who are insured via medical aid schemes accessible to them and their families as a result of employment within particular sectors; and those who can deploy foreign currency to gain access to international private health insurance schemes. Private insurance covers both hospital and general practitioner care.
5. A small foreign private sector which, given the poor tertiary-level medical facilities which have existed in Botswana until recently, has meant that both the public health system and the private system have accessed health provision in neighbouring countries. On average about 2 per cent of patients have been treated abroad per annum over recent years.

The move to develop the two tertiary hospitals and the setting up of the private hospital has significantly increased the availability of tertiary-level care within the country. However, it is likely that specialist foreign provision will continue to be used for many years ahead.

CENTRAL POLICY ISSUES

In assessing the impact which the private sector will have in Botswana, it is important to consider not just the financing of this sector and the issues surrounding the medical aid schemes, but also more general questions about the delivery of health services in Botswana. In any small country, the integration of health service planning between sectors is important. In Botswana, because of the severe human resource constraints, it is vital that the government should continue to play a dominant role in health planning. The issues facing Botswana fall into four categories: medical aid schemes and their contribution to health finance; the problems of cost-containment and efficiency; the role of the private sector; and, as a strand running through each of these, the problems associated with staffing health services.

Government policy which has encouraged the expansion of medical aid schemes has helped to begin to establish a viable private sector. However, since such schemes can only cover groups in formal employment, whole sections of the population are therefore excluded. At the same time, medical aid schemes are excluding certain conditions from cover, most notably Aids. Given the increasing demands which Aids will place on the health care system in the near future, the impact of this non-cover clause in medical aid will be to throw back a large number of very ill and very costly patients on to the already stretched public health systems.

The concentration of medical aid schemes within the formal employment sector will continue to disadvantage the poor who are likely to form an increasingly large proportion of the population. Additionally, if unemployment increases as a formerly buoyant economy weakens, fewer people may fall within the scope of the medical aid schemes and thus the viability of the private sector itself will be called into question with public health services coming under increasing pressure.

It is unlikely, given the small potential size of the market, that the commercial insurance industry will compete for private health care in Botswana as they are now doing in Zimbabwe and South Africa due to the failure of medical aid schemes. Competition therefore, except on a very small scale, is unlikely to play a major role in regulating the private sector. It will, however, be vital for the schemes to take a more pro-active approach to cost containment by negotiating new charging policies with the providers. Only very rudimentary attempts have been made to date to initiate these discussions.

The question must be posed as to whether, in a country with a population of 1.3 million, three medical aid societies are in fact necessary. On the one hand, it could be argued that a concentration of funds within one society would allow economies of scale in administration and also a more effective investment return. On the other hand, it can be suggested that only with an element of competition between schemes will effective measures be put in place to manage and control the costs of health care. Both schemes are starting to give thought to cost control.

As elsewhere in the world, rising costs are clearly observable over recent years. However, the options for cost control are not yet fully evaluated. At present, payments to providers are made on the 'fee for service' principle – a notorious mechanism for encouraging cost escalation. In addition, there has been little work on the monitoring of drug charges and the question of generic drug use. However, there is no doubt that the medical aid schemes will begin to negotiate various types of lump-sum agreements with, in the first instance, the new private hospital. Uniform fees in the sense of fixed payments for specific diagnoses seems the most likely way forward, or fixed annual fees covering specified ranges of conditions or treatments. To date, the hospital has negotiated with medical aid funds only over the 'hotel' aspects of its charges, that is, the daily rate per bed. However, work is going on to consider the question of drug charges, and negotiations on payment schemes are likely in the near future.

Control of prescription and drug charges will also be important. At present, medical aid schemes reimburse the costs of non-prescription, over-the-counter drug purchases. As there is almost complete deregulation in Botswana, patients can buy what they need from the pharmacist without needing to consult a doctor. In some cases physicians sell the drugs they prescribe.

It is clear that there are both allocative and operational inefficiencies within the health system which are mainly the result of the chronic human resource shortfalls. The current situation in Botswana is well summarised in NDP 7: 'A network of physical facilities has been developed which is now facing severe shortages of manpower.' The options available to Botswana to increase funding are relatively limited and in any case money in itself will not solve the problem of scarce localised professional manpower. In Botswana, while the government pursues a policy of primary health care, the demands of the tertiary sector, as in so many other countries, can distort the achievements of primary health care. In a country where it has proved difficult to provide professional manpower in the required quantities, infrastructural development has been pursued instead. The net effect of this is to spread human resources increasingly thinly with the main staff resource being concentrated at the tertiary hospital sector end of the spectrum.

Health investment has also been concentrated at the level of tertiary care – the point at which the supply of professional human resources is available. The ability of the system to allocate resources to primary health care has been limited by the shortages of trained staff. For example, the inability to supply sufficient numbers of health education and nutrition educators means that goals in respect of these areas of primary health care are not yielding the health gains expected of them. Capital funds are allocated to urban rather than to rural areas and while access to primary health care is widely available, demand for tertiary level care is increasing annually with a consequent upward pressure on the allocation of resources to this level.

However, despite these problems, access to health care in Botswana is much better than in other African countries. This is primarily due to the policies pursued by the government since independence and the fact that an integrated approach to health sector planning has been apparent in the actions of the Ministry of Health in coordinating development between public and private sectors, mission and mine hospitals.

There is clear evidence of operating inefficiency in relation to the costs of running hospitals and clinics which are underutilised. This can be seen most graphically in relation to underutilisation rates in some of the sectors of health care – most notably within the primary system, the mine hospitals and within the private sector. The introduction of high technology equipment – such as scanners – which remain underutilised, is another example of inefficiency. Charging policies at public hospitals for private patients are grossly inaccurate –probably only reflecting about one-third of the actual cost of provision. This is therefore an example of a further hidden subsidy to the private sector.

Overall, the impact of allocative and operational inefficiencies is that scarce resources do not necessarily contribute as effectively as they might to the goals of improving the health of Batswana and ensuring access and equity. The government has recognised that one of the major factors in improving quality and efficiency lies in improving the ability of the health services to manage. For example, there is a major programme in hand to improve the capacity of nurses to become senior managers. However, the delivery of the numbers of nurses trained in this way continues to fall far short of the target. In addition, wastage of resources occurs when patients themselves demand medical interventions which are unnecessary. This is well illustrated in respect of those insured by the medical aid schemes. Escalating costs as a result of wide-ranging tests and consultations prompted the medical aid societies to caution their members that should this level of demand continue, contribution rates would have to be raised dramatically. Initially, this threat has acted as a brake on claims. However, evidence suggests that in the public health system also, patient demands are for ever-increasing levels of intervention. There is evidence from elsewhere that free or very cheap medical services are more likely to lead to wastage than those where there is a clear linkage between the patient and the charge for service. Certainly in Botswana, demand for health care has increased over the last five years. However, this demand is increasingly for tertiary-level provision and has led to the underutilisation of primary health facilities.

It is likely that the private hospital itself will play a part in the development of managerial approaches to contain costs which may prove influential in relation to public services. 'The effects of privatisation on efficiency are ambigious' (Laffont and Tirole, 1993). However, the introduction of a small private sector which is likely to provide indicators of good practice to the public sector may well be advantageous. Evidence from studies in 50 countries has found that only in two countries was the cost of providing public services (particularly health services) less than that of the private sector (Mueller, 1989). The development of the private sector in Botswana could therefore have positive effects on the total package of health care delivery within the country. The private sector is aware of the need to address questions of efficiency and effectiveness and this managerialist climate may influence the debate which takes place within the public sector. Certainly, the government is aware of the need to raise management awareness among professionals and to train staff to fulfil roles as managers.

Perhaps one of the most promising features of the private hospital is its developing relationship with the public health system. This is still at a very early stage but suggests that the door is open for further cooperation in the future. For example, the private hospital participates in the government's immunisation programme by immunising 50 children each Saturday morning with vaccine supplied by the Ministry of Health and needles by the hospital. Other forms of partnership are being examined – for example, in the insertion of under-skin contraceptives. The hospital has taken a pro-active stance in relation to the question of staff development. It regularly invites visiting specialists to present papers relating to new developments and invites all local doctors to these. It recently ran a neonatal care Congress open to all doctors in the country and sponsored by a drug company.

One of the problematic areas for public/private relations has been the question of the purchase of new technology and in particular the purchase of the whole body scanner by the private hospital. This was a major investment for the private hospital at a time when NDP 7 had clearly targeted exactly the same purchase for the public health system. Given the small population of the country, it is generally thought that there is a need for only one scanner. The question now is whether the public sector will be willing to buy time on the private sector scanner, or whether it will insist on using public sector health resources to replicate a facility already in the country and presently very largely underutilised. Certainly the World Bank (1993) would endorse the utilisation of the private sector investment which could thereby free public resources for the primary and secondary levels of care.

Private sector development does have less beneficial consequences for public sector services. The most obvious problem is in the chronic human resource shortages which will continue indefinitely. While agreements are in place to counter the movement of trained staff from public to private sector, in a long-term context these might prove difficult to sustain. At present the private sector is very small. However, it is likely that if medical aid schemes begin to attract larger numbers of members, the private sector demand for medical staff may begin to impinge on the already understaffed public sector.

The question of government subsidies to the private sector is not one which has as yet prompted public debate. Subsidies take three forms: tax relief on employers' contributions to medical aid schemes; 'less-than-cost' charges in public hospitals for private patients; and the government's own contributions to the BPOMAS on behalf of its own employees which for 1994/95 is estimated at 10.9 m Pula.

It could be argued that the 'offloading' of responsibility for health care partly to the private sector is in fact quite a costly policy for the government. The main contribution of the development of the private sector is probably in increasing the pool of imported medical specialists available in the country. These – doctors, nurses, paramedics and technologists – would not have been attracted to work within the public health system. even had finance to employ them been available.

A dialogue needs to develop between the two sectors, not only over issues relating to management, but also over the opportunities which could be developed to share resources rather than duplicate them. Governments throughout the developing world continue to judge 'success' in more easily quantifiable terms such as life expectancy, rates of take-up of vaccination programmes, and so on. There is as yet little ability to judge managerial success – cost effectiveness in particular. The development of the private sector may provide a spur to increased managerial awareness within the medical community and to the development of useful information for cost control in the public sector. If such a climate does develop, the impact of the private sector will have provided a positive input into health care for Botswana.

CONCLUSIONS

A strong underlying theme in government policy in Botswana in relation to public services has been that all must benefit and have access. This underlying belief has, until very recently meant that there has been very little private provision of services – in both education and health. The government has been intent on ensuring that the provision of such services was within the control of the state and has been unwilling to see the establishment of either private schools or private medicine. Universal access to health care has been via a system of direct public financing rather than through a national health insurance system. User charges at the point of delivery have been no more than nominal.

However, Botswana has found, as have other countries, that the problems of constrained budgets and escalating costs in respect of health care in particular, require the consideration of alternative approaches to health care funding. Botswana's response has been to move towards a public/private sector health care mix – albeit on a very limited scale – and the reorganisation of the structure of government finance for health towards a more decentralised approach, based on the allocation of resources to districts. The experience of Botswana has important lessons for other countries where, to date, the state has assumed a pre-eminent role in the provision of health care. Certainly, Botswana has not restricted the growth of non-government health provision as have many countries in sub-Saharan Africa – most notably Malawi, Chad and Cameroon. On the contrary, the government of Botswana has developed partnerships with other organisations, most notably the Missions and to a lesser extent the mines in the provision of health care. What has been limited to date has been the involvement of the private sector at anything but the level of general practitioner care.

The government's current approach to dealing with the emerging strains within the system by encouraging the development of the private sector is one which finds favour with external funding agencies, particularly the World Bank (1987). However, a number of issues which accompany the development of the private sector have still to be addressed. Most notable among these must be the staffing problems of the public sector which may be exacerbated as the private sector expands. If the private sector develops as intended, the government will need to ensure that public health services do not become 'devalued' in the eyes of the consumer. It will be vital to ensure that public services are not seen as the poor relation of the private sector if the contribution of this sector to the health and well-being of the whole nation, particularly the poorer groups in society, is not to be diminished. This requires continued governmental commitment to public health services and a continuing role for government in health planning and finance. Only if this commitment, which is clearly evident to date, continues, will the system deliver effectively the objectives of health care for all.

NOTE

1. The article was written during a research visit to Botswana during 1994 and thanks are due to members of the Botswana Civil Service, the staff of the medical aid societies and others who provided time and information. The views expressed in the article are however solely the responsibility of the author.

REFERENCES

Bloom, G. and M. Segall (1993), *Expenditure and Financing of the Health Sector in Kenya* (Brighton: Institute of Development Studies, Commissioned Study, 9).

Central Statistics Office (CSO) (1993), *Statistical Bulletin, 18(2)* (Gaborone: Government Printer).

Cichon, M. and C. Gillion (1993), 'The financing of health care in developing countries', *International Labour Review* 132 (2), pp. 173–86.

Laffont, J.J. and J. Tirole (1993), *Theory of Incentives in Procurement and Regulation* (Cambridge, MA: MIT Press).

Ministry of Finance and Development Planning (1985), *National Development Plan 6* (Gaborone: Government Printer).

Ministry of Finance and Development Planning (1991), *National Development Plan 7* (Gaborone: Government Printer).

Ministry of Finance and Development Planning (1992), *Annual Statements of Accounts* (Gaborone: Government Printer).

Ministry of Health (1992) *Draft Health Manpower Plan for Botswana, 1992–2005* (Gaborone: Government Printer).

Ministry of Health/Centre for Health Economics, University of York (1988), *National Health Manpower Plan for Botswana 1988–2002* (Gaborone: Government Printer).

Mueller, D. (1989), *Public Choice II* (Cambridge University Press).

Republic of Botswana (1994), *Estimates of Expenditure from the Consolidated and Development Funds* (Gaborone: Government Printer).

World Bank (1987), *Financing Health Services in Developing Countries: An Agenda for Reform*, World Bank Policy Study (Washington, DC).

World Bank (1992), *Zimbabwe: Financing Health Services*, World Bank Country Study (Washington, DC).

World Bank (1993), *Investing in Health: World Development Report* (New York: Oxford University Press).

Part III:
Rural and Environmental Responses

10 Green, Brown and Red Issues in a Black Economy: Thoughts on Sustainable Development in Low-income Countries

Selected LDC's

James Winpenny

Q15
Q28 O13
Q21

INTRODUCTION

The recognition that a society's use of its natural environment may be a constraint to its long-term growth has given environmental economics a legitimate place at the table in development studies. The questions it raises, and the techniques it incorporates, have challenged all students of development. This is so despite the fact that the empirical relevance of some key concepts is untried, and the concept of sustainable development remains more of a talisman than a blueprint for policy makers.

This chapter reflects on the relevance of environmental economics to our thinking about development. Most discussions of sustainable development start from the abstract and work towards the concrete. Here we invert the process, starting with some thought prompted by recent personal experience in Africa, and placing it in the context of the conclusions of some notable recent empirical studies.

One is immediately struck by the importance of the link between population growth, agricultural adaptation, and the existence of the extensive frontier. Some recent studies, prompted by environmental concerns, have started to converge with an older tradition of development studies which addresses the conditions under which population growth will or will not be accompanied by development. This convergence is highly fruitful.

Let me briefly review the situation in five specific developing countries – Cameroon, Ecuador, Uganda, the Philippines and Kenya. The underlying questions I will be asking are: what factors explain the prevailing pattern of agricultural expansion?; what are its implications for the

169

environment?; and whether environmental economics offers any useful insights into this process.

CAMEROON

Much of Cameroon's recent agricultural growth has taken the form of expansion of the cultivated area. Traditional shifting cultivation – slash and burn – is still widespread. Within the next generation, on various plausible assumptions about population growth and fallow periods, the 'extensive' mode of cultivation will cease to be feasible (Tchoungui, 1995).

Symptoms of unsustainability are emerging in the shape of shortened fallow, extension of the cultivated area on to marginal and potentially erodible land, and the choice of annual crops, inputs and techniques carrying the risk of soil depletion and erosion. Moreover, this is to consider sustainability purely from an agricultural viewpoint; if other reasons for the preservation of tropical forest are allowed for, Cameroon must be much closer to the limit of sustainability.

The immediate causes of these symptoms are: growth in the farming population; growing and serious impoverishment of the rural population since the mid-1980s; entry of new farmers due to redundancies and loss of income elsewhere; shift of resources from tree to annual crops, necessitating use of new land in the short term; and finally, discouragement of intensive, and encouragement of extensive, modes of cultivation, due in part to the reduced availability of credit, fertiliser, and extension services.

The local population's recourse to environmentally-degrading practices may be a perfectly rational response to the prevailing land tenure, crop prices, marketing system, price and availability of fertiliser and other inputs, and credit and other farm support services.

In many regions, new land is available free of cost to the farmer, except for that of clearance and planting. The farmer does not normally compensate society or his/her neighbours for the costs of land use, including the risk of soil erosion and future depletion of fertility. These are externalities from cultivating new marginal land which do not feature in the costs of the user.

The converse of this is that many cultivators have insecure tenure on their land or are tenants, which is a disincentive for them to make long-term improvements, such as terracing, conservation, and tree planting. The combination of effectively free new land, and insecure tenure on existing land tilts the balance of attractiveness towards the extension of the cultivated area rather than the more intensive use of the presently cultivated area.

Farmers in all regions of Cameroon are acutely aware of changes in selling prices and marketing outlets for their cash crops. The decline in world prices for coffee, cocoa and cotton from 1985 onwards, coupled with the growing overvaluation of the CFA franc, led to progressive cuts in the official purchase price for these three major cash crops. After the devaluation of January 1994 these cuts were partially reversed, although the disorganisation of the marketing system has prevented some producers (for example, coffee producers in the North West) from benefiting from the recent price increases.

In the North West province the fall in coffee prices in the late 1980s led to the direct substitution of food crops for coffee plantations on erodible slopes, with clear environmental risks. In the East the fall in cocoa prices led to the abandonment of many plantations, and the decline in phytosanitary services has allowed disease to take root, perhaps irreversibly. Mature coffee and cocoa plantations confer important environmental benefits (shade, soil stability, organic matter for the soil, firewood, and so on), which have been jeopardised by recent policies.

Reform in the marketing system for export crops, which is essential in the long run, has added to confusion and uncertainty due to the recent fluctuations in world prices. The effect has been to weaken the incentives intended by the recent increases in the selling price. Recent economic problems of Cameroon have worsened transport and communication, and some of the adjustment measures have made the situation worse (for example, increased price of fuel, lower spending on road maintenance, sale of government vehicles). Hence producers' ability to respond to the recently improved price signals has been weakened.

Farmers' support services appear generally to have deteriorated as a result of adjustment. In the East, certain programmes and funds responsible for credit and the distribution of phytosanitary products, processing, credit and rural infrastructure have been dissolved. In the North West, a successful development authority project saw its activities suspended in 1993, causing its extension workers and credit agents to be laid off and its vehicles withdrawn. Its work in disseminating seeds, tree nurseries and other planting materials came to a halt.

Most output of the three main export crops comes from small farmers. Practically all the food crops are grown on family-size farms. The majority of these rely mainly on family labour, which may be supplemented with wage labourers during busy periods. Most farmers rely on traditional techniques: only a minority use fertiliser, and hand labour is the norm. Where topographical conditions permit, animals are also used in farm operations. The reduction in availability of credit has restricted farmers' use of bought-in supplies and wage labour.

Improvements in present methods – for example the more intensive use of existing land, diversification into new crops, upgrading planting materials – tend to rely on specific, often regionally-based projects, most of which have suffered directly or indirectly from the cut-backs in recurrent government spending.

ECUADOR

In Ecuador most of the growth in agricultural output over the last 25 years has come from the expansion of the farming frontier. This cannot continue for much longer, since virtually all land considered suitable for agriculture has already been cleared. Meanwhile, the frontier continues to be pushed back on to less suitable land, at one of the highest rates in Latin America (Southgate and Whitaker, 1992).

The necessary reorientation of agriculture towards an intensive mode of cultivation has been, and is still being, hampered by prevailing institutions and policies. Until the 1980s, economic policies were ruled by 'urban bias'. The overvaluation of the sucre due to the growth of oil exports penalised domestic prices received by producers of export crops. Imports of a range of foodstuffs were stimulated by the overvalued currency and in some cases by direct subsidies, at the expense of domestic farming.

The macroeconomic regime for agriculture improved during the 1980s, and agricultural output responded. However, the growth in output has come mainly through expansion of the farming frontier, for which various market and policy failures can be blamed: land rights are obtained by destroying natural vegetation; firms extracting timber, and agricultural colonists settling in cleared land, pay minimal rents; and lastly, the government exercises poor control over so-called 'national patrimonies', and individuals have a strong incentive to encroach on them before someone else does, without penalty. For all these reasons, if there is a choice between using land inside the frontier and land in agriculturally virgin areas, the latter will be preferred since it is available for use effectively at the cost of clearance.

Throughout the country, the rights of land users are insecure. This reduces their incentive to invest in land improvement and conservation, and limits their access to credit, which requires clear evidence of title. Land is prone to be expropriated in the name of land reform, which discourages serious investment. The national property registration system is inefficient and bureaucratic, and farmers know they cannot capture the full value of their land by sale or pass it on as a bequest, because of the delays and costs involved. This also reduces their stake in improvement and conservation.

Yet another factor militating against intensive land use is that standards of research and farm extension work are low. Little relevant agricultural research is conducted (for example, into new farming crops, techniques and systems) and partly as a result crop yields in Ecuador are well below regional standards. Low education levels among the rural population are another contributory factor. For such reasons, increased output has come disproportionately from expanded areas. Finally, labour legislation with the intention of safeguarding workers' rights and minimum wages has had the effect of discouraging paid employment in farms as well as other sectors. This limits the amount of agricultural transformation that can take place with hired labour, and also the creation of off-farm work as a rural safety valve and source of remittances.

In short:

in Ecuador, and in many other Latin American countries, agricultural land use conversion continues to be encouraged in the face of adverse natural conditions, both because a frontier property regime remains in place and because human-made inputs that substitute for land and other natural resources in the production of crops and livestock remain scarce. (Southgate and Whitaker, 1992, p. 50)

It should be noted in passing that the idea of the environment 'substituting' for other means of employment in poor communities, is a promising line of enquiry (Leach and Mearns 1992).

UGANDA

The South-Western province of Uganda is one of the most densely settled and farmed regions of Central Africa. It has fertile soil and a climate favourable for the cultivation of a full range of food crops. In a sense, it has become too attractive for cultivators. Land is farmed right to the top of the hill, without proper terracing, on slopes of 30–60 degrees. Watersheds are now mostly denuded of permanent vegetation. There are no proper estimates of soil erosion or slippage (though there is much anecdotal evidence), but the risk must be very high in view of the complete absence of the normal anti-erosion precautions. Farmers have traded on the high natural fertility of the soil, and little is done to restore its fertility.

Little land remains to be taken into cultivation, especially since several remaining forest areas have been declared protected areas. But there is little sign so far of moves towards intensive modes of cultivation. Plots are becoming smaller as they are sub-divided to accommodate family members. Holdings are typically scattered amongst a number of plots at different points on the slope, which spreads risk, but also makes intensification more difficult. New crops, for example fruit, are being encouraged under various foreign-aided projects, but their main motive is to replace income and goods forfeited by the virtual closure of forests to adjacent populations.

In this case, population growth has not yet triggered a process of agricultural intensification, despite the virtual closure of the option of expanding on to the external frontier of cultivation. Meanwhile, environmental risks are increasing by the day. Political and economic uncertainty has been the rule in Uganda over the last 25 years, and has not been conducive to people taking a long view, such as committing themselves to investment in land improvement. Rural poverty has probably increased, and alternative employment outlets have diminished – for example, internal migration, which was a traditional resort of the population of this region, is much diminished.

THE PHILIPPINES

Many of the Philippines' well-known environmental problems have been linked to economic structures established by the chosen pattern of industrialisation and recent measures of adjustment to excessive foreign indebtedness (Repetto and Cruz, 1992).

Soil erosion, for instance, can be traced to the expansion of the cultivation of erosive crops into marginally hilly areas by impoverished farmers to whom jobs in other sectors are denied or closed off. Upon further examination, rural land tenure remains highly unequal. The increment of rural population, swollen by economic migrants from the cities, has little option but to cultivate new areas rather than the most fertile of existing cultivated land, whose ownership is highly concentrated. Much of the problem arises from open access to communal property, such as state-owned forests, which are not properly managed and amount to a 'free' resource from the viewpoint of the user.

The development of off-farm employment has, in other countries, been an important siphon for surplus rural labour, as well as a source of remittances for investment in land and farm improvements. But the industrialisation policies chosen in the Philippines have promoted capital- and material-intensive industries and techniques, and have suppressed the growth of employment. Urban bias has ensured that Manila has attracted the bulk of investment and budgetary spending, and the rural economy has been squeezed in various ways. In the 1970s and 1980s it has been estimated that investment, net of resource depreciation, was negative in primary sectors (forestry, agriculture and fisheries).

Now even the growth of Manila is being throttled by the delay in tackling problems of congestion, pollution, water supply and sanitation. Meanwhile, the Philippines' population is growing at over 3 per cent per annum.

KENYA

A study in Kenya strikes a more positive chord, with strong echoes of earlier discussions of the link between population growth and agricultural intensification (for example, Boserup, 1990). Historical research in the Machakos District identified a number of factors accounting for the more intensive and productive use of land in the presence of population growth (Tiffen et al., 1994): first, increased market-orientation of farming, associated with the growth of population and incomes, and the spread of infrastructure; second, the availability of a wide range of economically and technically viable land-use options; third, the presence of an open society, with a broad, development-oriented leadership, and a relatively good educational system; fourth, growth in non-agricultural and urban sectors, to provide alternative employment, a source of savings for investment in rural areas, and a market for farm produce; and finally, a land tenure system under which customary law confers sufficient security for farmers to invest in the improvement and conservation of their land.

The more intensive use of land has not, in general, been at the expense of the natural environment. Erosion has been checked by the spread of terracing, extensive tree planting, and maintenance of soil fertility by the use of organic matter and artificial fertiliser. Indiscriminate livestock grazing has been reduced, even though the number of animals has risen.

In case this seems like a charter for laissez-faire, market-led development, it is worth dwelling on the responsibility of governments, and their donor backers, in getting this virtuous circle in motion. For instance, property rights and the role of customary law should be clarified, and not undermined. Transport and communication networks should be developed. A good basic education should be available, whether from state, community or private agency (the Kenya study revealed widespread payment of school fees). Research into new farming systems should be supported, with the maximum degree of farmer participation, and there should be adequate funding for extension services. Official and parastatal marketing channels for cash crops should be reformed, and scope allowed for the development of private and cooperative initiatives in marketing of output and merchanting of inputs. This is an active agenda for governments, and exceeds what many of them are now doing to create the conditions in which continued population growth is accompanied by a more productive agriculture.

REFLECTIONS ON COUNTRY EXPERIENCES

In all five of the countries reviewed above, rural populations are expanding rapidly, but only one of them appears to have made the transition to agricultural intensification. Ecuador, Cameroon and the Philippines are still locked into a system of agriculture in which increased output comes principally from an extension in the cultivated area. In South-West Uganda, there is little or no scope for expanding the geographical frontier of farming and the region seems poised to enter the transition to an intensive mode, though there is little sign of it yet. In the Machakos region of Kenya this transition appears to have been successfully made. What lessons can be drawn from this disparate experience?

It is no coincidence that the necessary agricultural changes have gone furthest in Kenya, where urban bias has arguably been least, and national economic policy-making has been framed with farming interests in mind. As a general rule, markets have been allowed to work to farmers' benefit, and public spending and investments have supported rural interests. In the other countries, by contrast, rural producers have been penalised in various ways, and their potential surpluses transferred to the rest of the economy. This has reduced both the incentive and the means for agricultural transformation and land conservation and improvement.

In a related vein, countries that have witnessed deepening rural poverty (for example, Cameroon, Uganda and the Philippines) because of past development policies or the shape of recent adjustment programmes have seen the worst environmental abuses. Dispossessed and impoverished people consume a disproportionate amount of common property resources, such as public forests, watersheds, pastures, wetlands and coastal fisheries – all potentially fragile environments (Dasgupta and Maler, 1990).

Alternatively, impoverished farmers see little alternative but to mine their own land at the expense of its longer-term productivity (Uganda).

A country's adjustment record is also relevant. The majority of poor countries – and all those considered above – have undergone structural adjustment at various times in the past decade. There have been few outright successes. As a generality, the restoration of some macroeconomic stability is a necessary, though by no means a sufficient, condition of sustainable use of the environment (Killick, 1991). Countries whose adjustment has been weak or flawed (for example, Cameroon) perpetuate the distortions and poverty that lie at the heart of environmental degradation. Adjustment that imposes disproportionate hardship on certain groups (variously, the rural poor, women, informal urban producers, and so on) risks creating a class of environmental vandals.

Important though successful adjustment is, one of the strongest messages coming from studies of the adjustment process is that the incentives to produce tradables which they contain are blunted or nullified by inconsistent measures. In Cameroon, for instance, farmers' ability to respond to better local prices for export crops (for example, coffee and cocoa) is hampered by the cut-back and effective collapse of most farm services – credit, extension, marketing, even transport. The scene painted by recent field surveys is of a rural hinterland increasingly isolated from urban life, in which the only government presence is the occasional tax collector. Externally-aided projects have been vital for agricultural development, and one of the most tragic results of the current fiscal crisis is that the government has withdrawn its counterpart funding from many of these projects, causing their collapse (Tchoungui, 1995).

One of the firmest conclusions to be drawn from the experience reviewed here is that property rights matter. If the users of natural resources are to care for their assets, and invest in their preservation and enhancement, they must have some confidence in their future rights to enjoy these assets. This does not necessarily mean the spread of freehold titles. In some countries (for example, Thailand) this has helped the cause of sustainable farm practices, and obstacles to titling have been adduced as harmful in Ecuador.

In other cases, such as semi-arid parts of Africa, it has been argued that titling is harmful and unnecessary (van den Brink and Bromley, 1992). Likewise, the inequitable distribution of agricultural land has probably hastened environmental encroachment in the Philippines. However, the example of Ecuador shows that half-baked land reform measures create uncertainty which carries its own environmental risk.

THE CONTRIBUTION OF ENVIRONMENTAL ECONOMICS

It has been observed, with some authority, that environmental economists are apt to take something that works perfectly well in practice and worry about how it works in theory (Baumol, 1991). As the old saw goes, 'that is all very well in practice, but how does it work out in theory?'

So it is with sustainable development. It is now fashionable to use the metaphor of capital stock to describe environmental assets (Pearce et al., 1989). On this view, the different kinds of environmental assets should be maintained so as to assure a continuing flow of environmental services to future generations. Applying this precept is complicated where population is increasing, people's appreciation of the environment is changing, or where the productivity of the environment can be affected by human actions.

Some critics turn the problem on its head, arguing that the size of the environmental resource base that we need to sustain should be decided after considering population change, intergenerational well-being, techno-logical possibilities, environmental regeneration rates, and the condition of the existing resource base (Dasgupta and Maler, 1990). Questions have also been raised about the empirical validity of the very notion of sustain-able yield, when applied to such key resources as tropical forests, wet-lands, fisheries, wildlife and agriculture. Practitioners may also have difficulty with the concept of the environmental compensatory project in the design and funding of public investment programmes (Markandya and Pearce, 1988).

On a more positive note, environmental economics has promoted – even if not invented – a number of insights and methods useful in the sort of cases considered earlier. For instance, incorporating environmental 'depreciation' into the estimation of national accounts has qualified the way national governments, and international agencies, view the economic performance of resource-based economies such as Ecuador and Cameroon.

Environmental economics has drawn attention to the importance of adjusting actual prices and values to 'internalise' environmental effects. A specific example of this is setting logging concession fees closer to the true economic rent (the stumpage value) of the wood. The fact that this rarely happens in practice is a major reason for the destruction of tropical forest (Repetto, 1988). In Cameroon, the impoverishment of the Forest Service has weakened its authority vis-à-vis the owners of logging concessions, and only a fraction of income due is being collected by the government.

The conversion of developmentalists to the virtues of the market over the last 15 years has its echoes in environmental economics. Exponents of the Green Market paradigm argue that getting prices 'right' is a necessary, though not sufficient, condition of sustainability. The job of governments is to tackle market failures, and to avoid adding policy distortions of their own (Panayotou, 1993). The evidence reviewed here is testimony to the environmental damage due to market and policy distortions, and the potential economic and environmental bonuses ('win–win' policies) from successful adjustment or, in the case of Kenya, from market-oriented strategies. But the cases also show the importance of the correct design of adjustment programmes to avoid internal inconsistencies. Likewise, market-orientation in the absence of other preconditions – such as secure property rights, or full capture of the economic rent – could make environmental degradation worse.

Finally, environmental economics has focused our attention squarely on property rights in explaining why farmers, pastoralists and other users of the environment act as they do. Security, whether of tenure, use or access, is important for the long-term care and enhancement of natural resources, though this is far from being a charter for privatisation and enclosure (van den Brink and Bromley, 1992). Environmental economics has also had much to say about common property, non-exclusivity and the environmental perils that are liable to ensue. Some environmental economists have drawn the premature conclusion that privatisation is necessary to arrest the degradation of the commons.

It has partly been due to the influence of social anthropologists and institutional theorists that we now recognise that communal management of common property resources does happen, and is often quite viable (for example, Ostrom, 1990). In this instance, environmental economists are like the aeronautical engineers who argue that, in theory, bumblebees can't fly.

In short, environmental economics has lent its growing weight to addressing some of the central concerns of development studies. This has been a constructive convergence, notwithstanding the claims of other disciplines in development studies that they have been tackling the same issues for years. As Oscar Wilde remarked, imitation is the sincerest form of flattery.

REFERENCES

Baumol, William (1991), Keynote Address to Annual Conference of the European Association of Environmental and Resource Economists, Stockholm.

Boserup, Ester (1990), *Economic and Demographic Relationships in Development* (Johns Hopkins University Press).

Dasgupta, Partha and Karl-Goran Maler (1990), 'The environment and emerging development issues'. Paper produced for World Bank's Annual Conference on Development Economics.

Killick, (1991) 'Notes on Macroeconomic Adjustment and the Environment in Winpenny, J. (ed.) Development Research: The Environmental Challenge, ODI, London, pp. 38–42.

Leach, Melissa and Robin Mearns (1992), *Poverty and Environment in Developing Countries: An Overview Study* (Brighton: Institute of Development Studies).

Markandya, Anil and David Pearce (1988), 'Environmental considerations and the choice of the discount rate in developing countries'. World Bank Environment Department, Working Paper No. 3.

Ostrom, Elinor (1990), *Governing the Commons: The Evolution of Institutions for Collective Action* (Cambridge University Press).

Panayotou, Theodore (1993), *Green Markets: The Economics of Sustainable Development* (International Center for Economic Growth/Harvard IID).

Pearce, David, Anil Markandya and Edward Barbier (1989), *Blueprint for a Green Economy* (London: Earthscan).

Repetto, Robert (1988), *The Forest for the Trees? Government Policies and the Misuse of Forest Resources* (Washington, DC: World Resources Institute).

Repetto, Robert and Wilfredo Cruz (1992), *The Environmental Effects of Stabilization and Structural Adjustment Programs: The Philippines Case* (Washington, DC: World Resources Institute).

Southgate, Douglas and Morris Whitaker (1992), *Development and the Environment: Ecuador's Policy Crisis* (Quito: Instituto de Estrategias Agropecuarias).

Tiffen, Mary, Michael Mortimore and Francis Gichuki (1994), *More People, Less Erosion: Environmental Recovery in Kenya* (New York: John Wiley).

van den Brink, Rogier and Daniel W. Bromley (1992), 'The enclosures revisited: privatisation, titling and the quest for advantage in Africa', Cornell Food and Nutrition Policy Program, Working Paper 19, January.

Tchoungui, R. et al. (1995) *Structural Adjustment and Sustainable Development in Cameroon*, ODI Working Paper 83, London.

11 Rural Development Models in China and Taiwan Revisited

Jerry V.S. Jones

INTRODUCTION

For the purposes of this study, the following villages and townships in mainland China were visited in 1994: Xipu, Litai, Liuzhuang, Linzhou (the location of the Red Flag Canal), Dazhai and Daquizhuang. Each at different times has acted as a model for rural development and played a key role in the evolution of rural development policy, and its various changes in direction. In Taiwan, the visit was to Hsi-lo township which is the location of the Ying-hsi irrigation system, one of the first to participate in the government-promoted consolidation programme that began in the early 1960s and is still going on. Consolidation consists of the re-laying and reconstruction of irrigation canals and farm roads to improve efficiency and access to fields, and at the same time negotiating the exchange and merging of land holdings so that each farmer ended up with one or two larger plots in the consolidated fields instead of the large number of small, scattered plots originating from the final land reform of 1952 (Shen, 1964, pp. 114–17).

Each visit incorporated a comprehensive tour of the various productive activities and interviews with local officials. The objective was to obtain sufficient data on the local economy to make comparisons with previous periods, as reported in the literature. The main findings are collected in Table 11.1 (pp. 188–91). It includes data on population, area under crops, time period when they acted as models and what they sought to demonstrate, the main agricultural and industrial activities, and other observations. In order to put these findings and the subsequent discussion into context, a brief history of each 'model' is given. The discussion focuses on the following issues: rural industrialisation and its effects on rural development and people's incomes; the question of self-reliance; the continuing role of collectivism; the significance of recruiting labour power for village enterprises outside villages; and the effects of more open markets. The aim is to draw lessons from the experience of China and Taiwan which might be applicable to less developed countries generally.

A BRIEF HISTORY OF THE VILLAGES AND TOWNSHIPS VISITED

Xipu

Xipu is located about 180 km east of Beijing. The village gained nation-wide publicity in the mid-1950s following the pioneering efforts of its poorest households working collectively to acquire the means of production which they lacked. Its history up to 1978 has been recounted by Maxwell (1979). During the 1970s, inspired by the 'Learn from Dazhai' campaign (see p. 184), a huge amount of earth-moving reordered the arable land into large, level and more regular fields, consolidating the approximately 2000 plots into 236. The largest plot became four hectares instead of only 0.0033 hectares before! One large field was created literally by moving a hill. People's incomes have increased dramatically since 1978, mostly from non-farming activities, and during the last few years most families have rebuilt or modernised their homes.

Litai and Liuzhuang

These villages, located about 600 km south of Beijing and some 40 km north of the Yellow River, are part of Qiliying township. This was one of the first to experiment, in the late 1950s, with confederations of coopera-tives, and is where they were first called 'people's communes' (Chu and Tien, 1974). The original driving force had been the need to bring together a sufficiently large workforce to dig a canal from the Yellow River and construct reservoirs and tanks to provide water for irrigation. Once formed, the confederations began to take on other responsibilities. These included, for example, the establishment of a flour mill; workshops to manufacture ball-bearings and other needed items; supply and marketing centres; and the administration of schools. Thus, calling them 'agricultural cooperatives' seemed no longer appropriate – hence the search for a new name. Litai and Liuzhuang were therefore among the first to demonstrate the huge potential of bringing together a number of cooperatives to enable the undertaking of larger-scale projects to improve agricultural productiv-ity, and diversification into other productive areas. This was also the inspi-ration for the ill-fated 'Great Leap Forward'. Following Mao Zedong's famous visit to Qiliying in 1958, when he promulgated: 'People's communes are good', the idea quickly spread throughout China (Strong, 1959). Liuzhuang is probably unique in China today in that it has retained fully the collective system of production.

Linzhou: the Red Flag Canal

Linzhou (formerly Linxian) is located in the foothills of the Taihang mountain range, about 600 km south-west from Beijing. The Red Flag Canal in Linzhou was first conceived in 1958–59 (when four neighbouring villages had just completed the rather more modest Tianqiao Canal, running below and roughly parallel to what was to be the Red Flag Canal, and irrigating roughly 300 hectares). It was a huge project, and, perhaps more than any other, demonstrated what large-scale organised labour could achieve under a confederation of cooperatives (or, in this case, in effect, a confederation of people's communes). Along with Dazhai, it became a major inspiration for many similar collective efforts in China to 'remove mountains' (after the famous fable – see Mao, 1965), and played a crucial role in the political struggles in the early 1960s following the disaster of the 'Great Leap Forward'. The struggle was essentially between the self-reliant approach to rural development championed by Mao Zedong, which, broadly speaking, was a continuation of the policies of the 'Great Leap Forward' in a modified form, and the more conservative approach, advocated by President Liu Shaoqi and associates, who favoured (even in the 1950s) a more gradual development of rural areas in parallel with the development of urban-based industries, markets, and educational and technical training facilities. The latter group, who within the political leadership were in a majority in the early 1960s, attributed the disaster of the 'Great Leap Forward' to too much involvement of farmers in idealistic and grandiose sidelines, to the neglect of operations essential to agriculture. Thus, to them, the Red Flag Canal, which was to involve the mass labour of 30,000 people (out of a total population of 700,000) was a hopeless and wasteful venture – a view endorsed by professional engineers. During the first year of construction alone, the provincial authorities issued orders for work to be stopped no less than four times (Anon., 1972).

However, the people of Linzhou were defiant and carried on regardless, and the whole project, including the vast network of secondary channels and so on, was completed in 1969. It required the damming of three rivers, and comprised a main canal of 70 km, and 1500 km of big and small channels, including 134 tunnels of total length 24 km, and 150 aqueducts of total length 6.5 km (ibid.). In addition, hundreds of small hydroelectric generators (ranging in capacity from a few tens of kilowatts, to 3000 kilowatts or more) were installed wherever there was a suitable drop. These provided power for workshops and lighting (ibid.; Science for the People, 1974). Furthermore, fish production was begun for the first time.

Dazhai

Dazhai is located in the 'loess-encliffed ravines of the Taihang mountains' (Marshall, 1979), about 400 km south-west of Beijing. It became famous in the 1950s and early 1960s. Using implements such as picks and shovels, the villagers transformed 4700 tiny, scattered plots in a barren and gully-scarred valley into broad, terraced fields. Using stones quarried in the hills, they built embankments in the gullies, and carried earth in baskets on shoulder poles to fill the gaps behind (Pien, 1972; Kuo, 1974; Maxwell, 1975; Marshall, 1979). Following the Third National People's Congress in 1965, which first promulgated the slogan: 'In agriculture, learn from Dazhai', the village became the key model for agricultural policy until the end of the 1970s. Between 1965 and 1973, Dazhai received more than six million visitors (and people still come to visit). Guest houses and conference facilities had to be built to cater for the large numbers. Furthermore, in 1975, following a national conference on 'Learning from Dazhai in Agriculture' (Anon., 1975), a nationwide campaign was launched to build 'Dazhai-type counties' (Hua, 1975). A second national conference on 'Learning from Dazhai in Agriculture' was held in December 1976 (Khan, 1984, p. 79). Presumably, in anticipation that the 'Learn from Dazhai' campaign would continue, the Shanxi Provincial authorities, in 1978, built a large meeting hall and hotel in Dazhai.

However, just one year later, agricultural policy dramatically changed direction, and the Dazhai model suddenly faced fierce criticisms (Anon., 1980a; Anon., 1980b; Zhou, 1981). For instance:

It was widely publicised that Dazhai never accepted any aid from the state. 'It had built itself up'. Not so. Between 1967 and 1977, the brigade got from the state 840,000 yuan, either in cash or in materials. The tiny village of Dazhai not only received enormous help in the form of material, funds and manpower from the state and various departments, but also at times sought assistance ... It is not unusual for the state and other departments to give help, but to falsely claim that no help at all was received and to create a 'model' with funds and material and then expect others to emulate without the same access to funds and material is downright dishonest. Moreover, such a model cannot be very persuasive. (Zhou, 1981, p. 25).

In fact, that Dazhai had received some state aid should not have been in dispute. Indeed, none other than Chen Yonggui himself, the long-time chairman of Dazhai (later promoted to high office at national level, including the positions of Minister of Agriculture and a Vice Prime Minister), had stated quite clearly some 15 years earlier that:

> The state has given us much aid – chemical fertilizer, machines, electricity, coal, and transport. And we have received much from other communes ... draft animals, tree seeds and saplings, timber and stone ... The central authorities and leading comrades from the province, area, county and commune have given us much concrete direction and help. (Marshall, 1979; p. 428)

Other specific instances of outside support have been documented by Marshall (1979). The extent to which that invalidates Dazhai as a model of self-reliant development depends on how one defines 'self-reliance', as will be discussed later.

During the 1980s, Dazhai almost became a model for the second time. Because of its high profile previously, and since the new policy was to some extent diametrically opposite to what it had been before (though clearly some, such as those in Qiliying township, were evidently able to 'bend the rules'), the authorities deemed it necessary to discredit Dazhai's past and demonstrate how much better off it was under the new policy. Hinton (1991) has shown some of those claims to be spurious, especially those related to income which, after discounting for inflation, had not risen at all. However, since then, data indicate that average per capita income in real terms has now increased, probably by about 40 per cent since 1978. Furthermore, there is some evidence to suggest that a compromise might have been struck between the old and the new, especially with the appointment of Guo Fenglian as Director of the Dazhai Economic Development Company (responsible for the development of the village enterprises owned by the villagers). Guo Fenglian had been one of the 'iron girls' in the pioneering days and, at the age of 28, as a disciple of Chen Yonggui, was elected as Party Secretary to succeed him when, as already noted, he moved on to higher positions.

Daqiuzhuang

Daqiuzhuang is located about 50 km south-west of Tianjin. Although described as a village, and it is most definitely in a rural location, Daqiuzhuang is, in fact, more like a huge modern industrial estate. The 'village' covers an area of some 7.4 km^2, and as many as 25,000 people from outside work in its various enterprises. Daqiuzhuang became the model for the 1980s, demonstrating what could be achieved with the new government policies. Previously, the people of Daqiuzhuang had been among the poorest in China. Like all villages in this area, agricultural development was severely handicapped by the high levels of salinity in the soil due to the high water table and the fact that the land was only a metre or two above sea level. Today, the land around Daqiuzhuang has been drained into ponds (used for rearing fish), and agriculture is highly mechanised involving 40–50 people only.

The process of change began in the late 1970s when able-bodied men of the village took up employment on construction sites in Tianjin and elsewhere. They saved enough money to purchase some small-scale pipe-making equipment for the manufacture of scaffolding tubes. This became the first village enterprise. The profits were used to invest in other metal-working equipment. This was repeated step-by-step over and over again, so that by the 1990s, production and the number of enterprises had expanded dramatically both in number and in scale (see Table 11.1). The 350 enterprises of today are organised in five main groups. All are subsidiaries of the Daqiuzhuang General Corporation, which is jointly owned by all members of the village. Sixteen of the enterprises are joint ventures with foreign companies (including companies from the United States, Panama, Germany, Australia, Hong Kong and Taiwan). In addition, one of the enterprises, in 1991, sold 4500 shares on the Tianjin stock market, which raised 90 million yuan (approximately £10 million at the time). An important factor in the development of Daqiuzhuang was the decision early on to buy in engineers and other expertise, offering high salaries, so that they could get the best possible professional advice. Today, they are housed in their own compound which has superior living conditions, including 4000 m^2 of living space (compared with an average of 80–100 m^2 for villagers). In a rather less orthodox method, in 1992, the then village chairman deployed 100 young villagers as 'exchange students' abroad offering 'bounties' to any of them who succeeded in marrying the daughters of foreign capitalists (Kaye, 1993). It is not known if this produced any results.

In general, it would seem that Daqiuzhuang was a little too successful, with economic power going to its collective head. Thus, the former chairman of the village, along with his son, six top managers, and eighteen 'village toughs' are now in prison for their part in trying to cover up the beating to death of a factory manager accused of embezzlement, and preventing police from Tianjin investigating (Anon., 1993). According to one report, this involved a pitched battle between 1000 armed police and nearly 300 villagers (Kaye, 1993). Not surprisingly, Daqiuzhuang has been quietly dropped as a 'model'. As it happens, this also seems to be what the villagers want. Possibly they fear that further unwelcome attention might jeopardise their present highly lucrative economy.

Hsi-lo, Taiwan: The Ying-hsi Irrigation System

Hsi-lo is about 200 km south of Taipei. The Ying-hsi irrigation system was first established more than 200 years ago. It is now part of the Yunlin Irrigation Association, which covers nearly 67,000 hectares of irrigated land. This is divided among some 500 irrigation groups, of which eleven are in the Ying-hsi system. So far, about 60 per cent of the irrigation groups within the Yunlin Irrigation Association have been consolidated. Ying-hsi, in fact, has undergone a second consolidation, in which the drainage channels have been narrowed and deepened to allow the widening of the farm roads so that they can accommodate larger vehicles.

Most areas practise various types of rotational systems, the most common giving two crops of rice every three years in a three-year rotational cropping pattern, embracing rice, sugar cane and miscellaneous/upland crops, linked to a three-year rotational irrigation system. Where enough water is available, two crops of rice are grown each year. Areas able to do that have been extended considerably over the years through the use of ground water to supplement the surface water. Water flows through paddy fields continuously, and farmers are charged on the basis of area irrigated and soil productivity. A growing constraint on the re-use of drainage water is the increasing problem of pollution, partly from domestic waste water, and partly from sedimentation, caused by the practice of a local gravel company washing the excavated gravel in the river before transporting it. As noted in Table 11.1, virtually all farmers in the Ying-hsi system work more or less full-time in other occupations, the few remaining as full-time farmers specialising in the intensive rearing of chickens and pigs.

EFFECTS OF RURAL INDUSTRIAL DEVELOPMENT

Thus, the first and most obvious observation in both mainland China and Taiwan is the extent to which agriculture has become a sideline occupation, such that employment in industries and other non-agricultural productive activities is now the main source of people's livelihoods. For instance, in Liuzhuang, agricultural production accounted for less than 20 per cent of people's income. In Daqiuzhuang, as a proportion of total income, it must

TABLE 11.1: *Data Collected on Villages and Township Visited*

Place visited	Population	Area under cultivation (hectares)	Period when acting as model	What model was demonstrating	Main crops
Xipu	1 379	260 (66 irrigated)	Mid-1950s	Advantages of forming primary cooperatives	Wheat, maize (inter-planted)
Litai	3 842	450 (most irrigated)	Late 1950s (as part of Qiliying People's Commune)	Advantages of forming people's communes	Wheat, cotton (inter-planted) fruit trees (apple, pear persimmon, walnut)
Liuzhuang	1 519	100 (most irrigated)	Late 1950s (as part of Qiliying People's Commune)	Advantages of forming people's communes	Wheat, cotton (inter-planted) fruit trees (apple, pear persimmon, walnut)
Linzhou	1 million approx. (incl. 17 townships and 536 villages)	53 000 (36 000 irrigated from Red Flag Canal plus 7 000 from ground water)	1960s and 1970s	Self-reliant financing of major projects through collective work	Wheat
Dazhai	530	200 (184 irrigated)	1960s and 1970s	Self-reliant financing of major projects through collective work	Maize

TABLE 11.1: *continued*

Other major farming activities	Main Industries	Other observations
Rice, millet, beans, potatoes, peanuts, fruit trees (70 000 apples, peaches, walnuts), chickens and pigs	Plastic bags; electric cables; several textile mills; vehicle repairs; several private enterprises	Land owned by village was allocated by lot in 1992 to be kept for 15 years; individuals responsible for all agricultural activities; all homes had colour televisions, 60% refrigerators, 40 households have IDD telephones
Chickens (30 000), pigs (2 000), dairy cows (100), mules and horses (20)	Nitric acid; textile mill; steel pipe rolling mill; fibre-board (utilising cotton plant debris)	Land ploughed, planted, harvested, and crops threshed and processed collectively; modern housing and outdoor amenities being developed according to a village plan
Chickens, pigs, dairy cows	Pharmaceuticals (penicillin, inosine and others – 700 people employed); three paper mills (utilising wheat straw); pesticides; milk processing	All productive activities carried out collectively; farming managed by team of 41 villagers + 19 tractors, seven combines, one light aircraft and other equipment; village where wheat/cotton interplanting first developed; people live in modern housing rent free, including water, electricity and air-conditioning; each household gets 12.5 kg pork and 50 kg fruit per year
Maize, cotton, rape, peanuts (mostly interplanted with wheat), vegetables, chickens, pigs	Huge number and very diverse, including: iron smelting; engineering; bricks; food processing; pharmaceuticals; textiles and clothing	Land ploughed, crops harvested (mostly by scythe) by individual households
Fruit trees	Coal mining; cement works (joint venture with Hong Kong company); knitwear and men's shirts	Land ploughed, crops planted collectively, seeds and fertiliser are free; irigation and harvesting carried out individually; orchard managed by village team under contract from village; some terracing work was being carried out collectively to claim new land; some former industries closed because unprofitable or causing pollution

TABLE 11.1: *continued*

Place visited	Population	Area under cultivation (hectares)	Period when acting as model	What model was demonstrating	Main crops
Daqiuzhuang	4 400	3 200 (most irrigated)	1980s	Advantages of production responsibility system	Wheat, maize (inter-planted)
Ying-hsi irrigation system	4 400 farmers	1 400	1960s	Advantages of consolidation (see text)	Rice, sugar cane

have been a fraction of that. The proportion of income from agriculture in Hsi-lo, Taiwan, was probably somewhere between that of Liuzhuang and Daqiuzhuang. Even in villages where industries were less developed, such as Xipu and Dazhai, less than half of people's income derived from agriculture.

Growth of Rural Incomes in Mainland China

In mainland China, it is clear from economic and other data collected in the villages visited that all have experienced significant increases in income since 1979. This can be directly related to how advanced industrial development is in their localities. Thus, from the data in Table 11.2, it is seen that Liuzhuang and Daqiuzhuang have advanced hugely more than Xipu and Dazhai, and with reference to Table 11.1, this clearly corresponds to the level of development of their industries. The changes that have taken place

TABLE 11.1: *continued*

Other major farming activities	Main Industries	Other observations
	Total of 350 industrial enterprises, 85% concerned with ferrous and non-ferrous metal fabrication. Others include: caustic soda and chlorine; furniture; building materials; paper and polyurethane products; transportation, catering and leisure enterprises	All land and industrial enterprises owned and managed collectively by villagers; 24 954 people employed from outside; farming carried out by 40–50 employees under five managers; all villagers have comfortable modern homes or apartments in landscaped gardens, rent free, including water and electricity
Vegetables, fruits, chickens, pigs	Almost all farmers work more or less full time in other occupations in various state or privately owned industries or other enterprises, or offices, either locally (including irrigation or farmers' associations) or further afield in towns	Rice is grown under continuous flow irrigation system, with pumps recycling drainage water, managed by Irrigation Association staff; all planting of seedlings done by machine by contractors, together with some harvesting; some groups of farmers had formed small cooperatives to cultivate papaya and citrus under irrigation

in Daqiuzhuang are particularly spectacular, progressing as it has from a very poor underdeveloped village to, in effect, a modern industrial estate in less than 20 years. Liuzhuang, on the other hand, was already relatively advanced in the 1970s and has clearly built on that base. Moreover, the fact that to this day the village has continued to operate entirely as a collective demonstrates, contrary to popular wisdom, that collectivism does not necessarily lead to economic stagnation – indeed, given the right leadership, quite the opposite (see further discussion below). Furthermore, it is interesting to note from the data in Table 11.2 that, in spite of the huge development of industry in Daqiuzhuang and the huge difference in the number of people employed, the output value per capita is actually higher for Liuzhuang. This implies that the productivity of labour in the latter must be at a higher level, or that a large number of employees in Daqiuzhuang are involved in services not contributing much to output value.

TABLE 11.2: *Data on Income of Villages Visited*

Village[1]	Population	No. of employees in village enterprises residing outside the village	Output value in 1993 (million yuan)	Output value per capita in 1993 (thousand yuan)	Average annual income (yuan)
Xipu	1 379	500	40	29	1 800[2]
Litai	3 842	100	65	17	1 850
Liuzhuang	1 519	1 360	2 300	1 514	38 400[3]
Dazhai	530	400	1	2	1 300[4]
Daqiuzhuang	4 400	24 500	5 600	1 272	95 000[5]

[1]   Linzhou is omitted because it is not a village, but a city with some 500 villages under its jurisdiction.

[2]   Estimate.

[3]   Of which wages contributed, on average, 6720 yuan. Data provided by village vice-chairman.

[4]   This figure is average income per capita, data supplied by deputy director of Dazhai Economic Development Company. For comparison, average wages for workers in the garment factory were 1800 yuan per annum. Furthermore, according to Shang and Shen (1994), the income of orchard workers (from that activity) was 2000–3000 yuan per annum, and 5000–6000 yuan for supervisors, and income from growing grain on an average-sized holding was about 1800 yuan (i.e. 450 yuan per capita for a family of four).

[5]   Average income per capita excluding that derived from agriculture, arrived at by dividing total net profits of the village-owned enterprises by population.

With regard to Xipu, although in terms of output value per capita the village is some way behind, comparing people's lifestyle and consumption patterns as described by Maxwell (1979) with what may be observed today, it is clear that significant improvements in people's income must have taken place, and this, again, can be correlated with the modest expansion of industrial activity that has taken place. Finally, Dazhai, although even further behind in terms of output per capita, with regard to income per capita it is quite similar to Xipu. It is estimated to have been growing in real terms during the last few years at about 10 per cent per annum, mainly as a result of the expansion of coal-mining activities. Once the new cement factory, and the planned second coal mine, are opened, it is likely that income will grow at a faster rate.

Effect on Agricultural Development

Although since the 1970s the productivity of agriculture in the villages visited has probably not improved much in terms of average yields per hectare, with regard to labour productivity significant advances have clearly been made, with many of the operations now fully mechanised, farmers using either their own or collectively owned equipment, or hiring from other farmers or employing contractors. The main exception, among the places visited, was the harvesting operations in Xipu and Linzhou (where households were responsible for all operations), and Dazhai (where ploughing and sowing were carried out collectively, but harvesting was not). The development of rural industries, therefore, could be assumed to have had a positive impact on improving the labour productivity of agriculture, as people sought to spend more time on other income-earning opportunities.

Furthermore, in the villages visited in both China and Taiwan, there appeared to be the beginning of a tendency for households to lease out their land (that is, that which was either individually owned or allocated by the village). The head of the team managing Dazhai's orchards, who contracts out his land to other farmers in order to concentrate on managing the orchard, believes that 'in the near future, China's agriculture will be modernized through specialized contracted management, as he is doing in the orchard' (Shang and Shen 1994). In both countries, this could be the means by which more far-reaching economies of scale could be introduced which are currently constrained by the complex pattern of ownership and allocation of small plots to individual households. Thus, as income from non-agricultural sources becomes ever more dominant, and that from agriculture increasingly insignificant, rural dwellers could be more likely to want to give up their responsibilities for agriculture, and, indeed, sell their interests in it. Moreover, this tendency could begin to accelerate as the older generation of farmers die because their offspring, many of whom already have stable employment in towns, might be more ready to sell or lease out their plots to those who wished to concentrate more on farming.

Allowing the process of transformation to larger-scale units to take its course gradually in this way could be a considerable advantage over the huge upheavals that have been experienced in other countries going through a similar transition – such as during the enclosure movement in Britain, or during the forced pace of collectivisation in the former USSR, or the wholesale expulsion of poor farmers from their land which is commonplace in many less developed countries. In all those cases, to a greater or lesser extent, people have been thrown off their land at a faster rate than industries and other employment opportunities could be created, leading to much human suffering with people being forced to live a precarious and exploited existence in towns or peri-urban areas.

A further major advantage of stimulating industrial production in rural areas is that it takes employment opportunities to where people are located, without a major upheaval in their lives, since people could remain in their established homes (which could be improved as their incomes rise) and in their communities. At the same time, as people found it more lucrative to spend more time in non-agricultural productive activities, this would be a stimulus to invest in improved agricultural productivity, for which they would increasingly have the means. This trend was clearly apparent in all the villages visited, having gone furthest in those where industries had been most developed.

Some Disadvantages of Rural Industrial Development

There are, of course, some major disadvantages of locating industries in rural areas – for some types of industrial production more than others. One is that it might be much more costly in terms of building the necessary infrastructure, such as water and electrical power supply, and transportation of raw materials and other inputs and of the products to markets. This was particularly apparent in Daqiuzhuang where the transportation costs of the materials coming in and of products going out must have been quite excessive compared with if these industries had been located near the manufacturers of the intermediate inputs or near a decent modern road or railway. On the other hand, the array of industries now established in Daqiuzhuang could stimulate the construction of an efficient transportation infrastructure, which, in turn, would stimulate the further development of industries in this relatively poor part of the country.

A second disadvantage, often, is that measures to control pollution and ensure safety might be more lax or even non-existent (though this could have the short-term advantage of reducing investment costs). However, an offsetting factor, evident in some of the villages visited in mainland China, is that since the employers were the villagers themselves and they lived in the community where the industries were located, they might be more likely to pressurise managers to install appropriate control measures, though often, unfortunately, after the problems had become apparent (that is, when people became conscious they were suffering from the pollution, or an accident had occurred). For instance, in Litai the villagers have become increasingly aware that their nitric acid plant is giving off noxious fumes (actually, it was not that bad) and, as owners, they had decided to employ contractors to modify the plant (as well as to install a district heating system for their newly constructed homes making use of the waste water used as a coolant in the plant). In Taiwan, by contrast, where the rural industries are privately owned, pollution control would depend more on popular protest limiting what owners of the enterprises could get away with, and, in some areas, this is causing the government to take a more active interest in pollution control measures. However, it is evidently a slow process, as witnessed by the failure of the farmers in the Ying-hsi system, as already mentioned, to do anything to prevent the gravel company from washing the gravel in the river which was causing their irrigation system to clog up.

A third problem, from an employee's point of view, is that employers might be able to get away with paying their workers less because the latter had few other employment opportunities, and were more isolated, thus limiting collective action that could be used to improve conditions. This would be less of a problem in the village-owned enterprises in China, since lower wages of workers would, in effect, be offset by higher profits at the end of the year and hence higher levels of income derived from dividends. However, that would not apply to employees coming from outside the village. Indeed, the villagers who owned the industries would have a vested interest in paying themselves less, alongside those from outside, in order to make more income in the form of dividends available to themselves at the end of the year to which those from outside the village would not be entitled. This issue is discussed further below. (In fact, it should be pointed out that China does have minimum wage legislation, but this has not kept up with inflation.)

Conclusion

The important conclusion evident from all the places visited in China and Taiwan is that rural development and income per capita in rural areas, and the improvement of people's livelihoods in general, is closely related to the degree to which industrial and other types of non-agricultural employment have been developed. That is because this raises the productivity of labour, which is probably the single most important factor determining people's incomes, as well as the rate of economic development.

Furthermore, it should be noted that such diversification of productive activities in rural areas has a stimulating effect on the economy as a whole, because the additional income provides economic demand for goods and services produced in other parts of the economy, which, in turn, generates economic demand for the wider range of products produced in the rural areas. This, essentially, is the driving force for economic development wherever it occurs. Underdeveloped countries elsewhere, therefore, have much to gain from a study of the recent experience of China and Taiwan in the field of rural industrialisation and adapting it to their own circumstances.

SELF-RELIANCE IN RURAL CHINA AND TAIWAN

As noted previously, critics of the Dazhai model have suggested that because the village received outside aid, that invalidated it as a model for self-reliance. However, whether that is so depends on what one means by 'self-reliance'. 'Self-reliance' does not necessarily mean the same as 'self-sufficiency' or 'autarky'. Indeed, being self-sufficient, apart perhaps from being unnecessarily costly, could mean that a community ended up being less self-reliant. For instance, a village or country that was self-sufficient in food could be highly vulnerable and dependent on outside aid if its harvest failed or if some other disaster struck, so that 'it would have bought self-sufficiency at the cost of independence and self-reliance' (Streeton, 1987, p. 39). 'Self-reliance', on the other hand, means having a 'diversified pattern of production and ... trade ... diversified by sources of supply ... by markets ... and by commodities and services, and ... ample [cash] reserves and access to lines of credit ...' (ibid.). Thus, if outside support facilitated those things, the village or country would have achieved self-reliance without being self-sufficient.

In the case of Dazhai, comparing the situation in the mid-1950s with that 20 years later cannot leave one in much doubt that its people had improved their degree of self-reliance, according to the above definition, beyond recognition. The outside support, in effect, was used to create higher levels of self-reliance rather than dependence. Moreover, the government and the country as a whole benefited because the combination of investments made by the villagers (in the form of labour power used to build the terraces and so on) and those made by the government, led to more grain and other goods being produced and more revenue from taxes which could be used to help other communities. Furthermore, the larger the number of villages and townships becoming more self-reliant in this way would mean the country as a whole would become more self-reliant.

However, it can be a thin line between government support leading to dependent development, in effect paid for by appropriating financial resources from other communities, and that which promotes self-reliance, the measure being how quickly the government 'gets its money back', say, in the form of higher revenue from taxes. For instance, if the figure of 25.6 million yuan given in aid to Xiyang county (in which Dazhai is located) to enable it to become the first 'Dazhai-type county' (Zhou, 1981) is to be believed, it would seem doubtful that this amount would have been repaid, in which case the critics would be justified that it could not represent a model for self-reliant development. Thus, if a government or other agency provides a great deal of aid to enable a village (or a county) to become a model, presumably in order to demonstrate what a village 'should' be like in the hope that others would follow, but for which the latter could not expect the same degree of support (because of lack of funds), then as a model the supported village would be of limited use indeed (see, for instance, Jones, 1983).

But the original model of Dazhai was not like that. The people of Dazhai themselves in the 1950s and 1960s carried out the transformation of the land, and only later came to the attention of the government, which decided to use it as a model. People came to Dazhai to see the achievements of the villagers *in the past*, that is, before it became a model, when there had been little or no outside aid, and before it had attracted the attention of the government. They came to see for themselves how the villagers had built the terraced fields, which are, indeed, impressive. (Nobody says that the villagers did not do that themselves!) This was the whole point: to encourage other people and villages to use their own resources to do similar things, and not wait indefinitely for the government to solve all their problems. And many were inspired to do just that, as is evident all over China (as even the critics of the Dazhai model in 1980–81 were prepared to admit), and in the process they became more self-reliant, thus validating Dazhai as a model of self-reliant development. This has been taken a stage further with the opening up of markets because this, in effect, accelerated the process of diversifying production and exchange (as will be discussed below), so that villages are very much more self-reliant today than, say, in the 1970s (at least that is the conclusion from the places visited in the present study).

Up to a point, a similar argument can be made for developments in Taiwan. People are, in effect, more self-reliant because, on the one hand, they now have the means (higher incomes) to procure the goods and services they require, and, on the other hand, the economy of Taiwan can supply those goods and services, either from domestic production or, because it has the financial resources, from overseas – that is, Taiwan as a whole is now relatively self-reliant in almost every sense. However, the present study has shown up one problem area. It would seem that rural communities do not have the capacity to undertake their own consolidation programme to rationalise the land-holding system, thereby increasing the efficiency of agricultural production. Thus, within the Yunlin Irrigation Association, 40 per cent of the irrigation groups had still not been consolidated, and the programme has been going on for more than 30 years. They are dependent, of course, on the government making the resources available, and because these are limited, it has meant a very long wait for some. In contrast to China, the Taiwan government did not encourage communities to do such things for themselves, and, of course, once several communities had had the work done for them, others would not see why they should be expected to do it for themselves. That is the difference between self-reliance and dependence.

THE CONTINUING ROLE OF COLLECTIVISM

Contrary to popular belief outside China, collectivism has far from disappeared in rural areas. In the places visited, this applied only to agriculture and a few other minor private enterprises. Moreover, even in agriculture, although land is now allocated to individual households (with the notable exception of Liuzhuang, and, stretching the point a little, also Daqiuzhuang – see below), many aspects of the collective system remain in place, not least the actual ownership of the land. Among the villages visited, only in Linzhou and Xipu were most agricultural operations the entire responsibility of individual households. Even here, households were only free to grow what they wanted up to a point, since they were still obliged to provide the state with a certain quota of grain (though they did not necessarily have to grow it themselves). In Dazhai and Litai, and of course in Liuzhuang, on the other hand, land was ploughed and planted, and in the case of the latter two, the crops harvested and threshed, collectively, utilising village-owned equipment. In Daqiuzhuang, too, agriculture was the collective responsibility of the villagers, but in this case was undertaken by managers and labourers employed from outside the village. In the case of industries, in all the villages visited, the major industrial enterprises were collectively owned, though in some cases as joint ventures with foreign companies (which could be a new trend away from collective ownership). Furthermore, much work on local infrastructure, including some road construction, maintenance of dykes and irrigation systems, and even the building of terraces in the notorious Wolf's Lair in Dazhai (a deeply eroded valley which the villagers have wanted to tame ever since the pioneering days in the 1950s), was being carried out by villagers acting as a collective.

However, a key difference now, compared with the regime before 1979, is that in all those collective productive activities the people are paid wages by the village collective, whereas before they would 'only' have received work points. Of course, the work points could be exchanged for money at the end of the year (and occasionally at certain other times, too), but it meant that the relationship between people's remuneration and their labour was much less immediate or direct then than it is now.

THE SIGNIFICANCE OF RECRUITING LABOUR POWER FROM OUTSIDE VILLAGES

Another key change in China since 1979, which is perhaps rather more controversial, is that the village-owned enterprises are now free to recruit labour power from outside the village (see Table 11.2 for its extent in the different villages visited). This means that the profits from their labour remain with the enterprise to the benefit of the villagers who own it. Thus, although the villagers who work in their enterprise might get the same remuneration as those employed from outside the village, the former would get additional income at the end of the year when the profits were distributed as dividends. Alternatively, and even more important, the profits can be invested in other productive activities, which, through the employment of more people outside the village, can generate more profits. This could go on ad nauseam as long as there were people from outside the village seeking work. This trend has gone to extremes in the case of Daqiuzhuang.

The tendency would matter less, perhaps, if there were a reasonable degree of quid pro quo. For instance, it was said in Xipu that as many people were finding employment in enterprises owned by other villages as were being employed in enterprises owned by the Xipu villagers, so that, in effect, villages would be helping one another's development, and, at the same time, there could be benefits arising from the increased mobility or specialisation of labour that might result. However, when the recruitment of labour is more or less one way, in which one or two villages in a given locality were doing all the recruiting for their industries, this, in effect, would hold back the development of industries and other productive activities in villages lacking them, and would mean that some villages would be developing at the expense of others, thus causing the latter to remain underdeveloped. In the case of Daqiuzhuang, it is quite clear that productive activity in neighbouring villages is virtually non-existent, even to the extent that they have sold their land to Daqiuzhuang. On the other hand, in this particular locality, it is equally clear that the huge number of people employed in Daqiuzhuang's village enterprises have a higher level of remuneration, and presumably have a better standard of living as a result, and are now more able to afford to buy a range of foods and consumer goods, compared with before.

In short, there are two opposing tendencies or possible outcomes arising from this new freedom to recruit and exploit labour power from outside the villages. On the beneficial side (at least in the short term) is that people can take advantage of developments taking place in enterprising villages rather than wait for constraints (whatever they might be) that prevent similar developments taking place in their own villages to be overcome. Thus, those employed in village enterprises outside their own villages are at least getting some additional remuneration to supplement their income from agriculture. Furthermore, by pooling their savings, during the course of time they could begin to acquire the financial resources to start the process of establishing industrial or other non-agricultural enterprises in their own villages (which was how the remarkable developments in Daqiuzhuang began). Moreover, the extent to which the standard of living in some villages is seen to be rising as a result of that could provide the stimulus for those villages left behind to do the same. On the other hand, over time, that would be likely to become increasingly difficult because those already on the bandwagon might already have captured the main markets, and, furthermore, would have more investment resources at their disposal to further develop their industries, perhaps by improving productivity so that they could undercut less efficient new entrants, or by diversifying production further thus depriving new entrants from producing non-competing products. In other words, the more advanced villages would carry on growing at the expense of those left behind, thus exacerbating the problem of uneven development. And that, in turn, could begin to hold back development everywhere, or make it slower than it otherwise would be, for the usual reasons (that is, investment growing too fast at the expense of growth of economic demand).

Another issue is that the reason some villages are unable to develop industries or other non-agricultural productive activities might not be through lack of enterprise but because of genuine technical problems, such as lack of natural resources, remoteness from significant markets, underdevelopment of local infrastructure especially transport facilities, difficult topography, population too sparse or with an unbalanced structure (that is, a low proportion of able-bodied, a high proportion of elderly, or the loss of young people to more lucrative opportunities elsewhere) so that there are extreme difficulties to build up the financial resources necessary to invest in new productive activities. Many villages in northern Shaanxi Province, for instance, suffer from some, or even all, of those problems, and, consequently, have remained underdeveloped (personal communication, 1994). A way to prevent people living in such villages from being exploited by other villages, as suggested by Hinton (1991) in the context of the mining enterprises in Dazhai, would be for neighbouring villages to form joint ventures so that all would be in a position to reinvest the profits generated by the workers (perhaps in proportion to the number recruited from each village). A problem here is that villages with plenty of initiative might be reluctant to share their entrepreneurship with those who were sluggish and who would benefit from the former's initiative at its expense. A way round that would be for employees from outside the village to be given a share of the profits of the enterprise at the end of the year either in the form of bonuses or dividends. Both arrangements would allow enterprising villages to continue to flourish but would be more fair and less exploiting, as well as provide funds for those living in other villages to begin to introduce new productive activities, all of which would raise income and ensure that economic demand would continue to expand and therefore further the process of economic development in all villages and beyond.

THE EFFECT OF MORE OPEN MARKETS IN CHINA

The opening up of markets for products from rural areas was probably the single most important aspect of the new policies in the 1980s – it enabled all the various investments made under the old regime to begin to bear fruit. The restrictions of markets previously, desperately held back the development of the collectively owned enterprises, but once free to discover markets for themselves it had the effect of stimulating one another's development because the process generated economic demand for products produced by others over an ever-expanding network. However, the point to be stressed here, which should be noted by policy makers in other countries wishing to learn from the Chinese experience, is that the freeing of markets was not the sole factor causing the remarkable developments since 1979. Thus, villages also had to have the means to invest in the diversification of production. This originated from the collective pooling of people's savings, and remains so. In other words, the two aspects are complementary to one another, and both were necessary in the Chinese context as there was no other significant source of finance in relation to the number of people. And the leadership in all the villages visited seemed to be highly aware of that (that is, they think in terms of self-reliance).

Another issue concerning the freeing of markets is that as long as the state was heavily involved in marketing, the government had the means to appropriate a part of the potential profits generated in rural areas (for instance, by keeping agricultural prices low). Some, but not all, would have been utilised for the purposes of economic development. Much was undoubtedly squandered on projects that produced few returns, as well as in various types of excessive consumption by the bureaucracy. Thus it can be argued, probably, that a significant portion of the potential profits originating from rural areas that accumulated at the state level held back rural development, and, by the mid-1970s, was beginning to hold back developments in all economic areas because economic demand in rural areas was stagnating or not expanding fast enough (see, for instance, Watson, 1983).

Finally, the freeing of markets and the introduction of the household responsibility system in agriculture had a dramatic effect in those areas where the cooperative system was not working well, which, according to a national survey made by young economists in 1980, were in a minority. Thus, in China as a whole, it was reported that only 30 per cent of the production brigades under the system of people's communes had been 'doing well', 30 per cent had been 'doing badly', and the middle 40 per cent had been 'holding their own, neither chalking up great successes on the one hand nor floundering on the other' (Hinton, 1991, p. 51). Anecdotal evidence confirms this view (ibid.). There could be any number of reasons why cooperative systems in particular localities were not realising their potential, ranging from poor or corrupt leadership, to members otherwise having insufficient incentives to use their initiative to improve efficiency and diversify production, or perhaps due to apathy generated by people being rewarded whether or not they worked properly. The extent to which the state appropriated potential profits from rural areas, already mentioned, would also have been a factor.

Thus, it is now clear that the proper working of cooperatives does depend to a considerable degree on a dynamic and far-sighted leadership, capable of mobilising people to achieve particular goals step-by-step as part of an overall strategy, and of organising a successful and fair system of division of labour, and that the most successful, including all those areas visited, had those assets in abundance. It was perhaps somewhat idealistic to suppose that a majority, or even a large minority, could be so fortunate in view of China's history. Interestingly, Hinton makes the point that most of the more successful cooperatives were in the north, in or near old liberated areas where 'the peasants first gave support to the Communist Party because it led the resistance war against Japan or the liberation war against the Guomindang' (1991, p. 51), whereas further south, where cooperatives were markedly less successful or worse (Anhui was the example given), the people had gone through no such history, and were liberated by northern armies, underwent land reform under outside leadership, then, without any trial period of mutual aid, were 'plunged into a land-pooling movement that leaped from the lower to the higher stage in the course of a few months'. For those areas where cooperatives had a mediocre history (the majority, according to the previously mentioned survey), the new open policy focusing on the household opened the way for many new initiatives to evolve. Meanwhile, it is noteworthy that the villages where cooperative production had been most successful, among those visited, have tended to preserve many elements of the old cooperative system (all in the case of Liuzhuang), perhaps making the best use of both worlds.

REFERENCES

Anon. (1972), 'Carved in the cliffs: The Red Flag Canal', *Peking Review* 15, nos 48 and 49, December.

Anon. (1975), 'National conference on learning from Tachai in agriculture', *Peking Review* 18, no. 38, September, p. 3.

Anon. (1980a), 'On the Question of "Learning From Dazhai"', *Beijing Review* 23, no. 3, January, pp. 6–7.

Anon. (1980b), 'No Deification of Dazhai Brigade', *Beijing Review* 23, no. 32, August, p. 5.

Anon. (1993), 'Rotten to the core: monopoly power leads to rampant corruption', *Far Eastern Economic Review*, 16 September 1993, pp. 16–17.

Chu Li and Tien Chieh-yun (1974), *Inside a People's Commune: Report from Chiliying* (Beijing: Foreign Languages Press).

Hinton, W. (1991), *The Privatization of China: The Great Reversal* (London: Earthscan Publications).

Hua Guofeng (1975), 'Mobilise the whole party, make greater efforts to develop agriculture and strive to build Tachai-type counties throughout the country', *Peking Review* 18, no. 44, October.

Jones, J. (1983), 'The Model Village Scheme of Northern Nigeria: A model for community development?', *Community Development Journal* 18 (1), pp. 68–74.

Kahn, A.R. (1984), 'The responsibility system and institutional change', in K. Griffin (ed.), *Institutional Reform and Economic Development in the Chinese Countryside* (London: Macmillan).

Kaye, L. (1993), 'Ugly face of reforms: model village defies police murder probe', *Far Eastern Economic Review*, 22 April 1993, p. 19.

Kuo Feng-lien (1974), 'The Tachai Road', *Peking Review* 17, no. 40, October.

Mao Zedong (1965), 'The foolish old man who removed mountains', in *Selected Works*, vol. III (English translation) (Beijing: Foreign Languages Press), p. 272. (From the concluding speech of Mao to the 7th Congress of the Communist Party of China, and first published in Chinese in June, 1945.)

Marshall, M.S. (1979), 'Red and expert at Tachai: A source of growth analysis', *World Development* 7, pp. 423–32.

Maxwell, N. (1975), 'Learning from Tachai', *World Development* 3, pp. 473–95.

Maxwell, N. (1979), 'A "Paupers' Co-Op" twenty-five years on: capital formation in rural China', *World Development* 7, pp. 433–46.

Pien Hsi (1972), 'The story of Tachai', in *The Seeds* (Beijing: Foreign Languages Press).

Science for the People (1974), 'The Red Flag Canal', in *China: Science Walks on Two Legs* (New York: Discus Books), Chapter 1, pp. 15–26.

Shang Ronguang and Shen Zhichun (1994), 'The non-anecdotal villagers of Dazhai', *Beijing Review* 37, no. 6/7, February, pp. 27–32.

Shen, T-H. (1964), *Agricultural Development in Taiwan since World War II*. (Ithaca: Cornell University Press, Comstock Publishing Associates).

Streeton, P. (1987), *What Price Food? Agricultural Policies in Developing Countries* (London: Macmillan).

Strong, Anna Louise (1959), *The Rise of the People's Communes* (Beijing: Foreign Languages Press).

Watson, A. (1983), 'Agriculture looks for "Shoes that Fit": The production responsibility system and its implications', *World Development* 11 (8), pp. 705–30.

Zhou Jinhua (1981), 'Appraising the Dazhai Brigade', *Beijing Review* 24, no. 16, April, pp. 24–8.

12 Conservation or Development in the Terai? The Political Ecology of Natural Resources in Nepal[1]

Katrina Brown

Nepal
013
028

INTRODUCTION

The reconciliation of competing demands for scarce natural resources often requires trade-offs between the needs for economic development and for environmental conservation. These trade-offs may be particularly acute in low income countries experiencing high rates of growth in human population. This is the case in Nepal, and this chapter examines the situation of the tall grasslands in the southern Terai region which comprise a rare habitat, home to a number of globally endangered species. However, these areas also provide other valuable resources, including grasses for thatch; cane for building, fuel and fodder; and wild foods for the local people. This chapter analyses the conflicts between different resource users, and identifies the interest groups and stakeholders within a political ecology framework. Various options for the conservation and development of the Terai, and the prospects for their successful implementation are suggested.

Nepal is a small landlocked country in Asia bordered by China and India. It covers 147,181 km², and has a population of approximately 18.5 million (CBS, 1993). Some 20 per cent of Nepal consists of subtropical lowlands, known as the Terai, which form a belt along the Nepalese-Indian border. From this southern belt, Nepal's land forms rise in successive hills and mountain ranges, culminating in the Xizang (Tibet) plateau in the inner Himalaya. These are shown in Figure 12.1. The Terai contains pockets of tall grassland, fragments of habitats which are believed to have covered extensive areas of the northern plains of the Indian subcontinent. These habitats are now confined to protected areas, five of which are in the Terai. These are the Royal Chitwan National Park,

Royal Bardia National Park, Suklaphanta National Park, Kosi Tappu Wildlife Reserve and Parsa Wildlife Reserve, and are shown in Figure 12.1. These protected areas cover a total area of approximately 2730 km^2. Within them the tall grassland, dominated by *Imperata*, *Saccharum*, and *Neranga* species, and the *Sal* (*Shorea robusta*) forest are habitat to a number of rare and endangered faunal species. These include the Asian one-horned rhinoceros (*Rhinoceros unicornis*), Bengal tiger (*Panthera tigris*), and Hispid hare (*Caprolagus hispidus*).

These areas have been identified as being of international importance for the conservation of these and other species (for example, Chitwan was declared a World Natural Heritage Site in 1984). In the past decade international pressure for the conservation of such areas has mounted, as evidenced by the so-called Earth Summit, the United Nations Conference on Environment and Development (UNCED), held in Rio in 1992. In response to UNCED, signatory states of the Convention on Biological Diversity are required to devise Action Plans outlining the status, threats and plans for the conservation of biodiversity. Incentives for developing countries to conserve natural resources take the form of both 'carrots' and 'sticks'. For example, the Global Environment Facility, the funding mechanism under the Convention, has the largest ever amount of funds available for biodiversity conservation (US$ 300 m up until late 1993: see Wells, 1994) which is supposed to assist developing countries to meet their commitments to the Convention. 'Sticks' include linking aid to so-called 'green conditionality' as described by Davies (1992).

It is likely that a 'business as usual' approach to conservation in the Terai is not sufficient to conserve its biodiversity, as the grasslands and forests are experiencing increasing pressure from other uses. The most important of these is the requirement for biomass, including grasses, fodder and fuelwood, by the human population which is increasing due to the ongoing process of migration from hill areas.

This study adopts a political ecology framework to analyse the competing demands on the grassland habitats. The following section outlines this approach. The historical context of the development and conservation of the Terai is explored, and contemporary perspectives on the wider political context are given. Local livelihood strategies, and the role of natural resources from protected areas are central to the study. Later sections then discuss some of the potential means of reconciling the competing demands made on the protected areas of the Terai, and whether such approaches represent a new paradigm of conservation with development. Davies (1992), for example, has identified two extreme views of environment and development: the 'environment-first', conservationist approach, and the

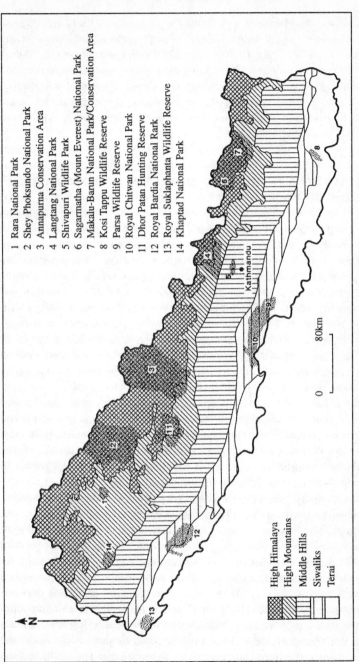

207

1 Rara National Park
2 Shey Phoksundo National Park
3 Annapurna Conservation Area
4 Langtang National Park
5 Shivapuri Wildlife Park
6 Sagarmatha (Mount Everest) National Park
7 Makalu–Barun National Park/Conservation Area
8 Kosi Tappu Wildlife Reserve
9 Parsa Wildlife Reserve
10 Royal Chitwan National Park
11 Dhor Patan Hunting Reserve
12 Royal Bardia National Rark
13 Royal Suklaphanta Wildlife Reserve
14 Khaptad Naitonal Park

Kathmandu

High Himalaya
High Mountains
Middle Hills
Siwaliks
Terai

0   80km

N

FIGURE 12.1: *Ecological Zones and Protected Areas in Nepal* 'food-first', development at whatever cost approach. Between these is what Davies describes as a 'battleground of compromise giving rise to a range of terms and conditions under which means are sought to reconcile the often-opposing goals of environmental protection and promotion of food security' (p. 152). Davies terms this a 'people-first' approach. It is within this battleground that this study attempts to identify the main conflicts and the feasible options for development and conservation of bio-diversity in the Terai.

THE POLITICAL ECOLOGY OF BIODIVERSITY CONSERVATION AND DEVELOPMENT

There is now a general consensus that policies aimed at conserving biologi-cal diversity are unlikely to be successful in meeting their aims unless full consideration is given to the competing uses of natural resources and the likely conflicts between users. Recent years have seen a proliferation of policy documents focusing on the relationships between local human popu-lations and protected areas (for example, Wells and Brandon, 1992; Kemf, 1993; McNeely and Miller, 1984). However, more fundamental issues of local empowerment and decision making are rarely addressed by the inter-national conservation agencies, and cynics might view the focus on local communities by some organisations as mere lip-service to a neopopulist development paradigm. Current initiatives on biodiversity conservation stress the *sustainable use* of biological resources and the implementation of *conservation with development* programmes (see Stocking and Perkin, 1992); indeed this is the language used in the Convention on Biological Diversity. Within the conservation and development discourse the battle-ground of compromise is contested by many different interest groups at many different levels between the extremes of the environmentalist and developmentalist lobbies as described by Davies, but also within the con-servation lobby itself. Two paradigms have been identified, one which represents a traditional preservationist view which sees conservation as largely a matter of protecting wildlife from human beings ('fortress conservation'), and a second which maintains that conservation can only be achieved through sustainable utilisation ('use it or lose it' is the slogan adopted by this view). These two extremes have been characterised by writers such as Child (1993), who refers to the preservationist and utilis-ationist views, and Machis (1992), as the bioethics-preservationist and the utilitarian. These different views are articulated to varying extents by the different interest groups identified in the present case study.

In order to be able to assess the development options for the Terai, there is a need to take full account of the competing uses of these areas – for conservation of biodiversity, and in contributing to the livelihood strategies of local people – and to consider the extent to which these needs are compatible or in conflict with each other, in order to develop workable solutions. This requires the identification of the interest groups and the main actors, the institutions which govern their behaviour, and an understanding of the wider political and social context of their actions. As Neumann (1992) points out, the establishment of a National Park is, in essence, a process of reallocation which involves the introduction of new social structures for controlling access to natural resources. This comprises an explicit shift in property rights, and is thus a political process. The analysis of conservation policies which include National Parks and other protected areas necessarily requires a consideration of the broader political economy context. This is highlighted by Abel and Blaikie (1986) who identify three major shortcomings in the conventional analysis of wildlife conservation. First, much of the writing on conservation issues considers itself to be *apolitical*, where the central issue needing to be addressed concerns the resolution of conflicts over scarce resources, an overtly political issue. Second, previous studies include little of the historic analysis which is essential to gain an understanding of contemporary problems. Third, most approaches contain a disciplinary short-sightedness, whether from a natural science, economic or social perspective, and fail to provide an integrated analysis which links human socio-economic and ecological aspects of the environment, conservation, and resource use. The use of natural resources at a particular place and time is the outcome of conflicting interests between groups of people with different aims (Abel and Blaikie, 1986) and therefore an understanding of these is required in order to formulate conservation policy.

The need for a broader analysis when seeking prescriptions for biodiversity conservation is highlighted in a recent study by Yonzon and Hunter (1991) of red panda (*Ailurus fulgens*) conservation in Langtang National Park in Nepal. A dairy development programme, sponsored by the government and international donors, used a series of incentives including loans and advance payments to encourage local farmers to supply milk to two factories producing cheese for the tourist market in Kathmandu. This development has resulted in a 95 per cent increase in demand for fuelwood (required by factories for processing) in the areas surrounding Langtang. There has been increased exploitation of the National Park for both wood and fodder which is directly threatening the red panda. The consequences of cheese production are likely therefore to include a deterioration in cattle health, loss of fuelwood, local extinction of some wildlife species such as the red panda, degradation of forests and pastures, and an increased risk of failure among small farmers. The key to red panda conservation therefore lies beyond the scope of conventional 'conservation' policy and is critically linked to agricultural development policies.

Political ecology has its origins in critiques of ecological anthropology and cultural ecology in the 1970s. The approach became well known through the work of Blaikie and Brookfield (1987) who explain that political ecology combines the concerns of ecology with a 'broadly defined political economy' (p. 17). Three main areas of inquiry have been identified in a recent analysis of the political ecology research agenda by Bryant (1992). These are the contextual sources of environmental change; conflict over access; and the political ramifications of environmental change. The current study is predominantly the second, in that it focuses on location-specific conflicts over access to and control over environmental resources. At the same time, it recognises the influence of the broader context (that is, at state, interstate and global levels), and also the evolving nature of the situation, where environmental changes, both inside and outside the location, have profound and direct implications for patterns of resource use by the various users (see Peet and Watts, 1993; Moore, 1993; and Neumann, 1992).

Neumann identifies three areas fundamental to the political ecology perspective: First, a focus on the land users and the social relations in which they are entwined; second, tracing the linkages of these local relations to wider geographical and social settings; third, historical analysis to understand the contemporary situation. Individual studies stress different aspects. For example, Amanor (1994) focuses on systems of local knowledge and innovation, and Peluso (1992) and Guha (1989) on peasant resistance, but commonly all studies include consideration of these three areas. The application of the political ecology approach to policy issues is demonstrated by a number of previous studies including those by Schmink and Wood (1987) and Abel and Blaikie (1986). In the case of Schmink and Wood, this involves examining policies to facilitate sustainable land use patterns in the Brazilian Amazon region. Their method of policy formulation involves a process of 'progressive contextualisation' of the existing system of resources use, and also requires an analysis of the goals of policy, their feasibility and scope for bargaining between different interest groups. Likewise, Abel and Blaikie identify interest groups in their study of conservation policy in the Luangwa Valley in Zambia and suggest ways in which current conflicts between different groups and uses can be overcome in a feasible management strategy which benefits local users and wildlife conservation objectives.

This study adopts a political ecology approach which concentrates on the livelihood strategies of local resource users, and the identification of different interest groups concerned with utilisation and management of natural resources, and the conflicts between them. The political and economic context, and historic aspects of conservation policy, and land tenure are examined. Key features of the study are the conflicts between different ethnic groups and different user groups, and their different modes of access to resources; historic role of migration and changing property rights; development of conservation policy in Nepal; and recent constitutional changes in Nepal. Following sections review these aspects.

Figure 12.2 presents a diagram illustrating the conceptual framework which shows the three areas of study: historical context; contemporary political economy; local resource use and its role in the livelihoods of communities adjacent to the protected areas. Issues specific to the Terai are illustrated for each of these three areas, and the common themes for investigation – access to natural resources, ecological impacts of different actions, and the needs of various interest groups – are shown in the centre of the diagram.

HISTORICAL CONTEXT

Nepal is one of the world's poorest countries, the seventh in the world, according to the 1993 World Development Report, with a per capita Gross

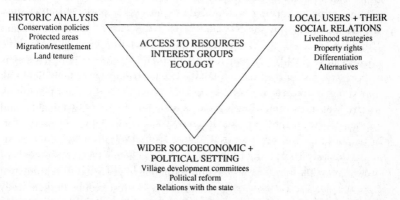

FIGURE 12.2: *The Political Ecology of Grassland Conservation in the Terai: A Conceptual Framework*

National Product (GNP) of only US$ 180 in 1992 (World Bank, 1993). Other indicators, such as literacy rates, life expectancy and infant mortality, show Nepal to be gravely impoverished, and the Human Development Report (UNDP, 1993) ranks Nepal 152 by its Human Development Index, a composite index of human welfare. However, these aggregate national indicators give only a broadbrush view which obscures significant regional differences within Nepal. The Terai region is agriculturally rich, and was relatively sparsely populated until 20 years ago. However, since the designation of protected areas in the 1970s, and with large immigration into the region from the mountains and hill regions, conflicts over land use have intensified. This section briefly discusses two aspects in setting the historical context; namely, conservation policy and development in the Terai.

Conservation in Nepal

Prior to the 1950s, Basnet (1992) describes self-interest and conservation as being traditionally linked in Nepal. Forests, for example, were used as a means of political protection – in the eighteenth century the Terai forest formed an effective barrier to Indian invasion, so the state had a vested interest in its preservation. These areas were also used for hunting by the Royal family, and indeed, the designation of the protected areas in the Terai was originally to provide hunting sanctuaries for use by the Nepalese Royal family and visiting dignitaries. Nepal was an essentially subsistence agricultural economy which was closed to foreigners until 1949. Population growth rates were low, and relatively little pressure was put on natural resources, including forests for timber production, and large-scale conversion of natural habitats for agricultural production.

Legislation governing National Parks and other protected areas was introduced in 1973 by the National Parks and Wildlife Conservation Act. This Act created the Department of National Parks and Wildlife Conservation (DNPWC), which was formerly an office of the Department of Forestry. Under the Act, the DNPWC has power to create and manage four types of protected areas: National Parks, Wildlife Reserves, Strict Nature Reserves, and Hunting Reserves. A later amendment gave the national government the power to recognise a fifth type of protected area in response to a newer proposal, called Conservation Areas. At present approximately 10 per cent of the land area of Nepal is under some form of protection (this is a reasonably high proportion; WCMC (1992, p. 460) cites the average for Asia as a little over 4 per cent, and about 5 per cent for the world, although the classifications differ; the WCMC records areas protected according to the pre-1994 IUCN (World Conservation Union) categories, and state 8 per cent for Nepal). Figure 12.1 shows the location of National Parks and Wildlife Reserves, and also the Annapurna Conservation Area, and Table 12.1 lists these areas.

According to Heinen and Kattel (1992a), Nepal is now considered a leader among developing nations with regard to conservation programmes and legislation; it was among the first Asian nations to develop national conservation legislation, sign the Convention on the International Trade in Endangered Species of Wild Fauna and Flora (CITES), and develop a national conservation strategy. The conservation policy has also followed the international tide and shifted away from a single species focus (identifying and legislating for the protection of endangered species, and for relocation programmes including the tiger relocation programme of the 1970s), towards biodiversity protection (for example, the designation of the Annapurna Conservation Area in 1988) (see Heinen and Yonzon, 1994). There is still, conservationists argue, a need for comprehensive biological inventories, and more information is required on the population dynamics and degrees of threat to habitats. In its most recent statement of policy, the Nepal Environmental Policy and Action Plan (HMG, 1993),

TABLE 12.1: *The National Parks and Reserves of Nepal*

Name	Location	Size km²	Date established
Koshi Tappu WR	E Terai	175	1976
Parsa WR	C Terai	500	1984
Royal Chitwan NP	C Terai	932	1973
Royal Bardia NP	Mid-W Terai	968	1976
Sukla Phanta WR	Far W Terai	155	1976
Shivapuri WR	Kathmandu Valley	114	1985
Khaptad NP	Far West Hills	225	1985
Makalu-Barun	E Himalaya	2 330	1991
Sagamartha NP	E Himalaya	1 148	1976
Langtang NP	C Himalaya	1 710	1976
Annapurna CA	W Himalaya	3 400	1988
Dhor Patan HR	Mid-W Himalaya	1 325	1984
Rara NP	Mid-W Himalaya	106	1976
Shey Phoksundo NP	Mid-W Himalaya	3 555	1984
	Total Area:	16 643	

SOURCE: Heinen and Kattel (1992b).

the government clearly links conservation and development (the subtitle of the document is 'integrating environment and development'), and lists the five aims of the government's environment policy as:

- To manage efficiently and sustainably natural and physical resources.
- To balance development efforts and environmental conservation for sustainable fulfilment of the basic needs of the people.
- To safeguard the national heritage.
- To mitigate the adverse environmental impacts of development projects and human actions.
- To integrate environment and development through appropriate institutions, adequate legislation and economic incentives, and sufficient public resources.

Protected areas remain a key mechanism for conservation policy. The five Terai protected areas were among the earliest to be designated soon after the enactment of the 1973 legislation. However, even the Royal Chitwan National Park, the first in Nepal, is only 21 years old. This means that resettlement is still within living memory, and indeed one village remains within the area designated and negotiations continue to relocate its inhabitants. In Royal Bardia National Park, extensions to the park in the last decade involved resettlement of numerous villages. In many of the protected areas the sites of old villages and cultivated areas are recognisable within the park by their vegetation (having a higher concentration of *Imperata*). In fact, this characteristic is part of the management conundrum, whereby human intervention may be necessary to maintain some types of grassland. The dilemma appears to be how that intervention is managed: by whom and for whose benefit?

Land Use and Development in the Terai

Before the second half of this century, the Terai was populated largely by indigenous Tharu people, who practised subsistence agriculture, supplemented by hunting, fishing and gathering of wild foods. According to Cox (1990) the Tharu had lived in the Terai for more than six hundred years and were possibly the first and only inhabitants of the region. However, little is known about the historic use of grasslands and their human ecology. For example, how regular and widespread were burning practices by indigenous people? In the last 20 years migration to the Terai has increased, following malaria eradication programmes which have made the plains a more hospitable place to live. Whereas between 1952/54 and 1971, the population of the Terai increased from 2.9 million to 4.3 million, representing

35.3 per cent and 38 per cent of the nation's total population respectively, in 1991 the Terai population numbered 8.6 million, some 46.7 per cent of the population. This rate of migration prompts Goldstein et al. (1983) to describe Nepal as moving from a mountain-rural to a plains-urban society at 'breakneck speed', with a redirection of development policy necessary to adjust (p. 64).

The migration to the Terai has been both legal (state-led) and illegal, encouraged by 'push-factors' in the hills regions which have experienced greater population pressure and apparent fertility declines as more marginal areas are taken into production (see Ives and Masserli, 1989; Thompson et al., 1986; and Metz, 1991 for a discussion of the 'Himalayan Crisis'). The *relative* fertility and land availability (Baral, 1986) have encouraged hill farmers into the Terai. At the same time, the designation of the National Parks and protected areas and the resettlement of people out of these areas, has put a 'squeeze' on the natural resource base, which was traditionally thought of as abundant.

With the large immigrant population, contested land rights and the designation of fertile areas for conservation, a highly skewed distribution of ownership of resources has resulted (Cox, 1990). Inequalities in land ownership and access to resources are exacerbated by some government policies, such as those setting land ceilings, and there are growing problems of landlessness in the Terai (Shrestha, 1990). According to Ghimire (1992) the most prominent of the landed classes currently retain land in the Terai as a source of supplementary earnings (the major part of income being derived from paid employment within the bureaucracy, urban business, or property speculation), or for maintaining an electoral base, rather than for productive use. This and other studies indicate that increasing impoverishment and differentiation among peasants in the Terai result from land use and the tenure arrangements.

CONTEMPORARY PERSPECTIVES: THE POLITICAL ECONOMY OF NEPAL

The previous section has outlined some historical perspectives on the conservation of natural resources and land tenure in the Terai, which have a bearing on the political ecology of the tall grasslands. At the present time, Nepal is in a state of comparative upheaval following significant changes in the political system since 1990. These changes have come about as a result of a popular political protest movement involving underground political parties, students and professional organisations, as well as significant sections of both the rural and urban populace. The most important changes involve the withdrawal of the Panchayat system (although according to Ghimire (1992) the traditions of the caste system and Hindu philosophy governing property laws, gender relations and legitimised socio-economic inequalities have not been challenged); a 30-year ban on political parties has been lifted and the king has taken a 'constitutional role'. Democratic elections (only the second in the history of Nepal) took place in late 1994, and resulted in the installation of a minority government. Although the government has pledged to institute land reform, at present the lack of a parliamentary majority makes it difficult for any radical policy to be enacted, and it seems likely that political instability will continue for some time.

These changes will have implications for the political ecology of the Terai grasslands, especially in terms of the organisation of local communities and the different interest groups using the resources from the protected areas. Table 12.2 shows the interest groups and stakeholders in grassland conservation and use, their scale of influence, sources of power, interests and aims, and means of achieving them. Although some users may be assumed to have the same aims and interests (for example, conservationists and tour operators profess an interest in conserving biodiversity) they may be far from complementary. Tour operators may have an interest in conserving habitats consisting of shorter grass, supporting larger grazing animals which are attractive to tourists. This may be in conflict with needs for scientific preservation of biodiversity where endangered small mammals require tall vegetation for cover (as demonstrated by Bell's study of Hispid hare in Suklaphanta Wildlife Reserve: see Bell, 1986 and Peet, 1994). In this case, conservation and tourism may not be complementary, yet they are often portrayed as such by the tourism industry which assumes large mammals to be indicators of habitat diversity, ecosystem health and stability.

LOCAL LIVELIHOODS STRATEGIES: THE ROLE OF COMMUNITY RESOURCES

When the protected areas of the Terai were designated in the 1970s, local people were resettled outside the parks, and also lost their rights of access to the resources of the parks (Heinen, 1993). These resources included grass for grazing, fodder and other needs such as thatch and building materials, use of wood for fuel and building, and many plants used for food, medicines and so on, and game and fish. Section 16 of the National Parks and Wildlife Conservation Act stipulates that park or reserve

TABLE 12.2: *Interest Groups and Stakeholders in Grassland Conservation in the Terai*

Group	Scale of influence	Source of power	Interests/aims	Means
Indigenous people	Local	very limited	livelihood maintainence; use protected areas for subsistence needs, minor trading of products; thatch, fodder, building materials, fuel, wild foods, plant medicines, hunting and fishing	subsistence farming, minor marketing; legal and illegal extraction of resources from protected areas
Migrant farmers	Local	limited	livelihood maintenance; use protected areas for subsistence needs: thatch, fodder, fuel, building material	cash farming plus subsistence; legal and illegal extraction of products from protected areas
Local entrepreneurs	Local	many hold official positions locally	profit; commercial; range of small enterprises tourist and non-tourist-based	small business enterprises, buying and selling to tourists
Tourist concessions	National/ some international	lobbying/may hold official positions	profit, commercial expansion; some of revenue may be earned overseas; control tourists staying in protected areas overnight	tourism revenues; concessions from government
Government conservation agencies	National	administrative and supervisory	conserving wildlife and facilitating tourist development	enforcing park boundaries; imposing fines

TABLE 12.2: *Continued*

Group	Scale of Influence	Source of Power	Interests/aims	Means
Conservation pressure groups	Local/National some international links	lobbying, may have personal contacts, international funding	Conserving biodiversity but with considerations for local livelihoods	lobbying, publicity
International conservation groups	International	international funding, 'green conditionality'	Conserving biodiversity; limited interests in human welfare	international legislation, lobbying
Central government	National	political and administrative	national development; economic growth	legislation, bureaucracy, budget allocation

authorities may permit the removal of natural products if such removal is deemed important for the management of the area. By way of compensation for the loss of access, the DNPWC allows local people into the parks for a limited period to cut grass and collect cane. This cutting period has been progressively shortened to span just two weeks during the dry season. In addition individuals belonging to ethnic groups who had traditionally lived by catching and selling fish may be given special permission at the discretion of the officer in charge to fish in the parks, but this varies in the different protected areas. The DNPWC does not offer any other form of compensation; for either crop or livestock damage, or even human deaths (there are acute conflicts with the rhino population in Chitwan, for instance, with more than ten deaths reported each year).

A number of studies have examined various aspects of the use of park resources and their role in local economy (for example, Sharma and Shaw, 1993), and park–people conflicts which have been highlighted in Chitwan by the work of Sharma (1990), Lehmkuhl et al. (1988), Nepal and Weber (1993), and Mishra (1984). Attitudes of local people to conservation were examined by Heinen (1993) in a study based in Kosi Tappu Wildlife Reserve. What particularly complicates this current study is the extent of differentiation within local communities (see Ghimire, 1992; Shrestha, 1990); migrant farmers, landless labourers, absentee landlords and indigenous groups, which further adds to the number of interest groups laying claim to the resources of the grassland.

The park resources used by local people play a considerable role in their livelihood strategies. Five major products are utilised: fodder; firewood; *khar*, thatchgrass (primarily *Imperata cylindrica*); *kharai*, reeds and canes used for building (mainly *Narenga porphorymina* and *Saccharum arundinacum*); and timber. A number of studies have attempted to quantify the amounts of biomass extracted from the protected areas; most of these have centred research on Chitwan (Lehmkuhl et al., 1988; Mishra, 1984; Nepal and Weber, 1993). Recent survey work in Royal Bardia National Park (Brown, forthcoming) shows that a significant proportion of the local population depends on park resources for thatching and building, and that indigenous Tharu people may be more dependent on these resources than migrants to the Terai region. In addition, people collect medicinal plants and various wild food, including mushrooms, roots, *nuro* and *siplikan*. A survey investigating local people's attitudes to the park (Nepal and Weber, 1993) indicated that firewood and fodder were ranked the most important products.

The legal collection of thatch and cane grasses is valuable to both individuals and the local economy. Lehmkuhl et al. (1988) calculated the gross value of these products, collected from Chitwan National Park in January 1986, to be in the region of US$ 451,836. The net value, with labour and permit costs subtracted, amounted to US$ 252,103, as shown in Table 12.3. The study also examined the costs of alternative building materials, and concluded that most villagers close to the park do not have enough capital to invest in other supplies, but they do have the time to cut their own grasses. The standard of living of these people would therefore be lower without access to park resources.

RECONCILING COMPETING DEMANDS – CONSERVATION WITH DEVELOPMENT?

Table 12.4 sets out some of the possible options for managing the Terai protected areas, assuming that conservation of biodiversity is one aim. If this were not the case, of course, the protected areas could be abandoned altogether. The Table identifies five different modes of implementation, which range, roughly along a continuum, from a strong protectionist to a utilisationist approach. Their key features, and also some of the problems they could involve are outlined.

Among the strategies are the designation of buffer zones around the protected areas, where limited exploitation of natural resources (the collection of renewable resources such as grass, cane and wood perhaps) is allowed. Such a strategy has been considered for Chitwan by Nepal and

TABLE 12.3: *The Value of Grasses and Cane Collected from Royal Chitwan National Park, 1986*

Product	of loads	Weight '000 kg	Value million Nrupees[1]	Value '000 US$[2]
Khar	162 592	6 406	4.55	206.9
Kharai	134 265	4 726	5.39	244.9
Total gross value			9.94	451.8
Net value[3]			5.46	252.1

SOURCE: Data from survey reported by Lehmkuhl et al. (1988)
NOTES: [1] Local price for Khar was 0.71 NR/kg, Kharai 1.14 NR/kg
    [2] Exchange rate of US$ 1 = 22 NR (1986)
    [3] Permit (1 NR pp/day) and labour costs (20 NR pp/day) subtracted

TABLE 12.4: *Management Options for Terai Protected Areas*

Mode of implementation	Features	Likely impediments
Strong protectionist	Stop access to park resources and strengthen enforcement of boundaries	High costs to local people Likely to worsen park–community relations Expensive in terms of enforcement and management
Business as usual	Cutting and burning of grassland during prescribed period only, but considerable encroachment and poaching	Evidence of environmental degradation, although long-term effects unknown Likely worsening of public relations Difficult and relatively costly to enforce
Intensive conservation management	Limited access to biomass resources; definition of core areas which are restricted, rotation of areas to be cut and burned each year, determined by 'scientific' criteria; possible joint-management with committees with community representation	Very expensive in terms of expertise, enforcement, planning and community relations Very difficult to police
Buffer zone outside park	Investment in community development and provision of alternative biomass outside park	Problems defining and demarcating the Buffer zone Revenue-raising ability and administration responsibilities unclear Very expensive in terms of time, expertise, community relations

TABLE 12.4: *Continued*

Mode of implementation	Features	Likely impediments
Conservation with development	Devolution of power to local people, involvement of community in park management Revenue raising and income generation projects through tourism and wildlife utilisation Investment in alternative biomass provision outside park/protected area	Who participates? problems likely in defining 'catchment' area Political impediments to full participation; lack of local NGOs and institutions? Very expensive, long-term solution Lack of valuable wildlife and other products to generate sufficient income (compared with, for example, CAMPFIRE), or appropriate tourism opportunities (compared with Annapurna Conservation Area) Administration and revenue raising unclear

Weber (1993), and is discussed more generally by Wells and Brandon (1993). However, fundamental problems – particularly with actual designation of the Buffer Zone; how revenue for investment should be raised; and how the area might be administered – have yet to be resolved.

Much of the literature on people–parks relations has focused on ways in which wildlife conservation can be made to pay and provide local people with income and thus an incentive to conserve rather than poach. This model has been used in Southern Africa by ensuring that revenues from safari hunting are captured by local people, for example through the CAMPFIRE project in Zimbabwe (Murindagomo, 1992) and in the Luangwa Valley in Zambia (Lewis et al. 1990). However, these schemes are successful partly because of the high value of the products (trophy hunting of elephant and other game animals) (Child, 1993), and it is not clear whether such schemes would be transferable to the Terai situation. Likewise, the possibilities for significantly increasing local benefits from tourism may be limited, as the type of tourism in the Terai protected areas, game viewing, may be less amenable to small scale operations than trekking in the Himalaya, where local initiatives are supported in the Annapurna Conservation Area (Hough and Sherpa, 1989; and see also Wells, 1993). Some preliminary research has been undertaken on the feasibility of these options (Heinen, 1990; Heinen and Thapa, 1988) but no schemes are yet under way.

Investments outside the protected areas may take pressure off resources inside them. Alternative sources of biomass, or alternatives products (for example the use of tiles instead of thatch for roofing), and the opportunities for developing local production centres need to be considered. However, the funding required would be considerable, and this would not be possible without outside assistance. More long-term solutions require effective participation of local people, so that they can become influential partners in the management of protected areas and their hinterland. The importance of participation is stressed by many, yet the barriers to its successful implementation are formidable. Current use of participation in the conservation and development discourse presents two extreme views. The first, as espoused by many of the conservation agencies, focuses on participation as a necessary input to facilitate the successful implementation of conservation policies. Participation is a means to an end (the conservation of biodiversity). The second, as propounded by grassroots activists and local non-governmental organisations (NGOs) views participation as a fundamental requirement, necessitating the empowerment and self-determination of local people, who define their own priorities. Participation is an end in itself.

Identifying the different interest groups is viewed as a first step to bring stakeholders together in an attempt to reconcile the competing uses. However, within the contemporary political context, doubt remains as to the feasibility of such a strategy given institutional, social and political barriers to effective participation in decision making and planning. It is clear from the above discussion that there can be no short-term, simple solutions to these complex issues of natural resource conservation. The next stage is to encourage the various interest groups actually to come to the table, or 'gather around the tree' (Child, 1993), and find consensus solutions in this battleground of compromise.

NOTE

1. The author acknowledges assistance from the Centre for Social and Economic Research on the Global Environment (CSERGE) which is a designated research centre of the UK Social and Economic Research Council. Funding for the UEA Tall Grassland Research Project in Nepal is received from the UK Department of Environment's Darwin Initiative for the Survival of Species. The author would like to thank Diana Bell, Nick Peet, Andrew Watkinson, Scott Perkin, Tim O'Riordan and Neil Adger for valuable comments made on earlier versions of this paper. All errors remain sole responsibility of the author.

REFERENCES

Abel, N. and P. Blaikie (1986), 'Elephants, People, Parks and Development: The Case of the Luangwa Valley, Zambia', *Environmental Management* 10(6), pp. 735–51.

Amanor, K.S. (1994), 'Ecological Knowledge and the Regional Economy: Environmental Management in the Asesewa District of Ghana', *Development and Change*, 25(1), pp. 41–67.

Baral, J.C. (1986), 'Nepal: Its Land and its Uses', in Last, F.T., M.C.B. Hotz and B.G. Bell (eds), *Land and its Uses – Actual and Potential* (New York: Plenum Press) pp. 523–34.

Basnet, K. (1992), 'Conservation Practice in Nepal: Past and Present', *Ambio* 21(6), pp. 390–3.

Bell, D. (1986), 'A study of the Hispid hare *Caprolagus hispidus* in Royal Suklaphanta Wildlife Reserve, western Nepal', *Dodo, Journal of the Jersey Wildlife Preservation Trust* 23, pp. 24–31.

Blaikie, P. and H. Brookfield (1987), *Land Degradation and Society* (New York: Methuen).

Brown, K., (forthcoming), Plain Tales from the Grasslands: The Utilisation of Natural resources in Royal Bardia National Park, Nepal. Paper presented to the International Association for the Study of Common Property Resources, Norway, 1995.

Bryant, R.L. (1992), 'Political Ecology: An Emerging Research Agenda in Third-World Studies', *Political Geography* 11(1), pp. 12–36.

Central Bureau of Statistics (CBS) (1993), *Statistical Yearbook of Nepal 1993* (Kathmandu: Central Bureau of Statistics).

Child, B. (1993), 'Zimbabwe's CAMPFIRE Programme: Using the High Value of Wildlife Recreation to Revolutionise Natural Resource Management in Communal Areas', *Commonwealth Forestry Review* 72(4), pp. 284–96.

Cox, T. (1990), 'Land Rights and Ethnic Conflict in Nepal', *Economic and Political Weekly*, 16–23 June, pp. 1318–20.

Davies, S. (1992), 'Green Conditionality and Food Security: Winners and Losers from the Greening of Aid', *Journal of International Development* 4(2), pp. 151–65.

Ghimire, K. (1992), *Forest or Farm? The Politics of Poverty and Land Hunger in Nepal*, (Delhi: Oxford University Press).

Goldstein, M.C., J.L. Ross and S. Schuler (1983), 'From a Mountain-Rural to a Plains-Urban Society: Implications of the 1981 Nepalese Census', *Mountain Research and Development* 3(1), pp. 61–4.

Guha, R. (1989), *The Unquiet Woods: Ecological Change and Peasant Resistance in the Himalaya* (Delhi: Oxford University Press).

Heinen, J.T. (1990), 'The Design and Implementation of a Training Programme for Tour Guides in Royal Chitwan National Park', *Tiger Paper*, April–June, pp. 11–15.

Heinen, J.T. (1993), 'Park–People Relations in Kosi Tappu Wildlife Reserve, Nepal: A Socio-Economic Analysis', *Environmental Conservation* 20(1), pp. 25–34.

Heinen, J.T. and B. Kattel (1992a), 'A Review of Conservation Legislation in Nepal: Past Progress and Future Needs', *Environmental Management* 16(6), pp. 723–33.

Heinen, J.T. and B. Kattel (1992b), 'Parks, People and Conservation: A Review of Management Issues in Nepal's Protected Areas', *Population and Environment* 14(1), pp. 49–84.

Heinen, J.T. and B.B. Thapa (1988), 'A Feasibility Study of a Proposed Trekking Trail in Chitwan National Park', *Forestry*, June, pp. 19–28.

Heinen, J.T. and P.B. Yonzon (1994), 'A Review of Conservation Issues and Programs in Nepal: From a Single Species Focus toward Biodiversity Protection', *Mountain Research and Development* 14(1), pp. 61–76.

His Majesty's Government (HMG) (1993), *Nepal Environmental Policy and Action Plan* (Kathmandu: HMG Environment Protection Council).

Hough, J.L. and M.N. Sherpa (1989), 'Bottom Up vs. Basic Needs: Integrating Conservation and Development in the Annapurna and Michiru Mountain Conservation Areas of Nepal and Malawi', *Ambio* 18(8), pp. 434–41.

Ives, J.D. and B. Masserli (1989), *The Himalayan Dilemma: Reconciling Development and Conservation* (London and New York: Routledge).

Kemf, E. (ed.) (1993), *Indigenous Peoples and Protected Areas* (London: Earthscan).

Lehmkuhl, J.F., R.K. Upretti and U.R. Sharma (1988), 'National Parks and Local Development: Grasses and People in Royal Chitwan National Park, Nepal', *Environmental Conservation* 15(2), pp. 143–8.

Lewis, D., G.B. Kaweche and A. Mwenya (1990), 'Wildlife Conservation Outside Protected Areas – Lessons from and Experiment in Zambia', *Conservation Biology* 4(2), pp. 171–80.

Machis, G.E. (1992), 'The Contribution of Sociology to Biodiversity Research and Management', *Biological Conservation* 62, pp. 161–70.

McNeely, J.A. and K.R. Miller (eds) (1984), *National Parks, Conservation and Development: The Role of Protected Areas in Sustaining Society* (Washington, DC: Smithsonian Institution).

Metz, J.J. (1991), 'A Reassessment of the Causes and Severity of Nepal's Environmental Crisis', *World Development* 19(7), pp. 850–20.

Mishra, H.R. (1984), 'A Delicate Balance: Tigers, Rhinoceros, Tourists and Park Management vs. The Needs of Local People in Royal Chitwan National Park, Nepal', in J.A. McNeely and K.R. Miller (eds) *National Parks, Conservation and Development: Role of Protected Areas in Sustaining Society*, (Washington, DC: Smithsonian Institution), pp. 197–205.

Moore, D.S. (1993), 'Contesting Terrain in Zimbabwe's Eastern Highlands: Political Ecology, Ethnography and Peasant Resource Struggles', *Economic Geography* 69(4), pp. 380–401.

Murindagomo, F. (1992), 'Wildlife Management in Zimbabwe: The CAMPFIRE Programme', *Unasylva* 43(168), pp. 20–26.

Nepal, S.K. and K.E. Weber (1993), *Struggle for Existence: Park–People Conflict in the Royal Chitwan National Park, Nepal* (Bangkok: Division of Human Settlements Development, Asian Institute of Technology).

Neumann, R.P. (1992), Political Ecology of Wildlife Conservation in the Mt. Meru Area of Northeast Tanzania', *Land Degradation and Rehabilitation* 3, pp. 85–98.

Peet, N., (1994), *Fire and Biodiversity Conservation in the Tall Grasslands of Nepal and North India.* (*Mimeo*, School of Biological Sciences, University of East Anglia.)

Peet, R. and M. Watts (1993), 'Development Theory and Environment in the Age of Market Triumphalism', *Economic Geography* 69(3), pp. 227–53.

Peluso, N.L. (1992), 'The Political Ecology of Extraction and Extractive Reserves in East Kalimantan, Indonesia', *Development and Change* 23(4), pp. 49–74.

Schmink, M. and C.H. Wood (1987), 'The "Political Ecology" of Amazonia', in P.D. Little, M.M. Horowitz and A.E. Nyerges (eds), *Lands at Risk in the Third World: Local Level Perspectives* (Boulder, CO: Westview Press), pp. 38–57.

Sharma, U.R. (1990), 'An Overview of Park–People Interactions in Royal Chitwan National Park, Nepal', *Landscape and Urban Planning* 19, pp. 133–44.

Sharma, U.R. and W.W. Shaw (1993), 'Role of Nepal's Royal Chitwan National Park in Meeting the Grazing and Fodder Needs of Local People', *Environmental Conservation* 20(2),pp. 139–42.

Shrestha, N.R. (1990), *Landlessness and Migration in Nepal* (Boulder, CO: Westview Press).

Stocking, M. and S. Perkin (1992), 'Conservation-with-Development: An Application of the Concept in the Usambara Mountains, Tanzania', *Transcriptions of the Institute of British Geographers* 17, pp. 337–49.

Thompson, M., M. Warburton and T. Hatley (1986), *Uncertainty on a Himalayan Scale* (London: Ethnographica).

United Nations Development Programme (UNDP) (1993), *Human Development Report 1993* (New York: UNDP).

Wells, M. (1994), 'The Global Environment Facility and Prospects for Biodiversity Conservation', *International Environmental Affairs* 6(1), pp. 69–97.

Wells, M. and K. Brandon (1992), *People and Parks: Linking Protected Area Management with Local Communities* (Washington, DC: The World Bank, The World Wildlife Fund, US Agency for International Development).

Wells, M. and K. Brandon (1993), 'The Principles and Practice of Buffer Zones and Local Participation in Biodiversity Conservation', *Ambio* 22(2–3), pp. 157–62.

Wells, M.P. (1993), 'Neglect of Biological Riches: The Economics of Nature Tourism in Nepal', *Biodiversity and Conservation*, 2, pp. 445–64.

World Bank (1993), *World Development Report 1993* (Washington DC: The World Bank).

World Conservation Monitoring Centre (WCMC) (1992), *Global Biodiversity: Status of the Earth's Living Resources* (London: Chapman and Hall).

Yonzon, P.B. and M.L.J. Hunter (1991), 'Cheese, Tourists and Red Pandas in the Nepal Himalayas', *Conservation Biology* 5(2), pp. 196–201.

13 Private Markets for Wastes: The Case of Calcutta

Anu Bose

INTRODUCTION

This chapter is an enquiry into the nature of the private markets in wastes in Calcutta, India, and is based on the author's doctoral research carried out between November 1991 and January 1994.[1] Wastes, for the purposes of this chapter, are defined as something which the current owner does not want. But almost everything that is thrown away, especially by affluent households, is useful to somebody, particularly in developing countries. Wastes are therefore a resource since they generate income for many thousands of marginalised households. In a scarcity-based[2] economy, like India's, there is always a high demand for low value products made from recuperated waste materials.

Calcutta, the old imperial capital of the British Raj, is now the capital of the state of West Bengal in India. The area under the jurisdiction of the Calcutta Municipal Corporation (CMC) is 18,556 km^2. The 1991 Government of India (GoI) census gives Calcutta's population as 4,400,000 with a weekday commuter population of 2,500,000.

Calcutta's municipal waste management system has the dubious distinction of being known as a textbook case of bureaucratic failure. There are no reliable statistics on the amount of rubbish generated or collected in the city.[3] The CMC's own figures (1993, unpublished MS) put it at 3100 metric tonnes per day. The CMC's quaintly named Directorate of Conservancy and Motor Vehicles which is responsible for the collection, transportation and eventual disposal of the wastes only manages to collect 2205 metric tonnes per day or 70 per cent of all the wastes generated (Government of West Bengal, Local Government and Urban Development Department, 1991 p. 1). The same publication estimates that 'private salvaging' or waste picking accounts for 10 per cent or 315 metric tonnes and 20 per cent or 630 metric tonnes lies uncollected. Bose and Blore (1993, p. 3) estimate that private recovery systems reclaim between

228

20 and 25 per cent and that 'the total turnover of the recycling operation is well over Rs 60,000,000 (£1,200,000[4]) and ... perhaps more than Rs 200,000,000 (£4,000,000)' (ibid., p. 12).

Calcutta's refuse does not contain a very high percentage of compostable refuse (41 per cent). Ash and silt, which are both non-combustible, comprise 27 per cent of Calcutta's rubbish. Combustible fractions, including paper and plastics, account for 12.05 per cent of the total weight. Paper accounts for 5.2 per cent of the rubbish and polyethylene/plastics 3.5 per cent.[5] The rubbish is dense because of the 'low percentages of non-putricibles [sic]' (Giri and De, undated, p. 8), and the moisture content is high at 41 per cent because of the humid climate and because uncollected rubbish lies open to the elements for days.

Calcutta may be unique in that it has distinct private markets for wastes and waste-handling services. The market for wastes can be divided into two: first, the trade in the rights of access to the wastes thrown into the roadside containers, and the second for the actual wastes at the dumping grounds. The market for domestic waste handling is unique to India and is as much a social as an economic institution. The CMC *mazdoors* (literally, 'workers', the lowest-level members of the public cleansing department) participate in all of the three markets in their various roles as private contractors, rentiers and auctioneers.

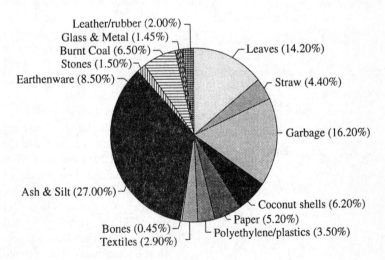

SOURCE: Calcutta Municipal Corporation, 1993.

FIGURE 13.1: *Physical Analysis of Calcutta's Wastes*

TABLE 13.1: *List of Items Found on Calcutta's Waste Heaps*

Brass
Bones
Batteries (dry and wet cell)
Stainless steel
Aluminium foil
Bell-metal
High Density Polyethylene (hdpe)
Low Density Polyethyelene (ldpe)
German Silver
Paper (several kinds)
Glass (clear and brown)
Cardboard
Iron
Rubber
Tin
Jute-waste
Earthenware shards
PVC
Leather

THE MUNICIPAL WASTE HANDLING SYSTEM

According to the Toronto-based researcher, Christine Furedy (1990), there are two different systems of solid waste management which operate in most developing country metropolitan cities: first, the public or municipal system, and second, a complex but wholly private system of waste-picking and trading. The two systems are neither discrete nor parallel but often work in tandem or intersect at various points. In fact, the phenomenon of private markets for wastes and waste management is wholly dependent on the municipal system.

The CMC's public cleansing system consists of 12,000 *mazdoors* and 1170 supervisory personnel deployed in a decentralised system spread over 15 boroughs with only the top-level managers at the head office. The manual labourers are backed by 140 dumper placers and tipper trucks and a few bulldozers and payloaders. The estimated total cost for the Directorate is Rs 52,300,000,000 or (£1,046,000,000) which constitutes 18.9 per cent of the total municipal budget. Road sweeping crews consist of three *mazdoors* who are supposed to work from five in the morning until noon under the direct supervision of a Block Sarkar.

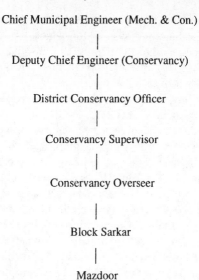

Chief Municipal Engineer (Mech. & Con.)

|

Deputy Chief Engineer (Conservancy)

|

District Conservancy Officer

|

Conservancy Supervisor

|

Conservancy Overseer

|

Block Sarkar

|

Mazdoor

FIGURE 13.2: *Conservancy staff structure, Calcutta Municipal Corporation*

The system used by the CMC is known as 'primary collection.' The *mazdoors* are required to sweep the streets, pick up the rubbish and transport it by handcart to the nearest container or on-road collection point. Since the late 1980s, the transportation of the wastes to the dumping ground has been partially mechanised on the advice of the World Bank and the Calcutta Metropolitan Development Corporation (CMDA) experts. Iron containers 6 m^3 in volume have been placed at selected points in the city to receive wastes from the primary collection. These containers are picked up by dumper-placers equipped with hydraulic lifting systems and operated by a driver and a *khalasi* (mate/assistant who is drawn from the ranks of the *mazdoors*) and transported to the dumping grounds at Dhapa on the eastern fringe of the city. The predominant method of disposal is by uncontrolled tipping at the 1,696.2 acre prime disposal site in Dhapa which was acquired by the CMC in 1866.

CASTE, OCCUPATION AND THE FORMATION OF A MONOPOLY

The market for the management of domestic and municipal wastes within the city was created by the convergence of two important factors: caste and demand for a particular service. 'Caste' according to Leach (1962,

p. 1), 'is a system of social organisation peculiar to Hindu India'. It is a highly complex and unique system for which there is a plethora of conflicting explanations. For the purposes of this chapter, the author has decided to utilise the occupational or functional theory of caste. Prasad (quoted by Jha, 1995, p. 64) has written that 'castes were more or less, occupational groupings and that the lower the profession of a group, the lower was its social status'. Therefore, the Brahmins or the priestly caste were at the top and the occupational castes at the bottom.

Even among the lower or Scheduled Castes[6] there are gradations depending on the hereditary tasks assigned to that group. The CMC Conservancy *mazdoors* are mainly drawn from the caste known as *Bhangi*. In the preface to his book *The Bhangi: A Sweeper Caste, Its socio-economic portraits*, Shyamlal (1992, p. ix) writes: 'Among all the traditional lower or untouchable castes found in India, Bhangi caste occupies the lowest of the low social status [sic].' This is because of their traditional occupational of night soil removers. (Gadgil, quoted by Shyamlal, 1992, p. 23).

In various contexts such as food, sexual relations and rituals members of higher castes are liable to be 'polluted' by either direct or indirect contact with a member of the lower castes. More importantly, according to Gould (1974, p. 293) the caste system fused occupational role and role occupant with respect to thousands of specialised tasks to such a degree that the person and the task are indistinguishable. This fusion of caste and occupation is known as the *bhai-bandi* system. Thus caste has both helped to create and guarantee an occupational monopoly for the *Bhangis*, in their dual roles as members of the CMC's Conservancy staff and as purveyors of certain caste-guaranteed services to private households. The latter role dates from the time when Calcutta had only service privies. Even today, no member of any other caste would consider applying to work for the CMC's Conservancy Directorate as a *mazdoor* for fear of becoming 'ritu-

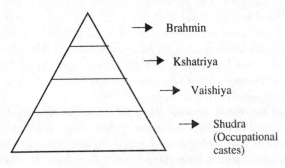

FIGURE 13.3: *The Hindu Caste System*

ally polluted' and being ostracised from his/her own caste group. Nor would a Hindu, Muslim or Indian Christian household conceive of engaging anyone but a *Bhangi* (or equivalent sub-caste) for cleaning toilets.[7]

The monopoly was further strengthened by the CMC's recruiting practices for *mazdoors*. First, under the panel system, *mazdoors*, at the age of superannuation, are allowed by the Schedule system to nominate their successors from their next of kin. Second, a great majority of the CMC Conservancy *mazdoors* are from the Chhotanagpore plateau of Bihar, a poor and underdeveloped part of India. This has provided the CMC with a homogeneous and stable workforce but over the years ethnic origin has been translated into yet another very effective barrier to entry into the CMC's Conservancy work force. Finally, the *bhai-bandi* system has been further entrenched with the formation of occupation-based and therefore caste-based trade unions for CMC *mazdoors*.

This situation is not unique to Calcutta. There are many other cases where closed ethnic groups have excluded outsiders from lucrative trades or contracts. In the UK there is the case of the Irish domination of the 'tat', or 'rag and bone' trade.

CMC *MAZDOORS* AS PRIVATE CONTRACTORS

The first market studied by the author, was for waste management services to private households. It is the oldest one and is now in decline. Until the end of the 1970s, Calcutta's housing pattern was one of individual dwellings, some with grounds, usually housing joint families.[8] Consequently there was a high and constant demand for the services of 'sweepers' in what was essentially a market protected by tradition and custom. It has been the preserve of the CMC *mazdoors* by virtue of both caste and tradition. The *mazdoors* contracted privately with upper and middle-class households in Calcutta to clean toilets, sweep the outside areas and take away the considerable amounts of rubbish generated by the household. These contracts with the householders on their CMC beat were verbal, or, to use Jagannathan's (1987) terms, 'implicit' or 'bilateral contracts' underpinned by the principle of mutuality which governs much of social intercourse in Indian society.

But in the 1980s housing patterns began to change drastically in Calcutta. Most of the large houses were demolished and replaced by highrise blocks of flats which usually employed one 'sweeper' who kept the common areas clean and removed rubbish daily from the individual flats. The demand for the services of private sweepers began to disappear accordingly. The *mazdoors* were forced to look elsewhere to supplement their wages which they did by transforming themselves from independent contractors to rentiers and auctioneers.

CMC *MAZDOORS* AS RENTIERS

There is very little discussion in the solid waste literature as to who owns the wastes once these have left the individual households. Bose and Blore (1993, pp. 3–4) are of the opinion that 'waste in Calcutta seems to have been accepted as private property at many points along the official cycle'. The CMC *mazdoors* were the first ones to stake their claim and at no point did the CMC challenge the right of its employees to appropriate these substantial quantities of waste.

Containerisation of wastes allowed the *mazdoors*, individually or as a group, to establish clearly delineated territories within their respective beats. The more traditional 'occupational entitlements' were then extended by the *mazdoors* to cover the containers on their respective beats effectively 'privatising' them without incurring any costs. Furedy (1990, p. 9) has also observed in other Asian cities that municipal cleansing and dumping-ground staff have established rights to dispose of a city's wastes.

Singh (1994, p. 146) has defined 'privatisation' as 'the creation and enforcement of private property rights' in what was essentially an open-access system. 'Property rights' are, according to Libecap (1989, p. 1), 'the social institutions that define or delimit the range of privileges granted to individuals to specific assets'. Eggertsson (1990, p. 34) has distinguished between three kinds of property rights: first, user rights, including the right to physically transform or destroy an asset; second, the right to earn an income from the asset and enter into contract over the terms with others; and finally, the right to transfer ownership rights of an asset in perpetuity. However, these rarely exist as discrete categories but are more liable to blend together.

The *mazdoors* undertook this 'privatisation' exercise because they knew that the containers housed a valuable resource stream which the pickers of Calcutta coveted. (*Mazdoors* had, as private contractors to affluent Calcutta households, sold waste materials they had separated from the households' wastes. Therefore, they were very aware of the demand, especially for all kinds of plastics and polyethylene.) The *mazdoors* were also aware of the high costs of policing their newly-acquired claims. It was therefore in their interests to pass on the costs of policing by trading the access rights for cash 'and other considerations' to the pickers in exchange for fixed rents.

Besides, CMC *mazdoors'* wages had risen sharply since independence in 1947 under pressure from the Government of India and from the conservancy unions. Under the circumstances, separating wastes and selling the collectibles was no longer worth the time and effort invested. It was more profitable to trade the access rights to the containers of waste.

Calcutta has always attracted resource-poor migrants from the hinterland and latterly from neighbouring Bangladesh. To them, waste picking was one of the few entry points into the labour market. Some 80 per cent of the author's sample, or 183 persons, confirmed that they had entered the labour force as waste pickers. In a scarcity-based economy such as Calcutta's, wastes have utility because they are tradable for cash. Competition for collecting wastes was intense with increasing numbers of people entering the market. Over half the pickers in the author's sample – 129 persons, or 58 per cent – believed that the entry of vast numbers of people into waste picking had increased competition for a finite amount of retrievables and recyclables. In fact, 25 per cent of the sample or 56 persons felt that their main competitors for the wastes were the CMC *mazdoors* themselves.

The pickers, as self-employed persons, enjoyed no labour-based entitlements to the wastes in the containers as the CMC staff claimed they did. They were outsiders or 'squatters' on the wastes generated in Calcutta who were allowed to pick on the sufferance of the police, the CMC *mazdoors* and Calcutta's citizens. The containers presented a challenge to the pickers. 'The problem was how to gain access to the hidden waste materials without entering those containers', a picker told the author. (The containers, which were not removed on a regular basis by the CMC, were full of rotting organic wastes which emitted methane and hydrogen sulphide. Pickers were afraid of entering them.) The more astute pickers realised that they needed to establish exclusive rights of access to a container somewhere in the city from which they could exclude others and from which they themselves could not be easily dislodged. Only then could they be assured of a continuous income stream in the shape of readily accessible retrievables and recyclables. Furthermore, they knew it was a 'seller's market' and that they could not, as individuals, bear the high costs of acquiring access rights. Nor could they police their claims without negotiating some limited cooperation arrangements with other pickers which could again create another set of costs. This confirms Furedy's observation that 'wastes and access to them are not necessarily free to collectors and pickers' (1990, p. 9).

Both *mazdoors* and pickers have their own reasons for considering Calcutta's wastes as a productive asset. Therefore, it is logical for a market to form around these since 'the existence of markets for productive assets is the most important feature of a market exchange system based on private property, capitalism' (Eggertsson, 1990, p. 37). In any situation where exchange occurs, transactions costs are incurred by the parties concerned. Schmid (1987, p. 95) has identified three distinct types of transactions costs: contractual, information and policing. Contractual costs are the costs of reaching an agreement with one other or several parties on a discrete or continuous basis. Time spent in bargaining is a good example of this. Information costs are the costs of acquiring information about product prices, and policing costs are the costs of excluding outsiders from the resource. Selling access to the wastes is a relatively cost-free activity compared to the acquisition of collective access rights. The latter exercise is both a complex and an uncertain undertaking and involves bearing all three of the costs in some measure.

The pickers' need for access to the waste coincided with the *mazdoors'* need to make up the shortfall in their incomes due to the shrinking market for 'personal or family sweepers'. The *mazdoors* were therefore willing to cede their acquired rights to the wastes, for a sum of money and 'other considerations'. Thus, both parties could reap material benefits from the containers: the *mazdoors* by allowing the pickers access to the waste in the containers and the pickers by converting the wastes into income streams for themselves. And some pickers and some *mazdoors* grasped the moment. This is consonant with the observation, 'It is the possibility of profits that cannot be captured within the existing arrangemental structure that leads to the formation of new (or mutation of old) institutional arrangements' (Davis and North, 1971, quoted in Libecap, 1989, p. 2).

In Calcutta it is quite common to find makeshift shacks and lean-tos clustered around the containers. This usually indicates that the rights of access to the wastes have been traded away by the *mazdoors*, but it is difficult to obtain any information about the exact nature of the 'arrangements'. The author was able, after several futile interviews, to inspire enough confidence in a group of pickers to obtain some information about the terms that their small group had negotiated with a *mazdoor* on the beat.

Six young male pickers had banded together about eighteen months previously and acquired the access rights to the containers. They had had to pay one of the *mazdoors* on the beat a sum of money[9] in return for exclusive rights of access to the wastes. The *mazdoor*, in return, was to dump the wastes collected on the beat outside the containers for the pickers to sort. Once this was done, the pickers were responsible for putting the unwanted, usually organic wastes, back into the containers as well as sweeping the area. The leader of the group also acted as custodian for the *mazdoor*'s CMC standard-issue equipment used for street cleaning as there were no CMC depots or centres where staff could store their equipment. The pickers had built their shacks around the containers in order to keep potential intruders away from what was now their 'patch'.

These cooperative arrangements have high contractual costs for the pickers, who must first negotiate sharing arrangements amongst themselves, then negotiate with the *mazdoor* and finally raise the sum demanded. Once the rights are acquired the group members have to invest time and effort in monitoring and sanctioning activities against shirking and free-riding within the group. Finally they have to police their newly acquired rights. If the costs of contracting among themselves or with the *mazdoors* are too high, no exchange takes place and the original 'owner' retains the use rights. But the pickers told the author that they were strongly motivated to find solutions to the problem of high costs, no matter how much time it took, because they knew that in the long run their livelihoods depended on the exchange.

Bromley (1991, p. 31) has remarked that the idea of transaction costs is 'culturally specific'. In the Indian context protracted personalised bargaining processes are seen as an acceptable investment of time, and as Geertz (1979, p. 215) has remarked, 'exchange skills are very elaborately developed' and it is very often the primary determinant of prosperity. If the pickers are successful at working out acceptable arrangements among themselves and with the *mazdoors* then both parties stand to benefit. The picker group that the author interviewed admitted that it had indeed succeeded in arriving at some workable arrangements within the group and with the *mazdoor*, albeit after a period of trial and error.

Gender, the author's research revealed, is an important factor in determining access rights. The picker group that the author observed was composed only of men. Households, however, function as single units for the picking, sorting and selling of wastes. Women and children often pick over and sort from the shares of the male heads of households who are group members. Female headed households consisting of divorced, widowed or abandoned women with young children were usually not part of these groups. Therefore, they were forced to devise their own methods for gaining access to quantities of wastes. The author interviewed two women at length who paid the *mazdoors* between Rs 25 (50p) and Rs 50 (£1) a month, which is the equivalent of one or two days income respectively, in return for which they were allowed to pick over an agreed number of handcart loads before the *mazdoor* tipped it into a container. This appeared to be an ideal arrangement, especially for women with young children, but it soon transpired that sexual services were often part of the contractual costs that the women had to bear. It was quite common, the women told the author, for the *mazdoors* to demand sexual services from the women. The women, in their eagerness to secure a steady supply of retrievables and recyclables, were often unable to refuse them.

In the case of Calcutta's wastes, the contractual arrangements arrived at between *mazdoor* and pickers are more favourable to the former. The group of pickers acquire only limited property rights to the containers in exchange for a sum of money and 'other considerations' usually imposed by the *mazdoor*. The access rights to the containers are given only in 'leasehold' and for a fixed period of time. The group of pickers have the right to appropriate all the retrievables and recyclables in the containers according to the sharing arrangements negotiated within the group. The *mazdoor*, on the other hand, is guaranteed a second income stream from the rents he collects from the picker group. As an added benefit, the *mazdoor* is able to reduce his CMC workload by shifting part of his tasks on to the picker group. The rights acquired are, as has been pointed out, neither absolute nor constant. They are a function of the pickers' own direct efforts at protection and of other people's attempts at capture. Thus, the CMC *mazdoors* have managed to transform themselves from private contractors to Calcutta's affluent householders into rentiers selling access rights to the wastes of Calcutta.

Furedy observes (1990, p. 9) that the rights to waste are 'unwritten rights'. This is indeed correct. The author would add an important qualification: that these rights can still be contracted for or negotiated. However, there are disadvantages inherent in unwritten rights. First, they are unenforceable in a court of law. De Soto (1989, p. 163) notes this is not only because informal contracts are generally oral but also because 'the parties are inhibited by the relative illegality of their activities'. But in Calcutta these rights are ultimately guaranteed by various powerful societal sanctions such as 'loss of face', noblesse oblige, ostracism and ultimately the threat of violence. As Alchian (1977, quoted by Eggertsson, 1990, p. 34) has noted, 'The rights of individuals to the use of resources (i.e., property rights) in any society are to be construed as supported by the force of etiquette, social custom, ostracism ... many of the constraints on the use of what we call private property involve the force of etiquette and social ostracism.'

THE *MAZDOORS* AS AUCTIONEERS OF WASTES

The market for wastes at the dumping ground is different to the other two markets described above because it is not the sole preserve of the *mazdoors*.[10] The *mazdoors* participate in it as part of a truck crew, and therefore all pecuniary benefits from the 'auction' are shared with the drivers of the dumper-placers and flat-bed trucks.[11] The market for wastes at the dumping grounds in Dhapa and Bantala is a long-established one. Both dumping grounds have long-time resident pickers and traders living in huts built on top of the rubbish heaps. This is also a common practice in Manila (Bubel, 1989) and Bangkok (author's field notes, February 1992).

The author was able to observe, but only from a distance, the ritual of the 'auctioning' of containers at the dumping ground in Bantala.[12] Each time a dumper-placer drove up, men and women emerged from the shacks perched on top of the hills of waste, and ran up to it. The first man to reach the dumper-placer would clamber on to the running board on the passenger side of the cab while others, mainly women, would stand on the ground beside it shouting and gesticulating. This was the start of a vigorous bargaining session and has been known to last over half an hour. Once the bargain was struck, hands would appear from the within the truck cab and money would be passed over. The truck would then bump off across the dumping grounds followed by women and children, with the successful bidder hanging on to the door giving directions. The truck would then grind to a halt on a certain 'patch' where usually another couple of men were waiting. Once the truck had emptied its contents on to the spot indicated by the men, they would fence it off with the flags and twine and the women would get to work sorting through the rubbish. The author also noticed that no windrows and bulldozers were in evidence. 'We have paid them off' a picker explained to us. 'They only come around once we have completely finished ... if they come at all.' Furedy, referring to practices in other Asian cities, cites Baldissimo and Lohani, (1988, in Furedy, 1990, p. 9) that 'pickers *may have* [author's emphasis] to pay police, municipal staff and field staff at dump sites'.

However, the author was frustrated in her attempts to investigate the amount a picker syndicate would pay to buy the rights to the contents of a dumper truck. Most of the pickers seemed unwilling to talk and gave vague answers such as, 'a lot of money', when questioned. Buddhadeb Chakrabarty of All India Institute of Hygiene and Public Health (AIIHPH) (personal communication, January, 1992) maintains that each container load is worth between Rs 50 (£1) and Rs 100 (£2), depending on the provenance of the load. Loads from middle and higher income areas command higher prices because they usually contain a higher percentage of retrievables and recyclables than those from poorer areas or from the city's markets.

The market for wastes at the Bantala dumping ground is characterised by a small number of potential buyers, all of whom are well-known to each other and to the CMC dumper-placer crews. But competition for the wastes is fierce and often ends in violence. Traders have effectively privatised the dumping grounds and divided it into private plots policed by their 'stables'[13] of pickers. The pickers who participate in the auction are merely acting as agents for the traders, and the wastes, when they are dumped, are therefore dumped on an individual trader's 'private property'.

CONCLUSION

The three markets described above appear to be very different in that the objects of exchange differ widely ranging from private waste management services to the rights of access to the wastes and finally the wastes themselves. However, they share one common characteristic: the involvement of the CMC *mazdoors*. In fact, the CMC *mazdoors* are the key actors in all three markets by virtue of being monopoly suppliers of waste management services to both the domestic and public sectors. The monopoly, however, derives from the fusion of caste and occupation which is a defining characteristic of Indian society. The monopoly is legitimised by the employment practices of the CMC.

The *mazdoors*, in the first instance, were contractors to the affluent households of Calcutta, selling their services for monetary and other considerations. In fact, the relationship of the households and the *mazdoors* reflected a venerable North Indian Hindu institution of *jajmani*. This is essentially an economic relationship which enables the castes to maintain their separate status and yet engage in meaningful relationships with others.

The change in Calcutta's housing patterns in the 1980s caused the market for 'private sweepers' to shrink. At the same time, the CMC introduced a system of roadside containers for waste collection. Some of the *mazdoors*, perceiving a void in the property rights to the wastes of Calcutta, extended their occupation and tradition-based monopoly to the wastes to cover the containers, effectively privatising them. This allowed the *mazdoors* to transform themselves, unchallenged, into rentiers and profit from the fierce competition that exists between pickers for wastes. The *mazdoors*' monopoly position is challenged only in the market for wastes at the dumping grounds since it is shared with the drivers of the CMC's trucks and dumper-placers. However, it is safe to assume that sharing arrangements have been negotiated between the partners in order to ensure the smooth functioning of the exchange process.

In conclusion, not one of the three markets described above conforms to the perfect market so beloved of neoclassicists. In fact, the three markets in Calcutta are, to use Preston's term, 'socially constructed'. That is, there is a 'complex network of local/social/political/cultural contexts' (Preston, 1994, p. 55) undergirding the exchanges.

NOTES

1. The thesis entitled 'Rich Pickings? The Political Economy of Solid Waste Management in Calcutta, India' is supervised by Ian C. Blore, Lecturer, Department of Development Administration, School of Public Policy, University of Birmingham, UK.
2. The author is indebted to Professor K.J. Nath, Director of the All-India Institute of Hygiene and Public Health, Calcutta, for the term.
3. Gourlay (1992, p. 25) quotes the UK Department of Environment as rue-fully admitting that 'There are *no* [author's emphasis] reliable statistics on wastes produced or disposed of in the UK with the exception of special wastes which are ... quantified to some extent'.
4. 1£ = Rs 50.
5. Calcutta's rubbish has recorded a 46 per cent overall increase in the combustible fractions, including paper, various kinds of plastics and polyethylene, in the 13-year period, 1970 to 1993, recorded by the Calcutta Municipal Corporation. Paper rose from 3.18 per cent to 5.2 per cent – a rise of 64 per cent. Plastics and polyethylene rose from a mere 0.65 per cent to 2.85 per cent – a rise of 338 per cent in the same period.
6. The lower castes are referred to as Scheduled Castes after the Government of India Act of 1935.
7. Article 15 (Fundamental Rights) of the Constitution of India forbids discrimination on the grounds of caste. In 1955, the Untouchability (Offences) Act was passed which made 'various types of untouchability' punishable by law.
8. Joint families are usually patrilineal and patrilocal. All members of the joint family, often encompassing three or more generations, live under the same roof, eat from the same kitchen and share in the property. Joint families are found among both Hindus and Muslims.
9. Measures of wealth, income and expenditure are often considered by informants to be sensitive information. (Christensen, 1993, p. 126) and they are therefore reluctant to divulge details of financial transactions.
10. *Mazdoors* assigned to conservancy transportation crews are often referred to as *khalasis* (drivers' mates/assistants).
11. In the days before containerisation, Calcutta's wastes were carried to the dumping grounds in flat-bed trucks with seven-man crews. It was quite common for the *mazdoors* to sort the collectibles from the wastes en route to the grounds. That market, some say, was controlled by the drivers.
12. The Bantala dumping grounds are hotbeds of criminal activity and a 'no-go area' even for the local police.
13. All the pickers who sell to the same trader are considered part of the trader's 'stable'. The waste trading confraternity have their own jargon!

REFERENCES

Barzel, Yoram (1989), *Economic Analysis of Property Rights – Political Economy of Institutions and Decisions* (Cambridge: Cambridge University Press).

Bose and Blore (1991), 'Public Waste and Private Property: An enquiry into the economics of solid waste in Calcutta', in *Public Administration and Development*, vol. 13.

Bromley, Daniel (1991), *Environmental and Economy Property Rights and Public Policy* (Oxford: Blackwell).

Bubel, Anna Z. (1989), 'Waste Picking and Solid Waste Management', in *Environmental Sanitation Reviews*, no. 30, December, (Bangkok: ENSIC, Asian Institute of Technology).

Calcutta Municipal Corporation (1993), *Solid Waste Management of the City of Calcutta, India: A Project Report on Promotion to Informal Waste Recycling and Reuse.* Unpublished MS.

Christensen, C. (1993), 'Sensitive information: collecting data on livestock and informal credit', in Devereux, S. and J. Hodinott (eds) *Fieldwork in Developing Countries* (Boulder, CO: Lynne Rienner).

de Soto, Hernando (1989), *The Other Path – The Invisible Revolution in the Third World* (London: I.B. Taurus and Co.).

Eggertsson, Thrainn (1990), *Economic Behaviour And Institutions* (Cambridge: Cambridge University Press) (Cambridge Surveys of Economic Literature).

Furedy, Christine (1990), 'Social Aspects of Solid Waste Recovery in Asian Cities', in *Environmental Sanitation Reviews* no. 30, December, (Bangkok: ENSIC, Asian Institute of Technology).

Geertz, C. (1979), 'The bazaar economy in Sefrov', in C. Geertz et al. (eds) *Meaning and Order in Moroccan Society* (Cambridge: Cambridge University Press).

Giri, Pabitra and Sulipi De (undated), *Solid Waste Management in Calcutta Metropolis.* Unpublished MS, Calcutta University Centre for Urban Economics, Calcutta.

Gould, Harold A. (1974), 'The Lucknow Rickshawallas: The Social Organization of an Occupational Category', in M.S.A. Rao (ed.), *Urban Sociology in India* (New Delhi: Orient Longman).

Gould, Harold A. (1977), in Schmidt, Steffen et al., *Friends, Followers and Factions: A Reader in Political Clientilism* (Berkeley: University of California Press).

Gourlay, K.A. (1992), *World of Waste Dilemmas of Industrial Development* (London: Zed Press).

Government of West Bengal, Local Government and Urban Development Department (1991), *Solid Waste Management in Calcutta: A Status Paper* (January).

Granovetter, Mark (1992), 'Economic Action and Social Structure: The Problem of Embeddedness', in Mark Granovetter and Richard Swedberg (eds), (1992), *The Sociology of Economic Life* (Boulder, CO: Westview Press).

Jagannathan, V. (1987), *Informal Markets in Developing Countries* (Oxford: Oxford University Press).

Jha, M. (1995), *An Introduction to Indian Anthropology* (Delhi: Vikas Publishing House).

Leach, Edmund (1962), 'What should we mean by caste?', in E. Leach (ed.), *Aspects of Caste in South India, Ceylon and North West Pakistan* (Cambridge: Cambridge University Press).

Libecap, Gary (1989), *Contracting for Property Rights* (Cambridge: Cambridge University Press).

Nair, P. Thankappan (1989), *Calcutta Municipal Corporation at a Glance* (Calcutta: Calcutta Municipal Corporation).

Nelson, Nici (1972), 'Women must help each other', in Janet Bujra and Patricia Caplan (eds), *Women United: Women Divided* (London: Tavistock Press).

Plattner, Stuart (1992), 'Economic Behaviour in Markets', in Stuart Plattner (ed.), *Economic Anthropology* (Stanford: Stanford University Press).

Preston, Peter (1994), 'The Political Economy of Trade', in Hans-Dieter Evers and Heiko Schrader (eds), *The Moral Economy of Trade Ethnicity and Developing Markets* (London and New York: Routledge).

Rao, M.S.A. (1974), 'Urbanization and Social Change', in M.S.A. Rao (ed.), *Urban Sociology in India* (New Delhi: Orient Longman).

Schmid, A. Allan (1987), *Property, Power and Public Choice: An Enquiry into Law and Economies* (New York: Praeger).

Shyamlai (1992), *The Bhangi: A Sweeper Caste. Its socio-economic portraits* (Bombay: Popular Prakashan).

Singh, Katar (1994), *Managing Common Pool Resource Principles and Case Studies* (Delhi: Oxford University Press).

Index

Index